ETHNOGRAPHIES OF EDUCATIONAL AND CULTURAL CONFLICTS: STRATEGIES AND RESOLUTIONS

STUDIES IN EDUCATIONAL ETHNOGRAPHY

Series Editor: Geoffrey Walford

Volume 1: Children Learning in Context – Editors: Geoffrey Walford and Alexander Massey

Volume 2: Explorations in Methodology – Editors: Alexander Massey and Geoffrey Walford

Volume 3: Genders and Sexualities in Educational Ethnography – Editors: Geoffrey Walford and Caroline Hudson

Volume 4: Ethnography and Educational Policy – Editor: Geoffrey Walford

Volume 5: Critical Ethnography and Education – Editors: Phil Francis Carspecken and Geoffrey Walford

Volume 6: Debates and Developments in Ethnographic Methodology – Editor: Geoffrey Walford

Volume 7: Doing a Doctorate in Educational Ethnography – Editor: Geoffrey Walford

Volume 8: Investigating Educational Policy Through Ethnography – Editor: Geoffrey Walford

STUDIES IN EDUCATIONAL ETHNOGRAPHY VOLUME 9

ETHNOGRAPHIES OF EDUCATIONAL AND CULTURAL CONFLICTS: STRATEGIES AND RESOLUTIONS

EDITED BY

BOB JEFFREY

Faculty of Education and Language Studies,
The Open University, Milton Keynes, UK

GEOFFREY WALFORD

Department of Educational Studies, University of Oxford, UK

2004

ELSEVIER
JAI

Amsterdam – Boston – Heidelberg – London – New York – Oxford
Paris – San Diego – San Francisco – Singapore – Sydney – Tokyo

ELSEVIER B.V.
Sara Burgerhartstraat 25
P.O. Box 211
1000 AE Amsterdam
The Netherlands

ELSEVIER Inc.
525 B Street, Suite 1900
San Diego
CA 92101-4495
USA

ELSEVIER Ltd
The Boulevard, Langford Lane, Kidlington
Oxford OX5 1GB
UK

ELSEVIER Ltd
84 Theobalds Road
London
WC1X 8RR
UK

First edition 2004

British Library Cataloguing in Publication Data
A catalogue record is available from the British Library.

ISBN: 0-7623-1112-6
ISSN: 1529-210X (Series)

♾ The paper used in this publication meets the requirements of ANSI/NISO Z39.48-1992 (Permanence of Paper). Printed in The Netherlands.

CONTENTS

PREFACE

Ethnography has become one of the major methods of researching educational settings. Its key strength is its emphasis on understanding the perceptions and cultures of the people and organisations studied. Through prolonged involvement with those who are being studied, the ethnographic researcher is able gradually to enter their world and gain an understanding of their lives.

Each volume of *Studies in Educational Ethnography* focuses on a particular theme relating to the ethnographic investigation of education. The volumes are closely linked to an annual two-day residential conference that explores various elements of ethnography and its application to education and schooling. The series of Ethnography and Education conferences began in the late 1970s, and was originally held at St. Hilda's College, Oxford University. The series later moved to Warwick University and back to the Department of Educational Studies, University of Oxford in 1996. Each year a broad theme for the conference is chosen and participants are invited to contribute papers. The conference meeting itself is a period of shared work: papers are pre-circulated to participants and critically yet supportively discussed. In their revisions for possible publication, participants are thus able to take account of the detailed critique offered by their colleagues.

The contributions presented in each volume of *Studies in Educational Ethnography* are of two types. Most are revised versions of papers presented at the annual Oxford Ethnography and Education conference, but each volume usually also includes some further specially commissioned pieces. They are selected on the basis of their high quality, their coherence as a group and their contribution to both ethnographic methodology and substantive knowledge.

The series recognises that the nature of ethnography is contested, and this is taken to be a sign of its strength and vitality. While the idea that the term can be taken to be almost synonymous with qualitative research is rejected, chapters are included that draw upon a broad range of methodologies that are embedded within a long and detailed engagement with those people and organisations studied.

Further details of the Oxford Ethnography and Education conference or the *Studies in Educational Ethnography* series of volumes are available from the Series Editor.

Geoffrey Walford
Professor of Education Policy, Department of Educational Studies,
University of Oxford, 15 Norham Gardens,
Oxford OX2 6PY, England geoffrey.walford@edstud.ox.ac.uk.

INTRODUCTION

Bob Jeffrey

The implementation of education policy, engagement with curriculum and the operation of pedagogic practices is a complex and recursive process. One of the main reasons for complexity is that policy, curriculum and pedagogies are initially constituted as broad packages that are created to provide programmes for all situations and contexts. For example policies concerning equity programmes have to be operationalised in relation to differentiated groups such as disability, gender, religion and class. The National Curriculum needs to be interpreted in terms of the cultures and experience of learners and adjusted accordingly, for example the literacy and history curriculum need to include perspectives relevant to the local culture. Pedagogies have often been formulated as if they were appropriate for all contexts and learners, for example, a child centred approach, but empirical research has shown teachers interpreting it differently (Alexander et al., 1992).

Teachers, learners, families and communities mediate, appropriate, subvert, and challenge the processes of policy implementation, curriculum engagement and pedagogic practices to make educational experiences more meaningful. These acts of agency exemplify the conflicts and incongruencies that exist within these processes, the coping strategies and resolutions adopted. In some cases local programmes are developed to take into account the context, e.g.: an early years school instituting a corporeal ethos where learners move around the school for lessons to maintain a physical dynamism that is inherent in young children (Jeffrey, 2001a, b). However, in others, learners can find themselves in tension with policy, curriculum and pedagogy (Pollard et al., 2000).

Examination of these educational processes using ethnographic methods identifies and characterises these tensions, in which the agent acts and provides

Ethnographies of Educational and Cultural Conflicts: Strategies and Resolutions
Studies in Educational Ethnography, Volume 9, 1–7

ISSN: 1529-210X/doi:10.1016/S1529-210X(04)09001-1

research findings that can be used to construct lasting solutions that are commensurate with complex situations. The identification of the failures of policy implantation, curriculum engagement and pedagogic approaches can be carried out using evaluations of objectives and outcomes (Reynolds & Farrell, 1996) by carrying out audits of conflicting teaching and learning contexts Ofsted (1995) or by recording the dis-satisfiers (Herzberg, 1971) of educational experience (Willis, 1977). Solutions can be proposed in response to these findings, for example, target methodology, reconstruction and redesignation of institutions – foundation schools, and palliative management such as counselling. However, these could be seen as simplistic solutions to simplistic analysis.

Walford's (2003, p. 4) comprehensive list of ethnographic methods indicates how ethnographic enquiry can show how policy, curriculum and pedagogy interact with teachers, learners, parents and communities.

(1) the focus on the study of culture;
(2) the of multiple methods and thus the construction of diverse focus of data;
(3) direct involvement and long-term engagement;
(4) the recognition that the researcher is the main research instrument;
(5) the high status given to the accounts of participants and their understandings;
(6) the engagement in a cycle hypothesis and theory building; and
(7) the focus on a particular case rather than on any attempts to generalize.

Ethnographic analysis based on data from across the research context brings out the nature of these interactions and provides opportunities for strategic development and effective solutions to conflicts and incongruency. Secondly, the data itself opens up possibilities for understanding learners' perspectives and strategic activity, for example, the quality of learning contexts (Rudduck et al., 1996; Rudduck & Flutter, 2000) and the creative management of learning by learners (Jeffrey, 2001). Those teachers and institutions that are receptive to different perspectives find themselves operating a recursive system that is able to develop and adapt to the interests and needs of learners (Jeffrey, 2003) a co-participative interaction (Emilia, 1996) a learner inclusive approach (Jeffrey & Craft, 2003).

The writers in this volume have carried out ethnographies that illuminate educational disjunctions, ambiguities and tensions, agency, strategic action and resolution. Their methodology enables them to show, in detail, how the incongruencies arose, how contexts affected interactions, what kind of agency was operating, the circumstances leading to resolutions. Six articles focus on educational inequality (Angus et al., Colton, Silva, Long and Volk, Walters, Williams and Gregory) two on identity development (Gewinner, Van Sluys) and we include three that discuss methodological issues of partisanship in researching equality issues (Hammersley, Hillyard and Hudson).

The broad conclusion across the equality papers is that compensatory programmes are not effective if they do not include attention to culture, identity and agency (Angus et al., Paul, Silva, Simon, Long and Volk and Williams and Gregory). Their analysis is that a multi-level approach is critical in reducing inequalities although where there is a reduction in inequality it may be at the expense of self-identity and cultural belonging.

In particular, five papers draw out the conflicts between narrow standardised pedagogies and learners cultural and individual interests (Angus et al., Long and Volk, Walters, Williams and Gregory) and two outline strategic action by either learners or researchers (Colton, Silva) and three illustrate some resolutions arising from the research contexts (Gewinner, Hudson and Van Sluys).

However, we begin with a methodological issue concerning partisanship in researching equality with papers from Hillyard and Hammersley who debate this issue by focussing on the work of Goffman and Becker.

PARTISANSHIP IN RESEARCHING INEQUALITIES

Hillyard argues that Irving Goffman's mixing of detailed study, an evocative writing style and interjection as social commentator can legitimately be defined as social science research because it highlights inequalities. His approach is seen not as a systematic model but as a appreciation of the rhetorical nature of ethnographic writing and argument, whilst maintaining a critical theoretical agenda. Debates over the legitimacy of partisan research and in particular critical ethnography are a feature of the last decade in education (Hammersley, 1992) and Irving Goffman, in particular, is held in high esteem for his work on inequalities which is why the debate at the Oxford 2002 conference was so pertinent.

Hammersley uses Howard Becker's article "Whose side are we on" (Becker, 1967) to show that, in spite of its use to advocate partisan research, he did not do so. Hammersley argues that research that promotes equality leaves no room for promoting some equity such as positive discrimination. It also precludes a position that recognises that there are always competing values. This is relevant, he argues, because it takes one value judgement as if it were scientifically validated compared with others, when research on its own cannot provide such validation and secondly it includes no argument as to why a particular value judgement is the most appropriate.

These arguments frame the rest of the papers in this collection. The writer/researchers are interested in equity issues but they range from those who engage in critical research to those who see ethnography as more of a presentation of complexity. It would limit our thinking around this issue if we were to try to designate the papers into one or the other. It is more fruitful to read all of them with this issue in mind to ensure that we gain, not only from the content of each article, but from a parallel reading of the methodological issue of how ethnographic research relates to social, political and educational inequalities.

CONFLICTS AND INCONGRUENCIES AND INEQUALITIES

Angus, Sunderland-Smith and Snyder point to inequalities in ICT provision, access and support across four wealth differing families in Australia and challenges an assumption that automatic access to ICT is a panacea for a reduction in educational inequalities. He identifies unequal provision and unequal supportive environments and at the same time raises the question of whether equality can achieved through ICT access to global discourses. This is done through close familiarity with families in the ethnographic tradition and the researchers provide rich analysis in the way they characterise the inequity.

Williams and Gregory's article is a case study of two schools with differing approaches and attitudes to its parents and learners. She concludes that in spite of the government's common curriculum, common pedagogic programmes such as the literacy and numeracy hour inequalities remain where the school intake is poorer and the school culture is less positive. This theme permeates many articles showing how centralised policies often fail in terms of equality because they are not broad enough to challenge other more determinist factors.

Long and Volk take up the same theme but focus on how reading programmes do not take into account family or cultural differences and consequently act to maintain inequality in literacy achievement. Their ethnographic work in both school and home enabled them to identify how parents could make more progress with their children's literacy because of their common cultural relationships. In doing this they also identified how learners use their cultural experience as a context for literacy progress.

Walters focuses more narrowly as she researches the activities of three Bangledeshi early years learners and how their agency assisted their educational development, mostly unbeknown to the teachers. She showed how they worked hard at "achieving achievement" and at the same time how they "hid" their incompetancies to the extent that their teachers regarded them as more proficient in some literacy and numeracy skills than they actually were. They protected their self-esteem. She concludes through these detailed observations of both school and family that the learners are seen as "Bangledeshi" pupils rather than as second language learners and that any resistance or diverting behaviours are seen as being situated in their cultural identity not in their special literacy needs. This article exemplifies Hammersley's problematising of equalities.

STRATEGIC ACTION AND INEQUALITIES

Paul continues an achievement inequality by focusing on Caribbean children and examining why positive action programmes have failed and concludes that his study of one primary classroom, its occupants and families, shows that the children were interested in achievement but that the relationship between the teacher and the pupils was a key factor. Taking up the need to be familiar with learner' cultures he further argues that teachers need to overcome or contain mythologies or cultural practices and beliefs that lead to confrontation and conflict. Using ethnographic methods of conversing with parents, pupils and teachers and carrying out detailed observations of classroom interactions he provides some insight into factors that need to be taken into account when addressing inequalities.

Silva, like Paul, concerned with spaces and interactions in classrooms containing learners of different cultures. She provides a three phased model based on the "acting subject" from conceptions by Anthony Giddens. She shows how students act to secure their position and identity but how specific discourses constructed with learners enable them to use their agency productively in the learning context. The three phases are building the model, the use of self-regulation through feedback and onto a resilient mode where the learner decides whether to let the environment act on him or her or to choose to act upon it but with the knowledge that these actions will be reflexively examined later.

RESOLUTIONS AND INEQUALITIES

Gewinner is also concerned with agency but her focus is on female secondary school students. In her research, however, achievement targets were met by the sample but at the expense of social and cultural identity. These students "internalised the dominant middle class social norms . . . they became socialised to a professional culture that would enable them to fit into various health professions." Gewinner shows the extent of their agency in adopting a new "position" (Davies & Harre, 1994) challenging correspondence theories that highlight inculcation (Sharp & Green, 1975). They were aware of the "paper" identities and even manipulated them "but sometimes they lost sight of the reified character of achievement identity." Her study of agency in the reconstruction of identities is particularly acute and informative. In Hammersley's terms the consequence of this equality programme was only one of a series of competing values and shows the necessity to acknowledge this in research programmes.

Van Sluys also shows focuses on agency with her study of a classroom of young children and literacy practices. She shows how the learners valued agency work in "risk zones" not just to improve their learning competencies but how these zones enhanced identities and how these enacted with improved literacy development. In these particular classrooms learners were less apprentices than participants in a co-participative discourse (Emilia, 1996) "They learn to take positions that call upon them to deliberate on their relationships between themselves, others and all available discourses." They were encouraged to try out different identities and consequently labelling of learners was diminished by this pedagogic process.

The highlighting of what might be regarded as positive successful practices to reduce inequalities is a necessary aspect of improving educational knowledge and can also be used to characterise theories, in this case of identity construction. So long as the ethnographic research outcomes are shown as situated other practitioners can "test" some of the ideas in their own contexts.

Finally, Hudson exemplifies a research practice which had positive results with the respondents of the research in spite of some constraints. She was researching thirty two secondary school student's experience of family and school life in a period of significant social change. This was intended to be a classic ethnography where she immersed herself as far as was possible in their lives and experiences to the extent of attending dances and being offered drugs. However, her husband was also the deputy head of the school the students attended and they were aware of this. Hudson shows how, nevertheless, she was able to build enough trust for the ethnography to be completed. Although her dilemmas and tensions are exemplified in the paper she also shows how the respondents deliberated about the situation and decided that they and the researcher could construct an appropriate research relationship as it was in their interests to do so. This article is not directly concerned with equalities or partisanship but with that other major issue for ethnographers, the engagement of the self and identity with the situation and the people one is researching. It is a recurring theme with ethnographers and can only add to a collection to have a further insight included.

REFERENCES

Alexander, R., Rose, J., & Woodhead, C. (1992). *Curriculum organisation and classroom practice in primary schools: A discussion paper*. London: HMSO.

Becker, H. (1967). Whose side are we on? *Social Problems*, *14*, 239–247.

Davies, B., & Harre, R. (1994). Positioning, conversation and the production of selves. *Journal for the Theory of Social Behaviour*, *20*(1), 43–63.

Emilia, R. (1996). *The hundred languages of children*. Reggio Emilia: Reggio Children.

Hammersley, M. (1992). Some reflections on ethnography and validity. *Qualitative Studies in Education*, *5*(3), 193–203.

Herzberg, F. (1971). Motivation-hygiene theory. In: D. Pugh (Ed.), *Organization Theory*. Harmondsworth: Penguin.

Jeffrey, B. (2001a). Challenging prescription in ideology and practice: The case of sunny first school. In: J. Collins, K. Insley & J. Solar (Eds), *Understanding Pedagogy*. Buckingham: Open University Press.

Jeffrey, B. (2001b). Primary pupil's perspectives and creative learning. *Encyclopaideia (Italian Journal)*, *9*(Spring), 133–152.

Jeffrey, B. (2003). Countering student instrumentalism: A creative response. *British Educational Research Journal*, 29(4).

Jeffrey, B., & Craft, A. (2003). Creative teaching and teaching for creativity: Distinctions and relationships. Paper read at *BERA SIG Conference* February, at The Open University, Milton Keynes.

Ofsted (1995). *The Ofsted Handbook: Guidance on the inspection of nursery and primary schools*. London: Office for Standards in Education.

Pollard, A., Triggs, P., Broadfoot, P., McNess, E., & Osborn, M. (2000). *What pupils say: Changing policy and practice in primary education*. London: Continuum.

Reynolds, D., & Farrell, S. (1996). *Worlds apart? A review of international surveys of educational achievement involving England*. London: HMSO.

Rudduck, J., Chaplain, R., & Wallace, G. (1996). *School improvement: What can pupils tell us*. London: David Fulton.

Rudduck, J., & Flutter (2000). Pupil participation and pupil perspective: Carving a new order of experience. *Cambridge Journal of Education*, 30(1), 75–89.

Sharp, R., & Green, A. (1975). *Education and social control*. London: Routledge & Kegan Paul.

Walford, G. (2003). Introduction: Investigating educational policy. In: G. Walford (Ed.), *Investigating Educational Policy Through Ethnography* (Vol. 8). Studies in Educational Ethnography. Oxford: Elsevier.

Willis, P. (1977). *Learning to labour: How working class kids get working class jobs*. Farnborough: Saxon House.

THE CASE FOR PARTISAN RESEARCH: ERVING GOFFMAN AND RESEARCHING SOCIAL INEQUALITIES

S. H. Hillyard

INTRODUCTION

The recent narrative, if not postmodern, turn within the tradition of ethnographic research has not eased difficult questions concerning how best inequalities can be researched by the social sciences. Whilst important additions have been made to traditional concerns with social class, race and gender, such as age (but not purely gerontology), disability and the rural/urban divide, epistemological questions remain over how theoretical and conceptual concerns about inequality also be met in field research.

One benefit of an appreciation of textuality is that the modes of representation available to contemporary researchers have opened up considerably (Atkinson, 1996; Stronach & MacLure, 1997). However, this is not to suggest ethnographers in the past have not successfully wedded style with substance. The paper uses the case of one such sociologist, Erving Goffman, to show how textual and rhetorical devices can be used to critically analyse institutional and interactional systems of inequality. Goffman is not presented as a model for future research, but rather as an example of how a research style can successfully challenge "hierarchies of credibility" and inequalities.

Ethnographies of Educational and Cultural Conflicts: Strategies and Resolutions
Studies in Educational Ethnography, Volume 9, 9–24

ISSN: 1529-210X/doi:10.1016/S1529-210X(04)09002-3

The aims of the paper are therefore two-fold. First, to argue that popular conceptions of Goffman's work as immoral (Gouldner, 1970) or merely concerned to voyeuristically catalogue social inequalities (Bennett, 1994; Marx, 1984) are misguided. The second, more general, comment is that the methodologies of a number of classical social theorists/researchers have come to be misconstrued. The paper uses Goffman as an example to demonstrate that the logic underpinning his methodology must be fully understood if contemporary social researchers are to use classical works in defence of new epistemological stances in relation to researching social inequalities. The chapter concludes with the suggestion that the identification of Goffman as a postmodernist is deeply misguided.

GOFFMAN'S SOCIOLOGICAL LEGACY

The passing of the twentieth anniversary of Goffman's death[1] has not allowed sociology sufficient time to reach an agreement on Goffman's legacy. His work has been both championed (Burns, 1992; Manning, 1976; Strong, 1983; Williams, 1986) and attacked (Dawe, 1973; Denzin & Keller, 1981; Gouldner, 1970) and, all the more intriguingly, both simultaneously (Erwin, 1992; Marx, 1984; Willmott et al., 1979). In spite of such disagreement, Goffman's popularity has not decline. The first text dedicated to his work emerged during his lifetime (Ditton, 1980), whilst others have drawn conclusions on the basis of an analysis of selected, core texts (Burns, 1992; Craib, 1978; Fine & Martin, 1990; Manning, 1976). His place among the classics has recently been affirmed by the publication of a four-volume collection of secondary commentaries on his work, which includes personal reminiscences and analyses of the sociological traditions present in his work (Fine & Smith, 1990).

The very curiosity his work attracts, during his career and to this day, is itself telling. Williams (1986) argues that "among older, more established faculty he is not taken very seriously" and furthers finds "more likely it is intentional" (Williams, 1986, p. 348). In contrast, Strong's (1983) obituary of Goffman, revealed the compelling nature of Goffman's sociology, when Strong recounts a rumour circulating among U.K. admirers of Goffman's work were considering seeking a grant to go and study his approach firsthand. Strong's (1983) obituary reveals one of the core reasons for the scrutiny and speculation Goffman's work provokes: that no consensus exists over the meaning or very consistency of his approach. This has, of course, only been accentuated by Goffman's refusal to offer a commentary of his own.[2] The attractiveness of Goffman's work is often attributed to his unusual method (Atkinson, 1989; Lofland, 1980) and his theoretical orientation (whether symbolic interactionist or structuralist) has been debated without resolution.

However, as the decades have passed following his death, the synergy between the *task* of his sociology and his *method* (in this instance I mean his writings, rather than his fieldwork) has become obscured. Fine (1999) suggests the very popularity of his writings has led the substantive content of his work to become under researched:

> The enormous number of citations of Goffman's work, while partly a reflection of his intellectual patrimony, is also a function of his role as an intellectual touchstone. The sedimentation of a writer's ideas into commonplace notions provides opportunities for later theorists to advance new readings.
>
> (Fine, 1999, p. 192)

Goffman is not alone in this. The work of other, classical sociologists have been revisited in order to establish the logic underpinning their arguments and, more fundamentally, whether they advocate the very positions that later scholars use to defend new work (Hammersley, 2000). My task here for Goffman is to attempt a similar exegesis for Goffman in relation to researching social inequalities. As such, the focus is fortunately narrowed, considering the size and breadth of Goffman's work when viewed in its entirety.[3] The perception of Goffman's: (1) writing *method* and techniques; and then (2) the place of a *political*, or moral, critique within his work is now considered. Following this, I re-evaluate different representations of Goffman. As often is the case, the analysis of one aspect of his work leads to a far wider appreciation and insight into the very task of Goffman's sociology, yet my intention is not to "free Goffman from some of the crude overgeneralizations that his colleagues have used in evaluating his writings,"[4] but to address the postmodern overtones identified within his work (Fine, 1999; Gauntlett, 2001; Hillyard, 1999; Manning, 1976). Goffman's approach is not held up to as *the* model for future research, but his critique of the "hierarchies of credibility" or structural inequalities (which he is often perceived to implicitly celebrate) and his methodological innovations are celebrated. The conclusion offered is that a greater appreciation of the methodological *and* theoretical connections in classical sociological works must not be neglected if ethnography and sociology are to continue to research social inequalities reflexively.

GOFFMAN: STYLE

The distinctive, instantly recognisable style of Goffman's work throughout his career has long been recognised (Fine, 1999). The style applies "bizarre" or "ironic juxtapositions" and avoids current writing conventions through a "combination of clinical approach, sensational content, deadpan stylishness" (Burns, 1992, p. 14;

Fine, 1999, p. 184). Goffman combines this with the use of "vignettes from the myriad microworlds of everyday life" in order to analyse seemingly "mundane little gestures" which successfully produced a "shocking effect" which served to open up a new world or field for sociological investigation (Manning, 1976, pp. 19, 16). Due, perhaps, to his focus on everyday situations and examples with which we are all familiar, "Goffman's original, jarring [. . .] [and] startling" writing has succeeding in reaching both an academic and "a popular audience" (Manning, 1976, p. 19; Willmott et al., 1979, p. 1).

Goffman's use of such techniques is far from arbitrary or a mere stylistic flourish, rather its carries a critical bite:

> Likely no two social scientists writing in English have been discussed more in terms of the significance of their style than Thorstein Veblen and Erving Goffman. In an age in which most social scientists seemed to want to *avoid* style (Mills, 1953, p. vii), these men embraced it. Both are said to write with a corrosive pen.
>
> (Fine, 1999, p. 182, original emphasis)

In his analysis of both Veblen and Goffman, Fine (1999) finds that Goffman's *style* of writing brings with it a social commentary, or rather, a critique based upon an "alienated cynicism" toward the social world (Fine, 1999, p. 190). Goffman's writings have likewise been argued to advocate sociology of "disenchantment," "cynical relativism" and, more generally, a "gamelike encounter-orientated sociology" (Manning, 1976, p. 20; Willmott et al., 1979, pp. 3, 5). Williams (1986) summarises this "essential ambiguity" within Goffman and notes that "some view him as a political radical, others view him as a middle-class conservative, while others view him as apolitical" (Manning, 1976, p. 13; Williams, 1986, p. 348).

The attractions and disagreements surrounding Goffman relate to different understandings of the *role* of this "unconventional" style of writing for making a particular comment on the social world. For example, is this "merely" a writing style or a critique of social inequalities? Burns (1992) advocates the former, viewing Goffman's "propensity for sardonic comment [. . .] is for the most part no more than an recurring undertone or an occasional throwaway remark" (Burns, 1992, p. 13). Manning (1976), other the other hand, argues that Goffman "conscientiously attacks" social conventions (Manning, 1976, p. 20):

> I believe that it is a conscious, deliberate choice of weapons by which to confront the fictional facades that constitute the assumptive reality of conventional society.
>
> (Manning, 1976, p. 19)

Therefore the task of unravelling Goffman's sociology is far from straightforward and abetted by Goffman's "tendency to make changes in centrality and definitions of concepts" and "almost systematic elusiveness" (Manning, 1976, p. 18). Similarly Willmott et al. (1979), in a comparative analysis of Berger and Goffman, set themselves the task of unravelling, what they term Goffman's "philosophical anthropology," in order "to expose the assumptions that inform it" (Willmott et al., 1979, p. 1). They concur with Manning (1976) that "in Goffman's case this is never explicit: it must be deduced from his comments about man's orientation to, and involvement in, social interaction" (Ibid.).

STYLE AS SUBSTANCE: GOFFMAN AND RESEARCHING SOCIAL INEQUALITIES

The secondary commentaries surrounding Goffman's sociology are generally split into two groups: the critics[5] and the admirers. The arguments of both camps are now evaluated in turn.

Fine (1999) identifies Goffman's focus lies with the interaction order and "the concern with how strangers are 'interpreted' and 'processed' in public situations is fundamental for Goffman" (Fine, 1999, p. 186). This very interactional focus, some argue, provides its own benefits:

> The popularity of the work of Goffman and Berger, it may be suggested, is very much related to their explication of their readers' everyday experiences and commonsense ideas about social life.
>
> (Willmott et al., 1979, p. 3)

Goffman uses the analogy of social life as a theatre (dramaturgy) suggest that appearances are presented or "staged." The seemingly mundane and banal interactions of everyday life, in this light, come to be highly significant. The very notion of the "presentation of self" and appearances can, simply, be just that has led Goffman's work has been argued to be cold and calculating. For, by implication, "irony is the footman/handmaiden of detachment" (Fine, 1999, p. 182). Hence Goffman's sociology comes to be viewed as distanced and lacking a critical bite by observing the interaction order and not a critique of its superficiality:

> According to Goffman, human action is non-alienated so long as it supports the prevailing consensus. By conceiving of alienation exclusively in terms of group cohesion, Goffman indicates that man is spared the experience of alienation so long as he gains the acceptance of others by sustaining the consensus.
>
> (Willmott et al., 1979, p. 2)

The contented social actor is the one able to "pass off" theirs as a presentable self. Willmott et al. (1979) critique goes further to reveal that Goffman's view of "real" consensus is merely "an optimistic ideal, and in any case not necessary for the smooth working of society" (Goffman, 1959, p. 20). In their view, it is the achievement of an ordered, rather than morally obliged, society that preoccupies

Goffman. The very identification of facework's role in the achievement of social interaction is too relativistic, even nihilistic, for Willmott et al. (1979):

> We describe the sociology of Goffman and Berger as cynical because it portrays social action as nothing more than the outcome of struggles to overcome meaningless and avoid social ostracism. Any conception of 'authentic action' or of a 'true self' is rendered illusionary by the revelation of the arbitrary and self-deceptive nature of social meanings.
>
> (Willmott et al., 1979, p. 2)

The implications of concentrating purely on face work and impression management, for some critics, is a denial of individual human agency:

> His sociology also provides continual witness to his acceptance of the inevitability of externally imposed order. Hence its omission of an essential constituent of the dilemma and of an adequate theoretical reflection of it – a serious concept of action and of an active, purposive, human agent.
>
> (Dawe, 1973, p. 250)

Goffman's sociology appears to deny the impact of structural forces upon action, whilst simultaneously presenting social actors as cultural dopes, than rational actors. However, there is amore profound social critique within his work if its conceptual implications are pursued:

> He claims that that which we take to be 'reality' [. . .] is quite simply the result of socialization within a given social structure. To this [. . .] he juxtaposes the weak, uncertain, somewhat befuddled human possessing the potential for humanity and dignity. Socialization, however, modifies humanity [. . .] *once we learn to accept conventional assumptions, and define events within that frame of reference, we lose a degree of humanity [. . .] We learn to accept what by a transcendental moral standard of judgement would be unconscionable*.
>
> (Manning, 1976, p. 19, emphasis added)

Here we come to see Goffman's dramaturgical sociology in a far more damaging light than the analogy between social life and the management of fronts. Goffman, rather, is suggesting that social life "actually a front, rather than merely *alike it* in certain respects. As a result, the need of the social actor to attend to their impression management becomes overwhelmingly compelling, for fear that their front will fail or be rejected:

> Berger and Goffman's voyeuristic revelation of our constructions and contrivances *appears* to debunk commonsense perceptions of social reality. Certainly, they highlight the relativity of belief and the presence of dramaturgical deceptions. However, in asserting the precarious nature of reality [. . .] the possibility of security is simultaneously rendered both problematic *and* obligatory.
>
> (Willmott et al., 1979, p. 4, original emphasis)

So here we see that accepting the importance of impression management has far deeper implications. The social actor begins to collude "in a working consensus that supports his [sic] social self. Once an attempt to secure identity is accomplished, security is primarily derived from the continuance of some form of attachment to social identity. Any threat to the maintenance of such an attachment is routinely perceived as a threat to self" (Willmott et al., 1979, p. 9). Rather than an image of the social actor able to actively select and control his own front, the situation rather becomes one in which the "cross of consistent characteristics" curtails alternative social identities.

The conclusion both Lofland (1980) and Williams (1986) ultimately draw in relation to Goffman's work is that his offers an existential sociology, in which "action is being: to engage in a particular type of activity is to be that kind of person, existence precedes essence" (Williams, 1986, p. 354). It is on this point that Goffman attracts the most severe criticism:

> Alienation is thus identified with the *faux pas* that disturb the working consensus. Goffman does not consider the possibility that dramaturgical conformity to the working consensus may *create* severe anxieties at the level of personal authenticity.
>
> (Willmott et al., 1979, p. 5, emphasis added)

In the eyes of his critics, Goffman offers only a superficial critique of social relations, which Goffman (1974) seemingly agrees with when he describes his is the business of watching people snore, rather than wakening class-consciousness. Alienation, within Goffman, becomes an entirely different with severe consequences:

> [In turning the] conception of alienation on its Marxian head, Goffman does not treat alienation as the devastating and debilitating experience of the automaton. Instead, he associates it with the failure to embrace social acceptance with cynical panache.
>
> (Willmott et al., 1979, p. 6)

It is as if to be alienation is merely to have failed to pull off a front, rather than to have been subjected to the fundamental inequalities present in social life.

The interpretation of Goffman considered to this point criticises his view of the individual and of society. The "person becomes a social construction – a manikin on which symbols can be hung – rather than a solid core that provides a basis for action" and any sense of social solidarity, which so concerned both Tönnies and Durkheim, is lost within a dramaturgical model concerned with facework (Fine, 1999, p. 187):

> Where Goffman departs from the Durkheim tradition is in his resolution of the tension between utility and morality [. . .] For Goffman, organic solidarity is denied by the manipulation of fronts; *contrived gestures provide a substitute for community; spontaneity is replaced by a conspiracy between members.*
>
> (Willmott et al., 1979, p. 12, footnotes 3, 4, emphasis added)

Ultimately, the critique here is that Goffman's is not a transformative model. He offers a commentary on the social world, rather than an agenda for change.

In the "absence of faith in the potential of human beings to transform the relationship between self and others" his denial of human and group agency appears complete (Willmott et al., 1979, p. 3). It is both cynical, disenchanted and "characterised in terms of self-interest, boredom, disappointment, oppression and precariousness. What Goffman and Berger provide is a developed articulation and, by default, *a theoretical legitimation of this condition* (Willmott et al., 1979, p. 3, emphasis added).

The dismissal of his approach, in this sense, seems epistemologically and irrefutably comprehensive. However, how have Goffman's many admirers dealt with the same issues that Dawe (1973) and Willmott et al. (1979) (to name but a few) find so problematic? In considering the success of Goffman's approach, the origins of his work in the nineteen sixties gains significance. In its historical context, his work's radicalism is better appreciated than from a contemporary perspective where the range of sociological inquiry had broadened so dramatically. As Fine (1999) reminds us, "the attitude that one brings to the work (and the expectation of the work as filtered through gatekeepers) affects one's evaluation" (Fine, 1999, p. 190).

Goffman's work can be placed in an historical period of "subversive writing, which became fashionable in the fifties. He explored pretension and embarrassment: the treatment accorded to the mentally handicapped, the defective and the mutilated, as well as the defensive strategies to which such persons resorted; failure, loss of face, and loss of dignity; and the vulnerability of everyday living and its underworld" (Burns, 1992, p. 14). In this sense, the topic Goffman chose for his attention directly engaged with instances where social actors are prone to failure, and consequently damage, in everyday facework and interaction. Manning (1976) argues this is vital to Goffman's sociology, for "one of his central concerns [is] the conditions [. . .] under which it is 'easy or difficult' to display, maintain, or retrieve a viable self" (Manning, 1976, p. 14). Goffman has therefore strategically selected the interaction order *because* it is the point at which success is won or lost and hence this is "where the action is."

Goffman's concern is not necessarily purely with the "underdog" *per se*, as fellow Chicagoan Howard Becker's work has often been perceived, but more generally "the 'common man' " and how he is constrained by those in authority (Manning, 1976, p. 14):

> With reference to the official self, Goffman is clear that they reside in roles. The concern with official and performing selves is, of course, clearest and most explicit in *Asylums* or more generally 'total institutions'. The papers on total institutions are documentations of the ways in which official selves are both attacked and laid on and of the ways in which performers deal with these assaults.
>
> (Williams, 1986, p. 354)

In this sense, Goffman is concerned with different conceptions of self. Therefore, the dramaturgical model is only *one* element of his analysis of social relations:

> The official self is conceived as existing apart from persons, persons only perform or play them out. The theatrical model is the most obvious rendition of the official self.
>
> (Williams, 1986, p. 353)

In addition, Goffman's work analyses the impact of institutional forces upon the self. *Asylums* (Goffman, 1961), for example, is seemingly about mental patients, but is actually about their keepers (Fine, 1999). Lofland (1980) unravels the layers of the conceptualisations of the individual within Goffman's work and finds three: the official self, the self-as-player and personal identity (or the conception of one's self). *This* is the distinction that allows the link between the self and a moral order to be made. People are attending, not only to their own needs, but also towards those of people around them. It is the very *ritual order* of interactional exchanges that imposes constraints upon the different conceptions of self Goffman identifies:

> Goffman's work undertakes to interpret everyday life as a 'ritual order' in which societies' central beliefs about the rights and character of persons are reaffirmed and revealed [. . .] people act in specific ways because of some hidden social constraint to do so. Society and its collective conscience, then, is not a big balloon in the sky, it is a deep, complex, moral arrangement in our everyday encounters, to help each other stage our personal realities.
>
> (Williams, 1986, p. 352)

The irony of Goffman's entire enterprise is his "stylized inversion" of the seemingly mundane everyday interactions becomes "the essence of social life. They should be considered as the empirical basis for constructing systematic social science" (Manning, 1976, p. 16). The task for Goffman is to expose seemingly assumed and taken-for-granted instances of interaction to be of rich, sociological importance. Goffman therefore established a new site of investigation for sociology, which he termed the interaction order (Goffman, 1983). Whilst there are connections between his concerns and those of his predecessors (which, again, is a point of some contention), his contribution lies in the linkages he made between what occurs in a social interaction, whilst holding a vision of a wider social system or structure:

> Goffman's work, like that of Simmel, Mauss and Durkheim, is an attempt to bridge situations and structures: his rendition of dramaturgical analysis interdigitates humanly-defined situations and rules in relation to social structure
>
> [. . .] *he attends to the primary quality of the situation as a structural entity.*
>
> (Williams, 1986, p. 351, emphasis added)

The challenge to establish the interaction order as a legitimate field for sociological investigation renders Goffman's choice of method particularly significant. That is, he is attempting to make visible social forms that are the invisible, because of their seeming normality. To borrow Simmel's metaphor, these are the hidden tissues of the everyday, organic working of social life. The techniques Goffman uses, of incongruous metaphors (social life as a drama, the psychiatric profession as the tinkering trades), can therefore be understood to be *strategic* in order to enable us to see otherwise. The metaphors are purposive, to extend the depth of our perceptions of social life, but also in the way they, in doing so, invite us to cast doubt over the order of things. Fine (1999) unravels the technique:

> Beyond irony lies satire – a trope that demands morality, exposing sham by extending it and taking it too seriously [. . .] In addition, humorous writing – irony and satire – is designed to *persuade* an audience [. . .] humour gains its power from the challenge that the author puts forth in a taken-for-granted world.
>
> (Fine, 1999, p. 182, original emphasis)

Therefore, we are able to see Goffman does attend to the contextual constraints upon face-to-face interaction and, in doing so, makes us a little nervous stripping away the very social forms we take as granted. We are shocked when people in officially sanctioned roles of authority, such as therapists, as revealed to act as agents of social control:

> People construct only a minimum working consensus, one which constrains interaction among team members situationally and reflects the authority of the interactants and the resources they can bring to bear upon actors who are discredited or whose performance is not accepted as legitimate.
>
> (Manning, 1976, p. 15)

Goffman progressively showed us the falsity and hypocrisy of social institutions and elites, by targeting power and significance of status symbols (Goffman, 1952), displays of public status (Goffman, 1979), the pressures and symbolisation of normality (Goffman, 1961). Therefore "Goffman's work is sensitive to 'structural' as well as 'situational' concerns and also to class, hierarchy and power" (Williams, 1986, p. 348). Goffman provides the focus (the microcosm) and method (satire, irony and perspective through incongruity) "to illuminate his view of the dynamics or the condition of the 'larger' social order" (Manning, 1976, p. 24). For Fine (1999), it is a highly complementary medium, in which Goffman's (and Veblen's) "analyses are given power, depth and resonance by the style in which they are put forward, the arguments are not only stylistic, but substantive" (Fine, 1999, p. 185).

The contribution of his sociology is recognised even by those who are generally critical, such as Willmott et al. (1979) who "*agree* with Goffman's thesis that in everyday life we do tend to manage fronts in order to maintain a working consensus" and that "certainly, the sociology of Goffman and Berger provides considerable insight into our experience of everyday life (Willmott et al., 1979, p. 7, emphasis added, 9). Whilst his methods failed to find merit in the eyes of one of his former students, they still saw "this was always a means to revealing some hidden and poignant truth. He offered a searing moral message regarding individual dignity" (Marx, 1984, p. 655).

The logic of Goffman's argument, Williams (1986) reminds, us is that "we should always be aware that his abiding concern was with the 'Interaction Order' and so consequently headings like structuralist and existentialist [. . .] must ultimately be seen as 'means' serving some higher goal for Goffman" (Williams, 1986, p. 354). However, Williams (1986) pays unequal attention to Goffman's early work to his final. In this final piece, Goffman (1983) offers an overview of the "Interaction Order." That is would prove so fruitful an area or something to which Goffman would be able to concentrate his entire career is a point he would have been able to foresee when he was writing *Presentation of Self in Everyday Life* (Goffman, 1959). It is the success of his cynical view of human nature as a phenomenon which is not to natural after all, that Goffman has come in recent years to viewed as a precursor to post modern analyses of society. The case FOR a postmodern reading of Goffman is now briefly entertained.

THE POSTMODERN GOFFMAN?

A wider view of Goffman's work, from which the moral critique of his work is appreciated sees that "Goffman's perspective ties together situation and structure: the rationalization of the world and the social psychology of the deracinated man" [sic] (Manning, 1976, p. 15). In this is a model of late modernity, echoing the loss of organic solidarity and therefore cohesion in Durkheim's sociology. However, the implications of Goffman's vision of social life connects with loss of centre or search for certainty in a mass society:

> Goffman's work, however, anything but a trivial or cynical exercise, shows just how fragile any social order is reveals to us the potential horror in a society where *the appearance of civility is just that*. [. . .] Goffman's writing contain a complex set of concepts relevant to the analysis of civility as well as a detailed depiction of the perplexing problems facing persons seeking self affirmation in mass society.
>
> (Williams, 1986, p. 349, emphasis added)

Whilst Goffman's own viewpoint and method is one containing a moral message, his portrayal of the social world is not positive and this aligns him with postmodern thought. That is, Goffman is negative in his vision, because he rejects the possibility of an absolute truth or standard. The seeds of this are visible in his use of dramaturgy:

> Goffman systematically argues against the utility of the quest for some standard against which truth or falsehood can be unequivocally judged. His view is that people's performances are judged not against absolute moral standards, but against relative standards such as the credibility of the performance given to a particular audience.
>
> (Manning, 1976, p. 19, footnote 8)

In this sense, the very conception of Goffman's work within interactional analysis comes under question, if the extreme implications are followed through to a relativistic stance. Whilst it is possible to recognise the postmodern themes within his work, there is enough evidence to draw back from re-positioning his work within the sociological traditions. The metaphor Manning (1976) employs to describe Goffman's balance between macro and micro concerns reveals that Goffman retains a central place for a core humanity:

> Goffman's rendition of dramaturgical analysis *interdigitates* humanly defined situations and rules in relation to social structure [. . .] to identify and illustrate the social significance of form of conduct, the symbolic cloaks in which we wrap ourselves [. . .] his less well-developed notion of a core of an abiding humanity shivering partially exposed 'beneath' these cloaks.
>
> (Manning, 1976, p. 15, original emphasis)

For Manning (1976), even Goffman's interest in structural concerns, such as the total institution, is used as a means through which the individual is shaped. This clashes with a postmodern system of thought, in which formal social arrangements and institutions are not see as concrete entities that offer individuals stability. The self in his later writing "becomes in later writings more a 'product' of 'social arrangement' than of others' imputations [. . .] The institution is seen as a foil *against* which a self is shaped" [original emphasis] (Manning, 1976, p. 17). Manning (1976) does not go as far as to suggest Goffman offers a consistent social theory of human action, rather he considers that "the task of testing, verifying, or establishing these notions (even if it were possible) would require a different sort of enterprise than that in which Goffman is engaged. A value of the work for sociology [. . .] lies [. . .] [as] a social critique and [. . .] [in] revealing the lacunae of arid and desiccated 'structural sociologies,' and the errors of excessive neoreductionism and mathematical hyperbole" (Manning, 1976, p. 23).

The importance of Goffman's legacy within interactionism seems secure for the moment. It is, nevertheless, vital to recognise his sociology is involved with critiquing "the consequences of the growth and erosion of Victorian morality are reflected in the moral chaos depicted in Goffman's sociology. Not solely a sociologist of middle-class life, Goffman is an appreciator and taxonomist of situations wherein he sees civility at issue" (Manning, 1976, p. 24). For it is here that we can understand postmodern themes emerge as "the class basis of society [. . .] erodes, many presumably "fixed" markers of social location vanish or are blurred (Manning, 1976, p. 24). In this, we can see Goffman "is a man of his time [but also] speaks eloquently and profoundly to our present conturbations" and that "his writing captures the changing tone of American life" (Manning, 1976, pp. 24, 13).

CONCLUSION

Goffman demonstrates one technique, which weds style to substance. For Goffman, the *method* becomes an essential part of the theoretical, or moral, *message*. The chapter has demonstrated that in Goffman's writings, more should be evaluated than his substantive argument, but also his rhetorical strategies – his very way of arguing. The chapter progressively revealed different visions of Goffman and attempted to correct misperceptions of Goffman's work as amoral and uncritical in order to propose that Goffman did indeed challenge 'hierarchies of credibility' and structural inequalities. His textual and rhetorical devices were a fundamental device in the achievement of delineating a new area for sociological investigation and the critical analysis of institutional and interactional systems of inequality.

The overarching intention of the chapter has not been to set Goffman up as a systematic model for future research. As noted by others, "Goffman sometimes rests his case with a series of definitions rather than analyses [. . .] and tends to present taxonomies and classification rather more than to seek to construct explanatory conceptual schema" and, therefore, following his conceptual thinking is highly problematic (Manning, 1976, p. 18). Goffman's contribution lies in the way its shows how a full understanding of his stance presents one way out of the cul-de-sac of the "narrative turn." That is, an appreciation of the rhetorical nature of ethnographic writing and argument, whilst maintaining a critical, theoretical agenda. The danger lies in misappropriating his sociology as a defence for new position. In doing so, the intrinsic connection between *rhetoric* and *theoretical critique* is lost:

> Intellectual fashions are dynamic, and, as fashions change, classic works acquire new meanings. [. . .] both Goffman and Veblen would acknowledge that intellectual objects [texts] are ultimately the basis for status claims and political dialogue for those with axes to grind [. . .] such a claim ultimately is a means by which audiences comfort and congratulate themselves in the toasty glow of 'classic' texts.
>
> (Fine, 1999, pp. 196, 197)

Goffman's sociology uses textual devices to great effect for his writing, but not as a means of moving towards a relativistic stance or epistemology. Unravelling the complexities of his approach, itself no straightforward task, can epistemologically ground his ideas and provides a more cognisant way to use his ideas to inform our own approaches towards researching inequalities. Goffman's contribution in this respect lies in his legitimising and new field of study and the pioneering method of "delineating the significance of the seemingly trivial objects consumed in our everyday life" (Fine, 1999, p. 185). The full implication and power of Goffman's new research area is recognised by Manning (1976):

> By tearing these items from one context and placing them in another, or, by contrast, making an absurdity of what appears to be quite 'reasonable;' he is reproducing for our appreciation the same process by which conventional society moulds, shapes, and in many cases dehumanizes powerless individuals. He consciously employs stark metaphors to show how brutally and inappropriately people are used in American society. If his rendition of the consequences of society's vicissitudes violates our sensibilities, which might (should) the experience produce for individuals who actually suffer them?
>
> (Manning, 1976, p. 20)

So hence, when we read Goffman, the depth of his critique, his style and social commentary becomes all the more richer and, hence, benefits our own perception into social and structural inequalities that characterise contemporary society:

> Among those who mingle with one another as colleagues in the profession of dentistry, it is possible to find some who have failed to become physicians and others who have succeeded at not becoming pharmacists or optometrists. No doubt there are few positions in life that do not throw together some persons who are there by virtue of failure and other persons who are there by virtue of success. In this sense, the dead are sorted but not segregated, and continue to walk among the living.
>
> (Goffman, 1952, p. 463)

NOTES

1. 19th November, 1982 (Williams, 1986, p. 367, Note 2).
2. There are two notable exceptions. Goffman (1989 [1974]) is an edited transcription of a conference presentation on research methods he had requested, as was his custom, not to be tape-recorded. Verhoeven (1993 [1980]) is an interview in which he offers reflections on his training at Chicago, but also refers to his approach and the status of his methods.
3. Lemert and Branaman (1997) offer the most accessible collection on Goffman, including both popular and neglected works, as well a catalogue of the extensive secondary literature surrounding Goffman's work.
4. Williams (1986) writes with particular reference to Gouldner (1970) and Dawe (1973).
5. Confusingly, some of Goffman's critics would also describe themselves as admirers of his work. However, for the purposes here, the division has been made on the basis of their commentaries on researching social inequalities.

ACKNOWLEDGMENTS

Thanks are due to the attendees who raised many questions and points at the Ethnography and Education conference, 2002, particularly to Bob Jeffrey for his perceptive comments and clarity of thought. David Clarke, of the Department of Psychology at the University of Nottingham, has been an outstanding source of insight into Goffman's life and work – and a great raconteur.

REFERENCES

Atkinson, P. (1989). Goffman's poetics. *Human Studies, 12*, 59–76.

Atkinson, P. (1996). *Sociological readings and re-readings*. Aldershot: Avebury.

Bennett, A. (1994). *Writing home*. London: Faber and Faber.

Burns, T. (1992). *Erving Goffman*. London: Routledge.

Craib, I. (1978). Erving Goffman: Frame Analysis. *Philosophy of the Social Sciences, 8*, 79–86.

Dawe, A. (1973). The underworld-view of Erving Goffman: Review Article. *British Journal of Sociology, 24*, 246–255.

Denzin, N., & Keller, C. (1981). Frame analysis reconsidered: Review essay. *Contemporary Sociology, 10*(1), 52–60.

Ditton, J. (Ed.) (1980). *The view from Goffman*. London: Macmillan.

Erwin, R. (1992). The nature of Goffman. *Centennial Review, 36*(2), 327–342.

Fine, G. A. (1999). Claiming the text: Parsing the sardonic visions of Erving Goffman and Thorstein Veblen. In: G. Smith (Ed.), *Goffman and Social Organisation: Studies in a Sociological Legacy*. London: Routledge.

Fine, G. A., & Martin, D. D. (1990). A partisan view: Sarcasm, satire and irony as voices in Erving Goffman's. *Asylums, Journal of Contemporary Ethnography, 19*(10), 89–115.

Fine, G. A., & Smith, G. W. H. (1990). *Erving Goffman*. London: Sage.

Gauntlett, D. (2001). http://www.theorycards.org.uk/card06.htm. Leeds, UK: Institute for Communication Studies.

Goffman, E. (1952). On cooling the mark out: Some aspects of adaptation to failure. *Psychiatry, 15*(4), 451–463.

Goffman, E. (1959). *The presentation of self in everyday life*. Harmondsworth: Penguin.

Goffman, E. (1961). *Asylums: Essays on the social of mental patients and other inmates*. Harmondsworth: Penguin.

Goffman, E. (1979). *Gender advertisements*. New York: Harper & Row.

Goffman, E. (1983). The interaction order. *American Sociological Review, 48*, 1–17.

Goffman, E. (1989 [1974]). On fieldwork. *Journal of Contemporary Ethnography, 18*(2), 123–132.

Gouldner, A. (1970). *The coming crisis of Western sociology*. New York: Basic.

Hammersley, M. (2000). *Taking sides in social research*. London: Routledge.

Hillyard, S. H. (1999). Goffman's reflexive imagination. In: G. Walford & A. Massey (Eds), *Studies in Educational Ethnography: Explorations in Methodology* (Vol. 2). Stamford, CT: JAI Press.

Lemert, C., & Branaman, A. (Eds) (1997). *The Goffman reader*. Oxford: Blackwell.

Lofland, J. (1980). Early Goffman: Style, substance, soul. In: J. Ditton (Ed.), *The View from Goffman*. London: Macmillan.

Manning, P. K. (1976). The decline of civility: A comment on Erving Goffman's sociology. *Canadian Review of Sociology and Anthropology*, *13*(1), 13–25.
Marx, G. T. (1984). Role models and role distance: A remembrance of Erving Goffman. *Theory and Society*, *13*, 633–648.
Mills, C. W. (1953). Preface. In: T. Veblen (Ed.), *The Theory of the Leisure Class*. New York: Anchor.
Stronach, I., & MacLure, M. (1997). *Educational research undone: The postmodern embrace*. Buckingham: Open University Press.
Strong, P. M. (1983). The importance of being Erving: Erving Goffman, 1922–1982. *Sociology of Health and Illness*, *5*, 345–355.
Verhoeven, J. (1993). An interview with Erving Goffman, 1980. *Research on Language and Social Interaction*, *26*(3), 317–348.
Williams, S. J. (1986). Appraising Goffman. *British Journal of Sociology*, *XXXVII*(3), 348–369.
Willmott, H., Knights, D., & Simm, J. (1979, January). A critique of Goffman and Berger's cynical sociology, University of Aston management centre. *Working Paper Series*, *122*.

SHOULD ETHNOGRAPHERS BE AGAINST INEQUALITY? ON BECKER, VALUE NEUTRALITY, AND RESEARCHER PARTISANSHIP

Martyn Hammersley

INTRODUCTION

There is a huge amount of social and educational research concerned with various kinds of inequality. Much of this research assumes that inequalities are a bad thing, even when it is solely concerned with providing information about the level and causes of inequalities of some particular kind.[1] Sometimes, however, this use of crude egalitarianism spills over into presentation of what can be read as practical value judgements. Ambiguity between factual conclusion and practical evaluation is frequently exploited, or at least allowed to prevail. As a result, evaluations seem to be expressed, and/or prescriptions for action proposed, with the implication that they are justified by research evidence. Yet, on its own, research evidence can rarely provide a sufficient justification for value conclusions (see Foster et al., 2000; Hammersley, 2003a). While on some occasions research evidence may be treated as pointing directly to value conclusions, there are always value premisses involved, as well as factual ones, and these will often be open to reasonable doubt and disagreement.

This tendency to present value conclusions as if they were research findings is especially common in qualitative research; and particularly that concerned with

---

Ethnographies of Educational and Cultural Conflicts: Strategies and Resolutions
Studies in Educational Ethnography, Volume 9, 25–43

ISSN: 1529-210X/doi:10.1016/S1529-210X(04)09003-5

educational inequalities (see Foster et al., 1996). Moreover, some qualitative researchers have explicitly declared that research should be partisan, this generally being taken to mean that it should side with the disadvantaged, the marginalised, or the underdog, and/or should resist dominant groups or "Power" itself.[2] In short, it is proposed that researchers oppose, challenge, and seek to eliminate inequalities. And, on the basis of this commitment, explicit presentation of evaluative and prescriptive conclusions is sometimes made an obligation; it is claimed that *not* to present such conclusions is to support the status quo (see, for example, Gitlin, 1994; Gitlin et al., 1989; Roman & Apple, 1989; Troyna & Carrington, 1989).

One of the sources to which advocates of partisanship among ethnographers sometimes appeal is Howard S. Becker's article "Whose side are we on?" (Becker, 1967). This article has routinely been read as declaring that researchers should be on the side of the underdog, of those at the bottom of what Becker refers to as the "hierarchy of credibility"; a hierarchy which determines whose views are likely to be taken as true, and which parallels hierarchies of power and social status. Yet this is not, in fact, the message of Becker's article, as the first half of this paper will explain. Moreover, it will be argued in the second half that partisanship – including opposition to "inequalities" – is undesirable in research.

BECKER MISREPRESENTED

I have shown at length elsewhere that the message of Becker's "Whose side are we on?" has typically been misinterpreted. While he has been portrayed as advocating researcher partisanship, despite his explicit disavowal of "value freedom" (Becker, 1967, p. 239) the methodological position he adopts in that article and elsewhere is close to a Weberian commitment to value neutrality (Hammersley, 2000, Chap. 3). The main part of Becker's article amounts to a sociological analysis of the conditions in which social researchers operate. He contrasts two types of condition, what he refers to as the non-political and the political situations. He argues that in both of these the researcher is likely to be accused of bias if he or she gives any credence to the views of those at the bottom of the credibility hierarchy. In the second – political – situation, where "the parties to the hierarchical relationship engage in organised conflict" (Becker, 1967, p. 241), the researcher will probably be accused of bias by both sides. Becker insists that, even in the face of such criticism, it is the responsibility of the sociologist to suspend acceptance of the credibility hierarchy, to explore the variety of views to be found within the context studied, and to assess their validity as sources of information about the world. In other words, the sociologist must be neutral in relation to the prevailing credibility hierarchy; and must be prepared to bear the charges of bias that will be made about his or her work as a result of this. The message here is that sociological researchers cannot avoid the danger of being labelled as partisan: it comes with the task.

Becker also acknowledges that the sociologist will probably be partisan in the sense of having more sympathy with some of those in the situation studied than with others. And, frequently, greater sympathy will lie with those at the bottom of the heap rather than those at the top. However, he insists that it is the duty of the researcher to follow rigorous procedures in order to try to avoid these sympathies biasing the research. He specifically warns against the danger of what he calls "sentimentality." He writes: "we are sentimental when we refuse, for whatever reason, to investigate some matter that should properly be regarded as problematic. We are sentimental, especially, when our reason is that we would prefer not to know what is going on, if to know would be to violate some sympathy whose existence we may not even be aware of. Whatever side we are on, we must use our techniques *impartially* enough that a belief to which we are especially sympathetic could be proved untrue" (Becker, 1967, p. 246; emphasis added).

Finally, Becker identifies a fundamental respect in which sociologists cannot avoid producing accounts that are partial, in the sense that they give attention to the views of some groups and not others. This is because the social canvas is simply too large.[3] He points out that:

> everyone has someone standing above him who prevents him from doing things just as he likes. If we question the superiors of the prison administrator, a state department of corrections or prisons, they will complain of the governor and the legislature. And if we go to the governor and the legislature, they will complain of lobbyists, party machines, the public and the newspapers. There is no end to it and we can never have a 'balanced picture' until we have studied all of society simultaneously. I do not propose to hold my breath until that happy day.
>
> We can, I think, satisfy the demands of our science by always making clear the limits of what we have studied, marking the boundaries beyond which our findings cannot be safely applied. [. . .] I refer to a [. . .] sociological disclaimer in which we say, for instance, that we have studied the prison through the eyes of the inmates and not through the eyes of the guards or other involved parties. We warn people, thus, that our study tells us only how things look from that vantage point – what kinds of objects guards are in the prisoners' world – and does not attempt to explain why guards do what they do or to absolve the guards of what may seem, from the prisoners' side, morally unacceptable behaviour.
>
> (Becker, 1967, p. 247)

In the final two pages of his article Becker makes quite clear that he believes the sole task of the researcher is to provide an accurate understanding of the phenomena being studied. He argues that in order to achieve this it is often essential to take account of the views of those who are at the bottom of the credibility hierarchy. However, he does *not* suggest that these views should be treated as more likely to be true than those of others. Even less does he propose that research ought to be designed to further their interests. In this respect, his position contrasts sharply, for example, with that of Harding (1992).

A more strident, and perhaps for that reason clearer, version of this position was presented around the same time by Ned Polsky, in a discussion of the need for criminologists to study crime and criminals from a value-neutral perspective. He writes:

> Many an anthropologist has been able to advance the state of knowledge only by keeping faith with people who radically transgress the moral norms of his society, that is, by refusing to turn-them-in to colonial officials and their cops, so I fail to see why the criminologist shouldn't do the same. Of course, if someone really wants to behave towards the savages as a missionary rather than as an anthropologist, if he really wants to be a superior sort of social worker or cop or therapist rather than a sociologist, there is no denying him this right; but at least let him own up to what he really is and stop fouling the waters of science with muck about 'the dual role of practitioner-researcher' [. . .] The social scientist has no business attempting to 'adjust' people to the moral norms of his society or any other.
>
> Max Weber, in emphasising that sociology must be value-neutral if it is to be genuinely scientific, long ago made the key distinctions between one's role as ordinary citizen and one's role as social scientist. Our allegedly sociological students of crime, however, have forgotten Weber's lesson if, indeed, they ever learned it.
>
> It is hard to blame them when they see other social scientists directly criticise Weber's fastidiousness about value-neutrality out of a gluttonous desire to have their cake and eat it, to be moralizers and scientists at once.
>
> (Polsky, 1971, pp. 141–142)

Further on, Polsky mentions a mode of sociological analysis, which he reports was suggested to him by Howard Becker, that "can prod us toward objectivity":

> [This] counterbalances the values of one's society – and the investigations by social workers or 'applied sociologists' of one's society – by using an 'anti-social' perspective, e.g. by viewing society as a 'problem' for the deviant rather than the other way round. Although the counterbalancing need not be restricted to criminology – one could, for example, sympathetically study the racist's 'problem' of how to check desegregation and increase racial discrimination – it is likely to have especially salutary effects there. This route to value neutrality I find adumbrated not in Max Weber's work but in Friedrich Nietzsche's *Genealogy of Morals*:
>
> It is no small discipline and preparation of the intellect on its road to final 'objectivity' to see things for once through the wrong end of the telescope; and 'objectivity' is not meant here to stand for 'disinterested contemplation' (which is a rank absurdity) but for the ability to have the pros and cons in one's power and to switch them on and off, so as to get to know how to use, for the advancement of knowledge, the *difference* in the perspectives and psychological interpretations . . . All seeing is essentially perspective, and so is all knowing. The more emotions we allow to speak on a given matter, the more different eyes we train on the same thing, the more complete will be our conception of it, the greater our 'objectivity'.
>
> (Polsky, 1971, pp. 143–144)[4]

What this extract makes clear is that, from the point of view of Becker and Polsky, the task of research is to produce sound knowledge of the social world; and both the principle of value neutrality and the Nietzschean "trick of the trade" (Becker,

1998) mentioned by Polsky are adopted in pursuit of that goal.[5] The credibility hierarchy is to be suspended not inverted, or at least only inverted temporarily for the purpose of "prodding us towards objectivity."

It is worth remembering that Becker and Polsky were writing at a time when there was very little social science work in the United States that was explicitly partisan in political terms, though there was much that took an implicit or explicit moral stance. And their writings – especially those of Becker – were an important stimulus to the "radical sociology" that emerged in the late 1960s and 1970s. However, along with Irving Louis Horowitz, Becker later criticised some of that radical sociology for putting politics before scholarship. What is required, he suggested, is not radical sociology but *good* sociology, arguing that the latter will have radical political implications and consequences (Becker & Horowitz, 1972). In short, while Becker and Horowitz, and Polsky, had Leftist political leanings, they insisted that research should *not* be designed to serve any political position. To make it do so, they insisted, amounts to deforming it; and, in fact, undermines its radical political potential.

Many recent qualitative researchers, including some in the field of education, have simply cited Becker in support of their arguments for partisanship, assimilating his quite different position to theirs (e.g. Mac an Ghaill, 1991; Troyna, 1995). As a result, they have misrepresented his views and have failed to take account of his arguments against partisan sociology. Moreover, it seems to me that the position adopted by Becker and Polsky is the correct one, in that they treat research as having only one immediate goal: the production of knowledge. (However, I think Becker is mistaken in believing that research has determinate political implications and consequences, "radical" or otherwise, see Hammersley, 1992, 2000). The upshot of this for investigations of educational inequalities is that, while the topic is an important one, there is no sense in which research ought to be opposed to such inequalities, with researchers challenging or aiming to eliminate them. And, in my view, the fact that much qualitative research in this field *is* partisan in this respect has had undesirable consequences.

QUALITATIVE RESEARCH AND EDUCATIONAL INEQUALITY

In Britain, the sociology of education was originally organised around the issue of social class inequalities in education, the focus being the impact of the 1944 Education Act (e.g. Floud et al., 1956). The methodological approach taken at that time was primarily a quantitative one, concerned with inputs to and outputs from the education system. In the late 1960s and early 1970s this approach was challenged, when qualitative research started to become dominant in the field. However, despite a stated concern by the "new sociologists of education" with "making" rather than "taking" research problems (Young, 1971), much of the qualitative work that has been done since then has continued to focus on educational inequalities. What has changed is the way these are theorised, and the *range* of inequalities brought into focus.

Where, under the guidance of the political arithmetic tradition, the primary concern had been with equality of opportunity to obtain a secondary education and its associated occupational benefits, research following in the wake of the new sociology of education has focused more on the role of schools in reproducing an unequal society. In other words, where previously schooling had been regarded as a progressive social force, now it is viewed to a large extent as a source of inequalities. In this context, both the official and the hidden curricula of schools were investigated; and their value was no longer taken for granted – indeed, a negative social function was often ascribed to them. Moreover, while there continued to be studies of social class inequality, for example concerned with the failure of the partial comprehensivisation of secondary schools to produce equality of opportunity (e.g. Ball, 1981), inequalities in terms of sex, race or ethnicity, and disability also began to be emphasised.

In this way, despite some important changes in orientation, inequality continued to be a dominant theme in educational research in Britain in the second half of the twentieth century. And this was despite the influence of symbolic interactionism and later of social constructionism. Indeed, it is striking that the radical theoretical orientation of these perspectives has rarely been applied to investigate how educational inequality came to be, and continues to be, constructed as a social problem.[6]

Now, there is no doubt that educational inequalities can be a genuine social problem, and that they ought to be addressed by research. Moreover, educational researchers have made a considerable contribution to recognising different kinds of inequality and to understanding their sources. However, the idea that it is the proper function of research to challenge or eliminate inequalities is false. And such an orientation has undesirable consequences: it increases the danger of bias, it exceeds the authority that research has, and it reinforces general cultural tendencies either to deny that value principles and judgements can be rationally appraised or to treat them as necessarily consensual once the effects of self-interest and ideology have been eliminated.

Encouraging Bias

It is important to be clear about the nature of bias. Having particular practical commitments or preferences does not, in itself, make a researcher biased. This is just as well, since all researchers will inevitably have such commitments and preferences. Moreover, there is even one practical commitment that is intrinsic to research, namely the pursuit of knowledge. Of course, to suggest that *this* commitment amounts to bias would make as little sense as claiming that someone in charge of recruitment to an organisation is biased because they have a commitment to equitable treatment of applicants. Rather, bias – at least in the form of motivated, systematic error (Hammersley & Gomm, 2000) – comes from commitment to some goal that is extraneous to research, in other words to some goal other than the production of knowledge.

Researcher bias can be conscious, but more usually will be below the level of consciousness. And it can go in a variety of directions, Right, Left, or Centre. However, the bias I am concerned with here amounts to a greater willingness to accept evidence documenting the existence of educational inequalities, or at least those believed to be inequitable, as against evidence which suggests equality or throws doubt on what was previously taken to be evidence for inequality.

An example of how this might occur is provided by Gillborn, when he argues that judgements of the validity of factual claims should take into account the differential costs of falsely accepting a knowledge claim or falsely rejecting it. He suggests that in the case of "the nature/nurture debate about 'intelligence' " the most sensible approach "is to assume no significant role for genetic heritability." This is because "if this belief is correct we avoid needlessly condemning countless young people to a second-class education and wasting incalculable human (and economic) potential. Alternatively, if the hypothesis is false we will have wasted resources on those who could not take full advantage. It is a value judgement that places human suffering and inequality against immediate economic concerns" (Gillborn, 1995, p. 60). What Gillborn proposes here might be a reasonable approach in practical policymaking.[7] However, it is not appropriate in the context of academic research, since policy recommendations do not follow automatically from factual conclusions. Moreover, to allow the assumed political implications or practical consequences of a particular knowledge claim to count in any assessment of its validity undermines the role that the research community should play in producing knowledge. Diversity in value commitments among researchers facilitates the elimination of error by forcing exposure of questionable taken-for-granted assumptions. Yet this process is blocked if, in response to criticism of their findings, researchers are allowed to refuse requests for further evidence on the grounds that they have simply adopted the factual conclusion that has the least damaging consequences from their own particular political perspective. Any research community which worked explicitly on this basis could not claim that it produces factual conclusions that are less likely to be false than those from other sources.

Elsewhere, some colleagues and I have documented in detail the existence of a bias towards "discovering" inequality in qualitative studies of educational inequalities (Foster et al., 1996). We argued that in this literature there is a tendency for evidence which could indicate discrimination on grounds of social class, sex, or "race" to be accepted at face value, and for questions raised about the validity or implications of such evidence to be dismissed. There is also a tendency to privilege the views of some groups against those of others; in other words, to invert rather than to suspend the conventional credibility hierarchy (Hammersley, 1998). We also noted a tendency to over-generalise conclusions about the existence of discriminatory orientations on the part of teachers, and to assume on very little evidence that discrimination is a key factor in producing social class, gender, or ethnic differences in educational outcomes. For example, it seems to be assumed that if an ethnic minority group does less well on average in outcome terms there must be discrimination against them within the education system (e.g. Gillborn & Gipps, 1996). Establishing the existence of inequalities, and showing their causes, is much more difficult than this approach implies; at least, if we are to produce evidence that would convince someone who did not already believe the knowledge claims we are making.

Exceeding the Authority of Research

While some ethnographers would deny that they claim any authority, such a claim is intrinsic to the pursuit of research, and especially to the publication of findings. If research could not offer greater likely truth than everyday beliefs or lay investigations, there would be no justification for it, and certainly no justification for its public funding. Authority, in this form, comes from expertise, rather than from official position. Indeed, even those who insist that the function of research is to "give voice" to the marginalised are claiming expertise and authority in determining who are marginalised and how their voices should be represented. Equally, those for whom the task of research is simply to subvert existing assumptions and social arrangements, or the social science knowledge they believe supports these, are claiming the expertise and authority to identify what needs subverting and to engage in that activity. Moreover, both these reformulations of the goal of research are parasitic on the existence of research as an institution devoted to the production of knowledge: if they were ever to destroy that institution they would destroy themselves.

There is nothing wrong, in principle, with claims to authority; and indeed they are a routine feature of everyday conversations, media discussions, etc. Here, they are often grounded in the speaker having witnessed some event, having a distinctive form of experience, being an occupational practitioner of a particular kind, and so on. What *is* wrong are false claims to expertise or authority, or claims to infallibility. All authority or expertise is limited, it is never all-encompassing. Thus, educational researchers can claim authority to produce factual knowledge – about what goes on in schools, colleges, and universities, for example – which is, on average, more likely to be true than knowledge claims from other sources. However, they cannot reasonably claim that the knowledge they produce is *always* more valid than that from other sources. Furthermore, they must be prepared to justify their conclusions by appeal to evidence, and also to provide information about how they carried out their research. Similarly, while researchers can reasonably claim to produce knowledge about the facts of what goes on in the education system, they *cannot* legitimately claim expertise, as *researchers*, about what is wrong or about what ought to be done. This is because the methodological procedures that researchers employ are only effective in relation to factual knowledge, and factual knowledge cannot, in itself, give us value conclusions.[8]

It is important to stress that for me, contrary to Weber, value conclusions are not outside the authority of social science because they are a matter of personal – and, in effect, irrational – choice. Rather, the point is that researchers, as researchers, do not have distinctive expertise for engaging in rational discussion about what is good and bad about the education system, and what should be done to improve it. Other people are equally well placed, and sometimes better placed, to do this. This is because, while research evidence is very relevant to such discussion, access to it is not limited to researchers; and, furthermore, it is not the only source of relevant factual information, practical experience is another. Moreover, as already noted, factual evidence, from whatever source, does not in itself validate value conclusions; and empirical researchers do not have distinctive expertise in appraising value judgements.[9] As a result, discussion of value issues – about what is right and wrong with the education system, or about particular policies or practices – must be open to equal participation by all, with no-one claiming general expertise.[10]

So, while educational researchers can claim fallible authority in relation to conclusions about the facts of what goes on in the education system, on the basis of research evidence, their authority does not extend to conclusions about whether what is going on is or is not desirable and what should be done about it. For this reason, researchers ought not to attempt to make their work serve educational or political goals directly; the sole goal of educational research is to produce factual knowledge relevant to educational policies and practices (see Hammersley, 2003b). To try to make it serve other goals, for example by drawing evaluative or prescriptive conclusions, is to exceed the authority of research; it is to extend the sociologist's role, in Polsky's words, to that of "missionary," "cop" or "social worker" (Polsky, 1971), or in Becker's terms to that of "moral entrepreneur" (Becker, 1973).

De-Valuation of the World

The final reason why a partisan commitment on the part of educational researchers to challenge educational inequalities is undesirable is that it discourages examination of value issues, and thereby leads to what we might call a de-valuation of the world. In other words, educational issues tend to be treated by researchers as if they were purely factual matters, and this encourages others to do the same. It reinforces a broader trend, often identified as characteristic of modernity, in which value judgements are regarded as either logically derivable from facts or as expressions of personality or mood that are beyond rational appraisal.[11]

This problem is illustrated by the way in which educational researchers use the word "inequality," and associated terms like "discrimination," "sexism," and "racism." It is very rare for any distinction to be drawn between inequality and inequity, yet the difference is profound.[12] An inequality is a factual matter: it is a difference between two phenomena, usually phenomena which can be ranked on the same scale. It may involve some category of person receiving more or less of something, achieving at a higher or lower level in some respect, etc., than some other category of person. By contrast, an inequity is an injustice, it amounts to a situation where someone has not been treated in a just way. Many inequalities are inequities, in terms of some value framework or other. But by no means all inequalities are inequities from all points of view, and some are not from any current point of view (for example, inequalities among students with blue and brown eyes). Moreover, not all inequities involve inequalities. The fact that girls have achieved at a higher level in English at 16-plus examinations since at least the 1960s cannot automatically be treated as inequitable, any more than can the fact that on average Chinese and Indian pupils currently seem to out-perform other ethnic groups, on average, in 16-plus examinations. Conversely, an equal distribution of resources to children with and without disabilities would not be equitable, on most definitions of equity – here we have an equality that is inequitable.

The failure to distinguish between inequalities and inequities is paralleled by the way in which the term "discrimination" is generally used. It is employed as a negative evaluation, as if what it represented were necessarily objectionable. It is against the background of this usage that allocation of unequal amounts of resource or opportunity to one category of person as against other categories on grounds of equity has come to be designated "*positive* discrimination." Yet, strictly speaking, discrimination, like inequality, is a factual matter. Whether it is good or bad is a separate question from whether or not it exists in a particular form in a particular situation.

All that research can do, then – though I would stress the importance of this contribution – is to describe and explain situations, processes, policies, etc., that are inequitable or discriminatory in some respect, *from the point of view of a given value framework*. In other words, any evaluations researchers put forward must be presented as conditional on acceptance of the particular framework employed, and without any suggestion that research can validate that framework.

The same problem arises, in a rather different way, with terms like "racism" and "sexism." These are even more obviously evaluative than "inequality" and "discrimination." What counts as racism or sexism depends on the definition of those terms employed; and which definition is appropriate is not something that research can determine – it depends on value judgements about what is and is not just. Yet these terms are used as if they referred to facts in the world that are open to identification by research; often with the confusing effect that, for example, racism is portrayed as the cause of racism.

What we have in the way these various terms are commonly used, then, is a confusion of fact and value, in which it appears that research can come to value conclusions. One effect of this is to obscure the point that there is more than one value framework in terms of which inequalities can be judged. Moreover, these different frameworks are not cultural incommensurables; indeed, they are often used by the same person on different occasions.

To illustrate, let us take a case where inequalities are found in the number of reprimands made by a teacher against black and white pupils in a class. Whether or not this is an inequity, and what type of inequity it is, depends on the value framework adopted, as well as on the facts of the matter. Indeed, the value framework determines what are and are not relevant facts. One could view it as an inequity in terms of distributional justice: that black pupils are being assigned more negative feedback on their behaviour by comparison with white pupils. However, probably more appropriate in this case would be the rather different framework of a retributive conception of justice. Here, we would need to know about the teacher's response to the same type or level of misdemeanour on the part of black and white pupils. Two factual questions need to be addressed: do the teacher's responses to different levels and types of misdemeanour match some specified definition of retributive justice?; and, if there is deviation from this ideal, does it show a bias against one or other category of pupil? On this retributive interpretation of justice, it is, of course, quite possible that despite differential frequency of reprimands in relation to "race," there is no inequity, or even that white pupils are being treated inequitably. Alternatively, we could well find that the discrimination against black pupils is even more severe than it originally appeared.

Furthermore, note that both distributional and retributive conceptions of justice are deontological: they specify the right to equal treatment in terms of some standard of fairness. An alternative, consequentialist, value framework could also be adopted. This would be concerned, for instance, with the *effects* of reprimanding or not reprimanding pupils. In these terms, even a tendency to reprimand one category of pupils less than another could be interpreted as unfair to that category, if it meant that their unacceptable behaviour was not being corrected, and as a result their chances of academic achievement were worsened compared to other groups.[13]

It is also worth pointing out that not only are there multiple interpretations of equity, but equity is not the only important value. Indeed, it is a value that cannot operate in isolation from other values: it concerns the allocation of some substantive good – such as education, welfare, future employment prospects, or fair treatment of deviance. And we cannot assume that provision or pursuit of each of these goods will always be fully compatible with one another, or with achieving equity; any more than achieving equity in one sense or respect will always be compatible with achieving it in others. Another lesson we can learn from Nietzsche is that there is no pre-ordained harmony of values; indeed, they will often be in severe conflict. It is this post-Enlightenment insight that lies at the heart of Weber's doctrine of value neutrality.

In summary, researchers focusing on educational inequalities often write as if all inequalities were inequities, and all equalities were equitable. More seriously, they write as if the inequalities they are discussing are *obviously* inequities and therefore in need of remedy. Furthermore, they treat "equality" as if it were the only or most important value, when in fact there are always competing values. And the result of not taking the diversity of value frameworks into account is that the value assumptions adopted remain implicit, the impression being given that what is produced is the only value-relevant account that could be given of the situations documented. Moreover, where (explicitly or implicitly) studies move beyond reporting factual findings about value-relevant inequalities to making claims about *inequities*, the result is the illegitimate promotion of some value interpretations at the expense of others. This is illegitimate, for two reasons. First, because it presents one value judgment as if it were scientifically validated compared with others, when research on its own cannot provide such validation. Secondly, it presents a value judgement without the supporting argument necessary to indicate why it is the most appropriate in the circumstances. Interestingly, this is analogous to the colonisation of the lifeworld by technical rationality of which Habermas and others have complained (see Habermas, 1984–1987), and to which one would have thought qualitative researchers would be especially sensitive.

Taking an even more radical position than Habermas in this respect, a number of other writers have argued that it is characteristic of modernity that value questions are treated either as merely irrational matters or as if they could be answered definitively by research.[14] Much qualitative research on educational inequalities perpetrates the latter myth, even when it denies any claim to science. Moreover, this leads to a failure to recognise value pluralism or to acknowledge that policymakers, practitioners, political activists, and citizens need to engage in value clarification, deliberation and discussion. Instead, the impression is given that what is right and wrong, better or worse, and what ought to be done, can be properly determined by research evidence.[15]

It is worth emphasising that what Habermas criticises as the colonisation of the lifeworld by a scientistic emphasis on technique continues to be influential. It is currently exemplified in the movement for evidence-based policymaking and practice. However, as I have indicated, I believe that the problem extends more widely than this, and takes in the "critical" tradition of research. Central to that tradition has been the idea that there is a single all-encompassing and harmonious set of ideals built into human social life, at least as a potential. This was explicit in the early writings of Marx, but became submerged in his later work; and continues to be implicit in much recent "critical" research in education and the social sciences. Moreover, this image is utopian, in the sense that it is a vision of a perfect society in which all of the problems that currently plague humanity are resolved.[16] Now the result of adopting such an ideal as the only standard of evaluation is that it will always lead to the conclusion that there is a very great deal wrong with the world. Furthermore, if one distrusts any sign of progress as reflecting the cunning of capitalism, sexism, or racism – as some critical researchers seem to do – then there will be a tendency to reach the conclusion that society is beyond redemption, or that worthwhile change can only be realised by a necessarily painful process of fundamental destruction and reconstruction. Yet, in fact, this ideal society could never be realised because human values are often in tension with one another; and, even if this were not so, we would probably never have the resources to satisfy them all.

In the field I am concerned with there, this "critical" orientation involves a focus on identifying inequalities against the background of an implicit ideal in terms of which all inequality, or at least all inequity, is abolished. Yet, it is in the very nature of inequality, and perhaps even of inequity, that this can never be achieved. Any equality in one respect implies inequality in another. Moreover, it is not clear that the various different interpretations of equity could ever all be achieved simultaneously, nor is it obvious how we could prioritise them in a rational way in abstract terms (see Hammersley, 1997). This means that more subtle, and explicit, evaluation is required of where progress has been made, and in what terms, or of where there has been growing inequity of particular kinds. This may still lead to a depressing sense of the incorrigibility of humanity, and to discouragement about the prospects for substantial improvement. But even if it does so, it should not lead us to reject present society as wholly discredited, in the way that Critical Theory encourages; in much the same manner as older religious utopianisms, some of which are unfortunately still current, in the shape of various kinds of fundamentalism (see Löwith, 1949). Rejecting the whole of current and past society as mere pre-history, as a precursor to some utopian new age, is irrational; whether in its older Marxist form, in its pessimistic Critical Theory version, or in the more coy post-structuralist or postmodernist manner of urging openness to "the other." And relying implicitly on some such notion in doing research about educational inequalities is likely to encourage not just distortion of research but also a false sense of the role of values in the world.

CONCLUSION

I began this chapter by discussing Becker's article "Whose side are we on?", noting that it is often wrongly treated as supporting researcher partisanship: as advocating the commitment of researchers to goals other than the pursuit of knowledge. In the second part of the paper, I discussed the way in which some ethnographers studying educational inequalities have assumed a partisan orientation, either implicitly or explicitly. They have tended to assume that inequalities are inequitable, for the most part drawing no distinction between equality, a factual matter, and equity, a matter of value judgement. I suggested that this has led to several undesirable consequences: a bias towards "discovering" inequality where the evidence for it is weak; a misuse of the authority of research; and a reinforcement of a widespread tendency to de-value the world.

Let me conclude by summarising the conception of research on which my criticisms are based. It is one that was largely taken for granted in the middle of the twentieth century, though rarely fully understood or adopted effectively. And it is one that is widely misunderstood today. It relies on the principle of value neutrality put forward by Weber. That term, like "value freedom," is an unfortunate one in some ways. It is often taken to imply the belief that research should be, and therefore can be, unaffected by values. And since this is clearly impossible, the principle of value neutrality is often dismissed as ideological, as disguising the values that actually inform a researcher's work. Yet this is a misreading of Weber that is as wide of the mark as the misreading of Becker's article I discussed earlier.[17]

For Weber, value neutrality is an ideal that researchers ought to strive to realise; it requires that values other than truth not be allowed to deflect research from its proper course – for example so as to avoid conclusions that are politically unpalatable.[18] As an ideal, it does not need to be fully realisable, even less to be known to have been fully realised. Furthermore, the influence of values other than truth is only ruled out insofar as it has negative consequences for the pursuit of knowledge; and even then subject to ethical limitation.[19] Background assumptions and values will often lead to interpretations of data that are true rather than false; they need not always be obstacles.

For Weber, commitment to the principle of value neutrality – to the production of knowledge as the only immediate goal and to rational pursuit of that goal – is intrinsic to academic research. We may choose to be researchers, or to investigate a particular topic, because of our political values. But once we embark on inquiry those values must not lead us astray from our obligation as researchers to maximise the chances of producing sound knowledge, or at least to minimise the chances of producing false conclusions. Furthermore, we must not make excessive claims for what research can deliver: it cannot supply infallible knowledge, nor can it tell us what is good or bad, or what is to be done, in terms of policy and practice.

At the present time, when there is so much talk about "evidence-based" policy-making and practice, it is crucially important that the limits to what research can provide, and the need for distinguishing factual and value questions, are recognised.[20] For researchers to exceed those limits, and to run these different types of consideration together, is not only to damage research but also to do a disservice to the democratic deliberation of public issues. Of course, value-loaded descriptions and explanations may often be more welcome to audiences who share the values concerned than carefully qualified factual accounts. But it is a responsibility of researchers to respect the distinction between facts and values, and to recognise the plurality of value frameworks that can inform discussions of policy and practice in the public sphere. If *they* do not do this, who will?

NOTES

1. This has long been true. See, for example, the introduction to Beteille (1969), and many of the articles contained in that book. This is one aspect of a more general confusion between social and sociological problems.

2. These are not, of course, the only forms that researcher partisanship could take. Furthermore, the arguments used to justify partisanship provide no basis for ruling out what might be regarded as more objectionable forms, such as those motivated by nationalism or racism, see Hammersley (2000, Chap. 1).

3. This relates to an important confusion regarding the notion of objectivity, one of the key meanings of that term being identical with Weber's usage of "value freedom." It is sometimes thought that "objectivity" implies a single "view from nowhere" that portrays everything exhaustively as it truly is. However, this is not essential, or defensible. There

can be multiple objective views of the same scene, each focusing on different features. It is frequently said that these views are *partial*, or that they capture different *aspects* of the scene, but there is a danger with such formulations: that they are taken to imply that such partial views are deficient because there is a single, "total" perspective which incorporates all aspects.

4. Polsky does not cite a translation (it may be his own) or a page number for the Nietzsche quote. However, it comes from the third essay of *On the Genealogy of Morality*, entitled "What is the meaning of ascetic ideals?", and occurs in section 12 of that essay. For what is in some respects a more illuminating translation than this one, see that of Diethe in Nietzsche (1994, p. 92). Note 4 above sketches the form of perspectivism to which Nietzsche was probably committing himself in this passage; though we should note that, as with Becker, there seems to be a residual belief in the possibility of a "complete" representation.

5. It is clear from what they write that Becker and Polsky are not prepared to go very far with perspectivism; but then, as this quote from "the anti-christ" himself indicates, Nietzsche did not consistently propose a simple relativism or scepticism, see Clark (1990).

6. For such an application, see Foster et al. (1996, Chap. 1). For discussion of the role of social constructionism in the study of social problems more widely, see Holstein and Miller (1993).

7. It should be said, though, that while taking account of the likely costs of different sorts of error is certainly a sensible consideration in practical decision-making, Gillborn's particular weighing of the costs on each side here is not very convincing. He assumes that providing different types of education for those judged to be of different intelligence can only amount to giving some a second-class education. He also neglects the fact that any resources saved by providing different sorts of education could be used to eliminate other sorts of suffering.

8. Methodological procedures can maximise the likely validity of conclusions only because research has a single immediate goal; pursuit of that activity can be evaluated in relation to this goal in a fairly determinate way that is not possible where activities involve combinations of goals. See Hammersley (forthcoming).

9. It might be argued that philosophers have such expertise. However, they do not have distinctive expertise in relation to handling empirical evidence. Furthermore, there is a difference between expertise in clarifying the implications of particular value principles and determining which are relevant principles in evaluating any particular case and what the priority should be amongst them in that case.

10. The situation is complicated by the fact that people have multiple identities. Thus, many educational researchers are also teachers (of one kind or another). However, this does not give such researchers any general authority since there are many teachers who are not researchers (as well as some educational researchers who are not teachers, in at least some senses). Furthermore, we might wish to distinguish between expertise in different fields of educational practice, at the very least in crude terms between teaching experience in primary, secondary, and tertiary education. On top of this, there are many other roles in relation to education that can provide practical expertise of one kind or another, including those of parent and pupil.

11. In terms of the latter position, it is often said that "everyone has a right to an opinion," with the implication that any attempt to appraise opinions must be viewed as an infringement of that right, or at least as simply another person's exercise of *his or her* right to an opinion. Such an argument undermines the possibility of rational opinion formation.

12. An exception is Gewirtz et al. (1995) book *Markets, Choice and Equity in Education*. They not only refer to equity as well as to equality/inequality but also distinguish between different interpretations of equity: between "desert-based" and "needs-based" conceptions. However, in the body of their book they continue to write as if inequality necessarily implied inequity, see the discussion in Foster et al. (2000, p. 217).

13. Of course, there are factual assumptions involved here: to the effect that reprimands correct behavioural tendencies (as well as value assumptions about what is and is not unacceptable behaviour). If, by contrast, one adopts the labelling theory of deviance, reprimands will be judged more likely to amplify rather than to deter future deviance. This illustrates how any value judgement depends on a *combination* of factual and value assumptions. There is a further complexity too: it is very likely that, in principle, any reprimand in a given situation would have a range of potential effects, across the spectrum from deterrence to amplification, varying according to stable, or perhaps even temporary, characteristics of the pupils concerned (see Gomm, 2001, p. 184). As a result of this, the same treatment may have differential consequences for different pupils. For all these reasons, coming to conclusions about what is and is not fair can be quite complicated.

14. The key examples are Leo Strauss and Alasdair MacIntyre, see, for example, Strauss (1953) and MacIntyre (1981).

15. Even before Habermas, Strauss, or MacIntyre, Weber pointed to the dangers of science exceeding its authority and stressed the importance of value clarification, see Bruun (1972).

16. Blumenberg (1983) argues that this arises from a tendency for modern ideals to "re-occupy" the position of medieval ideals, in this case the Christian salvation story.

17. For an excellent brief discussion of this aspect of Weber's position, see Keat and Urry (1975, Chap. 9). See also Bruun (1972).

18. Thus, Polsky notes that in one chapter of his book he "reports conclusions about highly erotic art that seem to be inescapable as a sociologist but that I personally regret having to report – because they give ammunition to censors, whom I detest" (Polsky, 1971, p. 143).

19. What I mean by "ethical limitation" is that while other values than truth should not be the immediate goal of inquiry, they *will* place limits on how that goal is pursued.

20. All value issues involve subordinate factual questions, but factual issues do not involve subordinate value questions. This is the case even though the pursuit of factual knowledge is based on commitment to the value of knowledge.

REFERENCES

Ball, S. J. (1981). *Beachside comprehensive: A case-study of secondary schooling*. Cambridge: Cambridge University Press.

Becker, H. S. (1967). Whose side are we on? *Social Problems*, *14*, 239–247.

Becker, H. S. (1973). *Outsiders* (2nd ed.). New York: Free Press.

Becker, H. S. (1998). *Tricks of the trade*. Chicago: University of Chicago Press.

Becker, H. S., & Horowitz, I. L. (1972). Radical politics and sociological research: Observations on methodology and ideology. *American Journal of Sociology*, *78*(1), 48–66.

Beteille, A. (Ed.) (1969). *Social inequality*. Harmondsworth: Penguin.

Blumenberg, H. (1983). *The legitimacy of the modern age*. Cambridge MA: MIT Press. (Translation of the 1976 edition, originally published in German.)

Bruun, H. H. (1972). *Science, values, and politics in Max Weber's methodology*. Copenhagen: Munksgaard.

Clark, M. (1990). *Nietzsche on truth and philosophy*. Cambridge: Cambridge University Press.

Floud, J., Halsey, A. H., & Martin, F. M. (1956). *Social class and educational opportunity*. London: Heinemann.

Foster, P., Gomm, R., & Hammersley, M. (1996). *Constructing educational inequality*. London: Falmer.

Foster, P., Gomm, R., & Hammersley, M. (2000). Case studies as spurious evaluations: The example of research on educational inequalities. *British Journal of Educational Studies*, *48*(3), 215–230.

Gewirtz, S., Ball, S. J., & Bowe, R. (1995). *Markets, choice and equity in education*. Buckingham: Open University Press.

Gillborn, D. (1995). *Racism and antiracism in real schools*. Buckingham: Open University Press.

Gillborn, D., & Gipps, C. (1996). *Recent research on the achievements of ethnic minority pupils*. London, Office for Standards in Education: HMSO.

Gitlin, A. (Ed.) (1994). *Power and method: Political activism in educational research*. New York: Routledge.

Gitlin, A., Siegel, M., & Boru, K. (1989). The politics of method. *International Journal of Qualitative Studies in Education*, *2*(3), 237–253.

Gomm, R. (2001). Would it work here? In: R. Gomm & C. Davies (Eds), *Using Evidence in Health and Social Care*. London: Sage.

Habermas, J. (1984–1987). *The theory of communicative action* (Vols 1 and 2). Cambridge: Polity Press. (First published in German in 1981.)

Hammersley, M. (1992). *The politics of social research*. London: Sage.

Hammersley, M. (1997). Educational inequalities. Block 5, Unit 1, Open University Course *EU208 Exploring Educational Issues*. Milton Keynes: Open University.

Hammersley, M. (1998). Partisanship and credibility: The case of anti-racist educational research. In: P. Connolly & B. Troyna (Eds), *Researching 'Race' in Educational Settings*. Buckingham: Open University Press.

Hammersley, M. (2000). *Taking sides in social research*. London: Routledge.

Hammersley, M. (2003a). Research as emancipatory: The case of Bhaskar's critical realism. *Journal of Critical Realism*, *1*(1), 33–48.

Hammersley, M. (2003b). Can and should educational research be educative? *Oxford Review of Education*, *29*(1), 3–25.

Hammersley, M. (forthcoming). Should social science be critical? *Philosophy of the Social Sciences*.

Hammersley, M., & Gomm, R. (2000). Bias in social research. In: M. Hammersley (Ed.), *Taking Sides in Social Research*. London: Routledge.

Harding, S. (1992). After the neutrality ideal: Science, politics and "strong objectivity". *Social Research*, *59*(3), 568–587.

Holstein, J. A., & Miller, G. (Eds) (1993). *Reconsidering social constructionism: Debates in social problems theory*. New York: Aldine de Gruyter.

Keat, R., & Urry, J. (1975). *Social theory as science*. London: Routledge & Kegan Paul.

Löwith, K. (1949). *Meaning in history*. Chicago: University of Chicago Press.

Mac an Ghaill, M. (1991). Young, gifted and black: Methodological reflections of a teacher/researcher. In: G. Walford (Ed.), *Doing Educational Research*. London: Routledge.

MacIntyre, A. (1981). *After virtue*. London: Duckworth.

Nietzsche, F. (1994). *On the genealogy of morality*. Cambridge: Cambridge University Press. (First published in German in 1887.)

Polsky, N. (1971). *Hustlers, beats and others*. Harmondsworth: Penguin.

Roman, L. G., & Apple, M. W. (1989). Is naturalism a move away from positivism? Materialist and feminist approaches to subjectivity in ethnographic research. In: E. Eisner & A. Peshkin (Eds), *Qualitative Inquiry: The Continuing Debate*. New York: Teachers College Press.

Strauss, L. (1953). *Natural right and history*. Chicago: University of Chicago Press.

Troyna, B. (1995). Beyond reasonable doubt? Researching "race" in educational settings. *Oxford Review of Education*, *21*(4), 395–408.

Troyna, B., & Carrington, B. (1989). Whose side are we on? Ethical dilemmas in research on "race" and education. In: R. G. Burgess (Ed.), *Ethics in Educational Research*. Lewes: Falmer.

Young, M. F. D. (1971). Introduction. In: M. F. D. Young (Ed.), *Knowledge and Control*. London: Collier-Macmillan.

ICT AND EDUCATIONAL (DIS)ADVANTAGE: CULTURAL RESOURCES AND THE DIGITAL DIVIDE

Lawrence Angus, Wendy Sutherland-Smith and Ilana Snyder

INTRODUCTION

Because access to new technologies is unequally distributed, there has been considerable discussion in Australia and elsewhere about the growing gap, the "digital divide," between the information-rich and information-poor (Bolt & Crawford, 2000; Castells, 2001; Companie, 2001; Gordon, 2001; Haywood, 1998; Negroponte, 1996; Nixon, 2001). Most schools have incorporated computers and Internet access into classrooms, partly in response to concerns about the gap between technology "haves" and "have nots" (Facer et al., 2001). Such concerns have led to high-profile information technology policy initiatives in the USA (Lentz, 2000; US Department of Commerce, 1999), U.K. (Selwyn, 2000), Australia (Foster, 2000) and other nations. Many families have invested in computer systems at home in order to provide their children with access to the growing body of information available through technology. Similarly, in an attempt to "redress the balance between the information rich and poor" by providing "equal access to the World Wide Web" (Virtual Communities, 2002),

Ethnographies of Educational and Cultural Conflicts: Strategies and Resolutions
Studies in Educational Ethnography, Volume 9, 45–66

ISSN: 1529-210X/doi:10.1016/S1529-210X(04)09004-7

the Australian Council of Trade Unions (ACTU), Virtual Communities (a computer/software distributor) and Primus (an Internet provider) in late 1999 formed an alliance to offer relatively inexpensive computer and Internet access to union members in order to make "technology affordable for all Australians" (Virtual Communities, 2002).

Drawing on a year-long, Australian Research Council supported study, this article examines the social circumstances of four families who accepted the Virtual Communities offer and acquired relatively low-cost computers for use in their homes. We acknowledge that "family" can be defined in many ways. In this research we investigated four nuclear families: one in which there is a single parent, the mother, and two children; one in which the heterosexual parents of one child are divorced; one refugee family in which the married, heterosexual parents have two children and, and one family in which the professional, married, heterosexual parents have two children. In the main study, the research team also elicited teachers' attitudes to the use of ICT in the schools that the participating children attended. Our aim was to find out how the technologies were used formally and informally in both school and home settings. We wished to examine the nexus between students' use of ICT in the home, referred to by Sefton-Green as "the digital bedroom" (2001, p. 164) and the school. In this paper, we wish to contribute to broad discussion about whether information technology can be used to "empower the information disadvantaged" (Companie, 2001, p. 11) and thereby make a difference to "the digital underclass" (Bell, 2001, p. 13).

It has long been assumed that families and family life have been affected over time by the various waves of "new" media such as radio, television, video recorders, computers, multimedia and the internet (Van Rompaey et al., 2002). The extent of use of relatively new information and communication technologies, for example, has been linked particularly with SES and education levels (Livingstone, 1999), although gender is also said to influence uptake of ICT in that men are likely to make the decisions to purchase the hardware and use it (Hellman, 1996). It also appears that when and if a family does decide to purchase new ICT, "it anticipates the effects that [such purchase] is likely to have on family life and the question of what is likely to be best for the children, in order to help prepare them for future careers and workplaces, is one that is frequently posed" (Van Rompaey et al., 2002, p. 190). It is also held that the "rapid diffusion and uptake of the Internet has been phenomenal" (Holloway, 2002, p. 51) compared with earlier media technologies such as telephone and television. In its latest survey on this matter in February 2001, the Australian Bureau of Statistics (ABS, 2001) estimated that in Australia computer usage is increasing in all socioeconomic sectors. The ABS anticipated that by the end of 2001 it was likely that every second household in Australia would have Internet access (ABS, 2001). As might be expected, higher levels of both computer and Internet access occur in households with higher incomes. Access is also higher in households with children under 18 years, and in metropolitan areas. In terms of gender, there are very small differences between adult male and female computer and Internet usage (ABS, 2001).

The rate and extent of uptake of ICT are said to be related to the bursting "new economies" (Garham, 2000), which are forms of "knowledge economy" (Brown, 1999; Garham, 2000) that are related to the "information society" (Facer et al., 2001). Indeed, so strong is the "rhetoric of inevitability" (Facer et al., 2001, p. 92) associated with the information age that Lacroix and Tremblay (1997) conclude: "It is as if there were only two possible kinds of future societies: information societies (the most modern and avant-garde) and the others, those that did not bite the information bullet and which will be condemned to underdevelopment." For governments, biting the information bullet has included promotion of educational policies in which educational institutions become "core institutions of capitalism" (Garham, 2000, p. 142) in order that the nation will remain, or become, internationally competitive in the global knowledge economy. According to this line of argument, the children of the digital generation (Papert, 1996) must be given access to the "information" in order to be future workers in the knowledge economy (Facer et al., 2001). So there are two particular concerns in countries like Australia about the digital divide: that people without access to the new technologies will not be part of the new economy/ knowledge economy/information age and will left behind; and that people will need ICT access in the new economy in order for the nation to be internationally competitive. That is, while individuals and families, particularly those already disadvantaged in terns of education and income, are at risk of "increasing their disadvantage through lack of access or skills to use this new technology" (Holloway, 2002, p. 56), then the nation is at risk of having insufficient trained human capital in the information age. The current policy assumption is that, like other differences between society's "haves" and "have nots," the lack of access to ICT can have negative effects on one's economic and social livelihood. This would imply that those who are "at risk" in terms of the ICT stakes are likely to suffer from other equity issues as well. In Australia, however, research on the digital divide has "has focussed on the divide that exists between non-metropolitan and metropolitan areas" (Holloway, 2002, p. 64).

There is a minority view that the vision of the information society and knowledge economy "bears little, if any relation, to any concretely and graspable reality" and therefore serves as an "ideology" (Garham, 2000, p. 140). Garnham claims that "rather than serving to enhance our understanding of the world in which we live, [such terms are] used to elicit uncritical assent to whatever dubious proposition is being out forward beneath [their] protective umbrella." The importance of young people being ICT literate, which is put forward in this view as inevitable, necessary and exciting, is therefore argued to be either simply hype or the assertion of particular capital interests. In criticising the hype, the view is sometimes put that the "digital divide" is not worth worrying about because it will soon heal itself because the technology, which is already spreading at a furious rate, is becoming increasingly cheaper and more efficient and more easily available (Companie, 2001). In terns of economic and political interests, the arguments are more complex. The central point, however, is the claim that increasing the availability of and access to ICT and the Internet will not solve the problems of the digital divide because the divide is caused by reasons of differences of culture, education, literacy, opportunity and social power as much as gaps in ownership of hardware and software. The divide, in other words, is closely related to same socio-political divide that influences the nature and quality of access to education, health services, wealth and power. The fact that, despite decreasing costs of digital access, the people who seem to gain "value" from it are largely the educated and affluent for whom the "information" can be put to good use and incorporated in their already extant social and cultural, as well as economic, advantages. From this perspective, "the Internet did not create a new social divide – it just exacerbates all the old ones created by poverty, isolation and poor education" (Griffin, 2000, p. 30). This is broadly the perspective that informs this paper.

This research deliberately examines different urban families and our emphasis is on issues of advantage and disadvantage. In a study like this of families at a local level, issues related to access require a textured account of the ways in which a number of interrelated critical elements and various dimensions of disadvantage come into play in different contexts. Indeed, to draw a simple dichotomy between the technology haves and have-nots in local settings is not particularly generative. It may be, as the findings of the study reported here suggest, that even when people from poor backgrounds manage to gain access to technology, they remain relatively disadvantaged. As Travers and Richardson (1993) argue, being poor or disadvantaged is more than a matter of income. We can experience disadvantage or advantage through dimensions of our lives such as the characteristics of the neighbourhoods we inhabit, access to the collective resources of the communities in which we live, as well as through our income, race, gender, social status, cultural group and so on. Research using the term "disadvantage" compares the circumstances of people or communities or places with others who are experiencing "advantage" or who are living in "average" conditions. "Being disadvantaged is thus an explicitly relative state, but the term also has a strong normative connotation. To be disadvantaged is to be unfairly treated relative to others" (Fincher & Saunders, 2001, p. 8). Most importantly for our study, research using "(dis)advantage" as a guiding concept refers to both advantaging and disadvantaging processes that cause the production and reproduction of advantage and disadvantage for different people in different situations.

METHODOLOGY

The research methodology was qualitative. We conducted case studies of the four families (three who gained computer and Internet access for the first time under the Virtual Communities scheme, and one that had had access for five years for comparison purposes). As it turned out, only two of the four families could be described as clearly "disadvantaged." However, the similarities and differences among the four families provided us with rich sources of data upon which to draw in our analysis and interpretation. Members of the research team visited each family a minimum of six times in their homes between mid-2000 and mid-2001. Family members were interviewed individually and together, and were observed using ICT. Additional interviews were conducted in parents' workplaces where appropriate. The schools the children attended were visited at least three times and the children were observed in various classes using computers. The research team also interviewed their teachers, the principal or assistant principal of the school, computer co-ordinators, English teachers and curriculum co-ordinators. Altogether there were over 60 interviews. Policy documents and school charters were viewed to help us understand the "mission statements" of the schools in providing computer technology. Two primary and two secondary schools were included in the study.

Each researcher worked with one family and the school attended by the child(ren) of that family. The researchers acted as participant-observers and took field notes in both school and home settings. Interviews with family members and teaching staff were audio-taped and transcribed. Some of the interviews with family members were conducted around the computer as one or more people worked with the technology.

THE PARTICIPATING FAMILIES

Sketches of the four families as they were in 2000–2001 are presented below.

The Rodriguez Family

Fernando and Luisa Rodriguez are political refugees from Chile. They came to Australia in 1988 and now live in a new housing estate in the outer-eastern

Melbourne suburb of Blue Hills. Fernando is a metal worker in a factory and Luisa is a childcare worker in a crèche. They have two children, Carmen, aged 11, who attends St. Cecilia's Catholic Primary school in a suburb 15 kilometres from Blue Hills, and Lydia, aged 5, who is in the pre-kindergarten group at the childcare centre where Luisa works. Both children are bilingual. Spanish is the language spoken at home.

Fernando explains: "Most of my English is factory English, you know?" He did not complete secondary schooling in Chile and has not attempted any study in Australia. Nonetheless, he badly wants his daughters to succeed in their education. Fernando does not use a computer at work, and says he uses the computer at home for emailing (in Spanish) people in Chile, accessing Chilean news websites, and following Chilean soccer results. He bought the home computer through the Amalgamated Metal Workers' Union for his daughters to use primarily for educational purposes. "Computer is everything now," he says. He is not adroit with the keyboard and has to think before finding the functions he needs. As the family never sits around the computer together (unlike the Browns and the Lakes, whom we discuss below), Fernando has to call either Luisa or Carmen to show him how to do things. During an interview with Carmen, the following exchange occurred:

> [Fernando comes in and looks on and smiles. He appears proud that Carmen is so competent on the computer]
>
> Fernando: You see? [gesturing that Carmen is operating various functions]
>
> Interviewer: Very quick. [indicating to Fernando that Carmen knows her way round the keyboard and is not fumbling keys]
>
> [Fernando laughs and gestures that he is not at all competent on the computer. He throws up his hands.]

The log book that the family kept over a three-week period had no entries to indicate Fernando had used the computer during that time.

Luisa studied French at school and completed her secondary education in Chile. Since arriving in Australia, she has taken Migrant English classes and completed Technical and Further Education (TAFE) studies in childcare. She uses a computer at work in the crèche she runs, including using the Internet to search for specific information (e.g. about Rubella). She says: "Everything computer is new for me... But if I want to communicate with my daughter I have to know about this, and I'm supposed to know more than her – because I'm the mother. I still believe that mums should know more."

Luisa was enrolled in a Bachelor of Education (Primary) course by Distance Education for a semester in 2000 but did not complete the degree because of pressure of family and work. She is very keen for her children to be economically successful in Australia and sees education as the way for them to achieve success.

She and Fernando seek "excellence" in education, which is why they are prepared to pay fees and send Carmen to a Catholic girls' school so far away from home. They believe St. Cecilia's is better than any of their local schools, but lately, Luisa says, she has been unhappy with the principal and is not sure she's getting "good value for money." Even so, Luisa says that sacrificing holidays and driving one car to save enough money to send Carmen to a private school is worth it because "it offers the best program and standards."

Carmen would like to become a veterinary surgeon and both parents are keen that she pursues this goal. She is a hard worker at school and the family rule is that she is permitted to use the computer only on Friday nights and weekends. She must finish her homework on other nights. She is able to demonstrate how she accesses the Internet, using the dedicated key on the Internet keyboard. She borrows CD-ROMs from the school library and uses the computer to listen to music or goes on to the Internet to use email. She shows a picture she constructed using Crayola which she calls "Lazy Days" – explaining that it's what she sees when she lies down: "a river and background and other things." She also borrows books from the library and is reading *Hitler's Daughter*. Carmen's classroom teacher describes her as:

> Orally very good and as for her written skills, she's got quite a flair – a natural flair for English, actually. She's a very interesting writer. She can write lots of genres and can swap over very easily . . . She's one of the ones who is really keen to read out in class and also loves to be chosen for Mass – being involved in some sort of way in the school assembly.

The Brown Family

Jenny Brown is a single mother living on benefit payments and raising her two children, Brad, aged 14, in year nine and Lizzie, aged 12, in year 7. They live in a modest council house in Greenacres, a suburb in north-western Melbourne about 12 kilometres from the CBD. Both children attend Greenacres Secondary College. Jenny, turned 33 in 2000. She did not complete secondary school and, apart from a short stint as a sales assistant before Brad was born when she was 17, has never had a job. Her father, who retired from the Vehicle Builders' Union in 1999, took advantage of the Virtual Communities offer and leased a computer package for himself and one for Jenny and her children. The computer and the TV are in the "lounge room." During our visits, both were on.

Brad and Lizzie have no contact with their biological father who walked out on Jenny two weeks after Lizzie was born. They regard Tony, with whom Jenny had a de facto relationship for almost ten tears, as their dad. Jenny's father says his motivation for leasing the computer package was to provide his grandchildren with another source of entertainment and amusement. Wendy says she is interested in its educational benefits for Brad and Lizzie:

> I mean, they're the future and they're gonna take over everywhere and so it was like well, it will definitely help them look up things. They'd always been comin' home with different projects or whatever and it sounds silly, but sayin' that such and such got an A, or that she got this from the computer or that from the computer, and it just seemed like there was so much more that they could get from the computer.

More than any other activity, all three are using the computer to go to chat rooms: all three say how they enjoy meeting people from a range of countries, backgrounds and different ages. When asked how they determine whether the person to whom they are speaking is being truthful, all say confidently that it is always easy to tell. Lizzie illustrates:

> One guy goes: 'Oh I'm 16. How old are you?' I go: 'I'm 12', and he goes: 'Oh, I'm 12 too.' I go: 'Why did ya say you were 16 then?' So he goes: 'So people would accept me and talk to me.'

Lizzie says she can tell someone's age by the way they "speak" in chat sites: "He just talks like, more adulty, instead of little kid talk sort of thing." Brad adds: "You find little kids blow kisses to each other and that sort of thing, whereas adults don't." Jenny adds: "Kids say things like 'What's up?' and just different things."

Jenny says she can quickly tell if people are what they "say" they are:

> There are ones that you don't trust and you'd more or less pick that up as soon as they say hello to you, just from different things they say, so it's normally: 'All right, thank you very much, goodbye, gotta go'. Whereas the others, I mean, the others you can be picky and choosy and it's like, 'no, speak to someone that sounds a little more genuine'.

When asked how she supervises her children in these situations, Jenny says:

> Oh yeah, we sit there often and actually watch each other and 'have a look at this one' and like, 'yep, this one, you know straight away he's going to be a right sleeze'; and yep, 'ta ta, alright, see ya later'. We just close, that's what we do.

Lizzie adds:

> A couple of times, I've seen like these people come up to me and they go: 'Oh hello.' And I go: 'Oh hi.' And they go: 'Do you wanna cyber (have cyber-sex)?' and I go: 'No, I'm only 12.' And they go: 'Oh you're old enough.' And I go: 'No! I'm not.'

Jenny sighs:

> They ask all the time, all the time, male and female, it doesn't matter. I mean you have people click on ya and you know straight away they're the people, you know just straight away, 'no thank you, goodbye'.

While someone in the family is using the Internet, someone else is watching TV or playing with the Play Station. If Brad wants to listen to music that he's downloaded from the Internet, he goes to his room and uses headphones.

Jenny claims the computer has "changed our life." The virtual world of chat has become her social focus and she relishes the friendships and relationships that have developed from it. She says: "I feel like I've got friends on the computer. There's friends I can talk to, have a laugh with." Jenny had been almost housebound for years – just going shopping at the local supermarket is a major expedition as both kids have to assist and carry as many bags as they can. Now, after being energised by having friends "in the computer" after years of "feeling like a nothing," Jenny is talking for the first time about getting a job: "I mean, you start evaluating, like, what have I been doing with meself and what am I going to do? It's amazing what chatlines can do!"

Lizzie Brown wants to be a clothes designer. Her teachers describe her as quite skilled with technology, but a rather quiet and shy student. Various teachers describe her as "a nice kid," "quiet," "probably below average," and "a pleasant student who needs to be helped." Lizzie wishes teachers would "just to stop tellin me off." At home, she uses the computer for email, plays on Internet sites such as Virtual Dog, Barbie.com and fan sites, and uses chatrooms a lot. She is very competent in the chatroom environment and has created images of herself (avatars) to represent her physically in the virtual world.

Brad Brown "hates school." He says: "I hate wakin up for it. I hate goin to it. I hate comin home and havin work for it . . . just everyfin about it. I just hate everyfin about school." Although Greenacres Secondary College is a big school, Brad is described as the sort of student "every teacher knows." He was "kept down" at the end of year 7 and made to repeat. Failing year 7 is very rare, even in schools like Greenacres that have a relatively low level of academic success. In his repeat year, in what Brad remembers as the "best time since kindergarten," he was sent for a term to a special centre for students who teachers cannot manage and who have been withdrawn from classes because of behavioural problems. But despite being perceived as "a loser" and as a serious discipline problem by teachers, Brad is highly competent with the computer at home. He is the one relied upon by Jenny and Lizzie to troubleshoot when the computer breaks down. He says: "When somefin happens, I know straight away basically." He says he uses the computer for everything: "I just go on it, muck around, talk to my friends, get car pictures, download songs – I do everyfin on it." He also accesses sites for job searches and uses email and chatroom functions. In contrast to his home use of computer technology, Brad asserts: "I didn't learn nuthin at school from the computer." Then reconsidering: "I had infotech classes and I gotta admit I learnt somethin but I've never used it – mailmerge!"

The Lawford Family

Helen and Brendan Lawford are recently divorced. Brendan is a communications manager for a union body and Helen is a corporate assessor for a multinational power and resources company. Both had been actively involved in union activities during university days prior to Helen being employed as a bureaucrat (ultimately at Senior Executive level) in public sector administration in Victoria in the late 1980s and early 1990s. She explains that she began this career before completing her teaching degree:

> Interviewer: You didn't go into teaching?
>
> Helen: Ah, no. No, I've never taught... I think by the time I finished my degree, I was working for John Cain [then Premier of Victoria], advising him on Women's Affairs, and before I'd graduated I was being paid more than a Principal.

With a change in political power in 1992, Helen moved easily to a higher-paid position in the private sector. Brendan hints that the strain in their marriage may have been partly due to his perception of a change in Helen's political values. Brendan still works for the union is committed to the cause. His grandfather was a Labor Party Senator in Federal Parliament. The couple have a six-year-old daughter, Angela, who is in grade 1 at the inner-city Rosewood Primary School. Angela lives with Helen in the family home (which houses the computer), and her father has a flat nearby where she stays two nights a week. Brendan purchased the computer through his union to use primarily for work at home. Now Angela has almost exclusive use of it. Helen brings her laptop home for work purposes.

Helen has an unusual background for such a corporate high flier – quite similar in fact to that of Jenny Brown. Helen's parents were among the wave of British immigrants in the 1950s who settled in a brand new satellite city just north of Adelaide, near other working class suburbs like Happy Valley and Paradise. The city was founded to accommodate workers in a huge new General Motors Holden automotive plant. There was plenty of work on the assembly line as production was cranked up during the post-war boom years. Few of the kids who attended schools like Satellite High completed their secondary schooling, much less went on to higher education. Helen did both. She recalls a major defining moment in her life – what she calls her "Big W experience," which occurred when she had been working during the summer school holidays at a large "Big W" supermarket and must have impressed her superiors. At fifteen, she was offered full-time, continuing work at the store – an offer most of her friends would have jumped at. The offer caused her to seriously consider where she was headed. She talked it over with her parents and recalls thinking: "I'm fifteen and not pregnant. Perhaps I might amount to something!"

Brendan and Helen are both computer users; both have jobs that demand a high degree of computer competency; both regard the computer as an integral part of Angela's education. They bought her first computer program when she was four years old because it was "the best little program around and it was all about mouse skills." It is apparent that six-year-old Angela is highly computer literate and competent. She observes: "The fun things are where you go somewhere and you see all these addresses . . . on the train, in the car, and I put them in my head and when I come home I go to the computer and I search them." Helen says: "I know she's learning; when she thinks she's playing (on the computer) I know she's learning." At the same time, both parents emphasise the importance of books. Helen insists that Angela "is a very, very good reader and reads at above average levels."

Angela is extremely bright, good-natured, proud of her computer skills and willing to display them. She says the computer has displaced the TV as her main source of entertainment and recreation. Her appraisal of television is that the programs can be divided into "babies' TV" and "mummies' TV." Neither now interests her. The large TV rests quietly in the corner of the jam-packed living room until late evening when Angela is in bed and Helen might watch something to help her relax. The focus for Angela is the computer. She loves playing with her CDs and, best of all, with Barbie.com, her main recreation these days.

The Lake Family

The Lake family live in the inner-city suburb of Kilvington and the two girls, Felicity, aged 15, in year 11 and Sally, aged 13, in year 9 attend City High School. Sara and Ray Lake both have postgraduate degrees (arts, management and labour relations law for Ray; arts and law for Sara) and hold senior trade union positions. They bought the computer primarily so they could work at home, and for the girls' schoolwork. The family members see the computer as a tool for work or research but stress the superiority of books and their love of the world of paper-text. For instance, during family discussions around the dining table, at which family members linger after meals, someone will often reach for the Britannica to settle a dispute or look up information relevant to dinner-table conversation. While actively downplaying the importance of the computer and their ICT skills in general (Ray: "I'm never sure where to put the petrol in"), all members of the family are exceptionally competent technology users. Sara uses the computer for webpage construction and "time-consuming fiddly work and email" and Ray "to type things, format a letter . . . use the Internet and email."

Felicity says, and her parents agree, that she has used computers, mainly for games, since she was two. She uses Hotmail a lot. She is a member of a band that meets on weekends and finds that Hotmail is very useful for making arrangements. Sally has used computers at school from an early age and enjoys games and emailing friends. She says she's good at Internet searches and downloads images for projects but, when asked about how much she uses the Internet for research purposes, she gestures to the Britannica volumes on the shelf behind her to indicate that she more often refers to them. In fact, the status of the Encyclopedia Britannica in the house has become something of a family joke:

> Sally: The other day I was looking up old song lyrics [on the Net but] I usually just go to the library or into the dining room . . .
>
> Interviewer: And get the Britannica out.
>
> Sally: Yeah!

Family members claim that there is no real competition to use the computer, although certain activities are prioritised. The hierarchy of need is: work, homework, general Internet searches and then games, but the general consensus is that the computer is used 80% of the time for games. No-one uses chat programs, but everyone in the family emails the grandmother in Adelaide who is described as "an email addict."

The favourite family computer activity is playing *Civilisation*. Sally describes it as "a particularly addictive game" and adds: "Sadly, this is what I do most of the time." She likes to play the part of "someone like Catherine the Great, but called Bob – easier to remember." She says: "I like the building and starting a civilisation. Mum goes on and she builds – like, she's building the first space program which is going off to Alfa Centoria." The family consider this game feeds their love of history and culture. They jointly espouse the notion that paper-text literacy in the form of books is superior to computer literacy forms, but they are aware that, as Felicity says, "unfortunately, the computer is necessary."

DISCUSSION: SYMBOLIC CAPITAL AND COMPUTER TECHNOLOGY

In examining the attitudes of the participating families to the use of computer technology at home and school, we found it useful to consider the concepts of cultural access and deprivation. We use Bourdieu's notion of symbolic capital (Bourdieu, 1990) to help us understand the social, political and cultural relationship between the families, notions of livelihood, and their external environments. Bourdieu (1990) considers that "capital," the kinds of resources that can give one social and economic advantage, can be of different forms. He argues that individual actions are shaped (but never totally moulded) within social, political and economic contexts that mediate power relationships among people. According to Bourdieu (1990), there are tangible forms of durable capital, such as money and quantifiable assets, which he terms "economic capital." These are directly transposable. They are, Bourdieu (1990) claims, the most efficient forms of capital because they can be readily transferred or exchanged. In addition, Bourdieu (1990) conceives notions of non-material forms of capital, called "symbolic capital." These forms of capital enable individuals who possess them to open or close doors to material success and power.

One form of symbolic capital is social capital, which Bourdieu defines as "a network of kinship (or other) relations capable of being mobilized or at least manifested" (1990, p. 35). For example, Jenny Brown says her life has been "changed by the computer" as her social network, which confers upon her greater confidence and self-esteem than she has felt for many years, is now that of Internet chatrooms where she feels she is a valued member. The final type of symbolic capital, and the main one we use in this discussion, is Bourdieu's (1990) notion of "cultural capital." Cultural capital includes all the attributes, including education, literacy, and social graces, with which an individual is endowed. An example of cultural capital is the desire of some of the parents (Lake, Lawford & Rodriguez) that their children attain excellence in education. In the case of the Lakes and the Lawfords, this expectation would seem realistic enough. Indeed, although we must emphasise that nothing is pre-ordained about social futures and one cannot with any accuracy predict social and economic success, good educational outcomes would seem a normal and "natural" consequence of Felicity's and Sally's and Angela's "inherent" skills, networks and "insider" knowledge of what counts as education, knowledge and culture. This is all part of their social and cultural identities. Their backgrounds and easy familiarity with the education world (although Helen had to win such familiarity the hard way) enhance their cultural capital way above that of the Rodriguez family in which the parents, particularly Luisa, are striving to enhance their children's cultural opportunities and identities through private education. But the Rodriguez family is in turn way ahead of the Browns in the cultural capital stakes. Differential cultural capital provides the families with differentiated resources and options in the pursuit of educational, vocational and social opportunities. Some aspects of the forms of cultural capital may be glimpsed in the families' engagement with computers.

All four families acknowledge that the computer is a tool for accessing information that can be processed into knowledge. Such access to knowledge is a form of cultural capital as defined by Bourdieu (1990). All families agree that using computers in the home is of educational benefit to their children. The Lake family, however, prefers the hard copy of Encyclopedia Britannica as a source of information but admits that "unfortunately, the computer is necessary." The Rodriguez and Lawford families consider computer skills and technology as one means of opening doors to future higher education and economic sectors. The extensive computer use of both Helen and Brendan Lawford in their work attests to their understanding that increased computer competence is advantageous in the cultural and economic capital stakes. Although Luisa and Fernando Rodriguez are not highly skilled users of computer technology, they are determined that their daughters will be. For all of them, there seems to be a clearly perceived relationship between computer competence and educational success. Yet the relationship between the schools, the children and the four families is complex and variable.

For example, Angela Lawford quite likes computing classes but is disappointed that "at school [speaking slowly and choosing words] you don't get to choose what you do. They actually show you what you're meant to be doing and we're meant to be working on [that]." Angela spends most time at Barbie.com and sites to do with witches and fairies. She enjoys spelling and number games that could be regarded as school-like. The recreational computer activities of the Lake girls could also be regarded as school-like. As a family they love playing "Civilisation" (which accounts for the majority of time spent on the computer) and looking up on the Internet ingredients from interesting restaurant dishes or the botanical names of plants – although their preference is for the hard-copy Britannica. The Brown children, however, derive pleasure from decidedly un-school-like computer activity. Principal among these is chat. There's also music downloading and searching for car information and images (Brad), and celebrity news, magazine and fan sites, and virtual dog (Lizzie). One of the few times Brad spoke with enthusiasm about anything (except his job) was when he said:

> I love the . . . when I go on the Internet, well . . . yeah, and like, I'll save a few pictures to my file, like car pictures, pictures of cars, and soon as I'm offline or whatever, ya know, I'll go into paint, open file, yeah, and put a car picture. And if, like, I put a car picture, I can like chop the roof off, make it smaller, make the wheels fatter, like modify it. Yeah, it's fun. (laughs)

For all of these young people, as Facer et al. (2001, p. 106) put it:

> the active computer user outside school is forced into the position of novice learner within the school environment and, at times, actively required to 'forget' the skills learnt in the home.

In Brad's case, as seen above, the response at school to his Internet skills was particularly crude and dismissive.

One startling difference between the Brown family and, say, the Lawford family, is the way the families, indeed the school communities, are perceived within the respective schools. Angela Lawford is discussed fondly by her teachers, who are impressed by the level of support she receives from her extended family. Helen Lawford knows each of Angela's teachers by their first name. One says of Angela:

> Whenever we have a special function at school either one or both parents are here and that often extends to the grandparents as well. And whenever we have special activities for the children, it might be the crazy hair day or whatever, there's always the support to make sure that Angela is decked out in the appropriate hairdo or whatever. Ummm... parent-teacher interviews is always both [parents] attending, and just a general interest. So a lot of that sort of support.

Helen has harmonious contact with the school, where she feels welcomed, as part of her routine. Jenny Brown, however, asserts: "the only times I've contacted the school is when [Brad's] in trouble." She has no rapport with teachers at all. Jenny is an "outsider" where Helen is a valued "insider." This raises issues about how different "parental voices" (Vincent & Martin, 2002) are "heard" and listened to in schools.

Angela's current classroom teacher, Alan West, feels he knows Helen Lawford well enough to appreciate her "rapport in the classroom":

> I'm confident to say, you know, 'Go away and don't come back!' I guess I have that confidence and rapport and I enjoy her company and she enjoys mine.

As far as Alan is concerned: "[Angela's] like the perfect student, the ideal child." Over at Greenacres Secondary College, however, you can't find anyone with a very high opinion of Brad or Lizzie Brown. But there's not a high regard for the community either. In response the question, "how would you describe Greenacres Secondary College," Mr Hall says:

> Well, a lot of strugglers. A lot of families that put education well down their list of priorities. Certainly not all. There are parents who do care and who really do try and help the school, but then at the other end we have quite a few that education is way down on their list and that rubs off onto their kids. There's nothing. I mean we get a lot of animosity no matter what we do from the parents towards the school.

Even this teacher, who Brad says knows him best, expresses little knowledge of Brad's family: "They're basically working class stock. Apart from that I really don't know." According to the Deputy Principal at Greenacres Secondary College, Lyn Wagner:

> Technology comes number one. It's used as a kind of marketing technique because we give our year 7s a really intensive computer program. We make a big thing of the fact that we have four operational computer rooms.

But despite computer education being a "big thing" for marketing purposes, teachers have very little sense of which or how many students have computers at home; indeed teachers' estimates vary from "perhaps up to 25%" to "at least 75%." Greenacres is regarded by the Principal, Rob Earlwood, as "disadvantaged" because, he says, 60% of families exist on some kind of government benefit. He believes that schools "have a corporate responsibility to our kids" and must train students for jobs not yet in existence, particularly "the acquisition of knowledge and technology." Technology, it would seem, might be the salvation of the masses. Mr. Earlwood says the problem for Greenacres is lack of overall funding and extensive social problems in the area. He says: "for a lot of our kids, the only stable person in their lives who has a values system is their teachers."

The general attitude displayed to the working-class community of Greenacres, and to the Brown family in particular, seems consistent with Reay's (2001, p. 335) conclusion that:

> In Bourdieurian terms, the working classes both historically and currently are discursively constituted as unknowing, uncritical, tasteless mass from which the middle class draw their distinctions . . . [by] representing the children of the poor only as a measure of what they lack.

For example, none of the teachers we spoke to knew that Brad or Lizzie had a computer at home. When informed of this fact, one teacher volunteered:

> I'm certain that most of the time [Brad's] on the computer he's searching the Net, it's for pleasure not for anything educational. You know the sites that . . . Brad's heavily into skateboarding for instance. As a teacher I have a computer at home for my kids. When my kids use the computer I like to oversee it and see exactly what they're doing. But who knows what Brad is doing!

Here, within a "powerful blaming discourse" (Reay, 2001, p. 338) the Browns are constructed as "others," as being of a different world to the teachers. They and their neighbours are viewed as disconnected from education in ways that the school can't really do much about.

At the gentrified Rosewood Primary School, things have changed a lot in the past decade or so. According to the Deputy Principal, Rob Grey:

> When I came to this school, you know, we had about five [%] professionals and the other ninety-five [% of families] would be blue collar and unemployed and the whole range. Now there would only be five [%] non-professional. It has been virtually a complete reversal and we are attracting the sort of middle-class Anglo-Saxon into the school.

The suburb of Rosewood has a very high proportion of Vietnamese and North African families. Rob says that "most Vietnamese go to the Catholic school" and that other immigrant families tend to use the school nearest the Housing Commission flats "where they feel more comfortable." He says that computing is important to his school's clients, but that "we highlight our music and the facilities and the programs." He adds: "We're pretty well in line with the parents."

Another difference between the Browns and Lawfords is the ease with which school and home, work and play, are integrated – particularly in terms of information technology. Brendan and Helen Lawford value both computer and traditional forms of literacy highly as part of the cultural capital they wish their daughter to absorb. The fact that Angela Lawford was using her first educational software package at the age of four indicates that her parents are keen for her to become a competent computer user. Brendan has the necessary insider knowledge. He says: "I knew that the school she was at had computer studies and having some sort of basic click and drag search ability to start with means she's at a level that means she's not going to be behind as soon as they sit down at the screen." Helen Lawford is equally keen that Angela access paper-text literacy skills. Angela, aged 6, has read (with parent assistance) all the Harry Potter books.

The Lawfords articulate the view that playing on the computer is akin to learning computer competence, and are happy about Angela's computer play. Both parents are comfortable with Angela accessing different sites such as Barbie.com. Helen surmises, "I know that typing out the invitations [for her Barbie.com party] she's learning. As long as I know which sites she's going to, I'm very relaxed about playing." Jenny Brown also supports the view that a computer at home is important for her children, "to help them look things up." The reality is, however, that little schoolwork is done on the computer in the Brown house. It is generally used by Brad and Lizzie for downloading songs, email and, particularly, chatroom activities. Although Jenny conceives of computers as "the future and they're gonna take over everywhere," she does not insist the computer at home be used for school work, as does Luisa Rodriguez.

As far as the children in the study are concerned, there is much more happening in their lives than school. The children in all the families use the computer at home largely in an extension of activities they already enjoy and, in most cases, are good at. Time spent on the computer at home is mainly for pleasure not work. The possible exception here is Carmen Rodriguez whose computer time is severely rationed. She is permitted to play on the computer only at weekends when all homework has been completed. In the Rodriguez house, the computer is for education not play. Carmen does play some games, however, and uses Crayola for art work.

Luisa and Fernando regard a high level of education, and integration of computer technology into that education, as vital for successful penetration of barriers to cultural and economic power. They explain: "We want our children to be better than we are." They are adamant that Carmen and Lydia will obtain better, higher paid jobs than they, themselves, have and are fully supportive of Carmen's dream of becoming a veterinary surgeon. Luisa, in particular, regards using knowledge and credentials as vital to improving the life chances of her children. There is a slight desperation about academic success which is putting Carmen under some pressure to avoid failure. It is unlikely that she will ever experience the casual assumption of academic success that pervades the Lake girls' personas. For Felicity and Sally Lake, it would appear (although we repeat out caution that nothing is pre-ordained about social futures) that the "decision" to be successful at school and proceed to university is, as Ball et al. (2002, p. 54) put it, "a non-decision." It seems part of a "normal" and expected social trajectory. For Carmen, however, it would seem a similar decision has been deliberately made for her by Luisa, but this "active" decision is more problematic. The family lacks the social and cultural resources and supports that are available to the Lawfords and Lakes.

Unlike Luisa Rodriguez, Jenny Brown is not at all desperate that her children attain high levels of education and thereby increase their cultural capital and their opportunities of acquiring greater economic capital. Yet, perhaps surprisingly, the least hazy "imagined future" of all the young people is Brad Brown's. From his first interview Brad spoke of his plan to leave school at the end of 2000 (although he would be only in year 9) and get an apprenticeship. This was aiming very high in Brad's world (although not so high for the other families) and he was advised at school that such a move would be impossible for him. One teacher said: "I actually mentioned to him, a lot of times now, you need a minimum of year 11 for an apprenticeship. Otherwise they're not even going to look at you." Brad was adamant, however. He would turn fifteen by the end of the year and no one could then make him go back to school. He said he would prove to everyone, including his family, that he *could* get a job and that he would not conform to the expectation of others that he would become a layabout dole bludger. In the event, Brad did achieve exactly what he said he would achieve. He explains:

> The day after [we last spoke] I organised to go up [to the crash repairer's] and we went up there and I spoke to the boss and he said, 'Yeah come in tomorrow and we'll give you a test try'. And I went, 'Oh all right'. And that [next] day they just said, 'Don't worry about the test try, we'll give you an apprenticeship now'.

In terms of where he had set his sights, Brad has achieved huge success against the odds and bypassing the usual institutional frameworks. Apprenticeships are like gold dust among Brad's peers, even if the work can be dirty and dangerous. He's on track to becoming a skilled tradesperson and, eventually, as Brad sees it, to having his own spray painting or crash repair business. This boy, who was a "discipline problem" and a failure at school, has been able to use his limited capital – including a rev-head network, an uncle in the automotive trade and Jenny's ex-de facto who is a motor-bike fanatic – to make contacts in the business in which he has now scored the kind of apprenticeship he always dreamed of.

Of the people in the four families, the person who spent most time on the computer in the home was, by far, Jenny Brown. She uses it almost exclusively for chat with a voraciousness that suggests she may be making up for lost time spent with little social contact. This use of Internet chat has enhanced her personal symbolic capital and enabled her, a once socially isolated and housebound woman, to engage with other people and feel pretty good about herself. But it has not so far enhanced her social power. Jenny uses the computer to chat with and to email her new friends "in the computer." The virtual world of chat and email has become her social capital. Her children have also become engaged in the virtual world of chat, which has a curious relationship to their off-line social world. For Jenny in particular, and to a lesser extent Lizzie, the life "in the computer" is a polished and improved version of their "real" life, an idealised extension of what they do and would like to do, and which, to some extent, fills what is lacking in "real" life. But the engagement in this partial world is active, creative, and requires imagination and multiple judgements as cyber relationships and situations are negotiated. Much time is spent discussing avatars and identities, relationships, realities, emotions and truth. As Webb (2001, p. 562) explains: "Virtual identities are embodied, sensuously experienced and contingently rhythmic and mobile. If you wish, we *write identity* through them." Potentially (and this is something we hope to do more work on), it could be said that in such chat activity the capacity to "produce" identities, representations and alternative realities, rather than just be consumers of computer games and Web-based information, might become an empowering and enriching activity. But at present, in the Brown household, it looks like fantasy and escapism.

Overall, compared with the Lawford and Lake children, and also with the Rodriguez girls, Brad and Lizzie Brown have experienced greater inequalities of access to resources and life chances, making the reproduction of disadvantage more likely. Yes, they have a computer and Internet access in their home, making them part of that rapidly expanding group, at least in Australia, of the technology "haves," but that's where the similarities with the other children in the study more or less begin and end. We need to ask, therefore, how useful it is to talk about technology "haves" and "have-nots." Our data suggest that we require an expanded, reconceptualised understanding of "access" and its relation to equity. Access cannot be seen merely as a matter of having a way to use computers and a connection to the Internet. "Access" needs to be rethought as a much more complex and multileveled social goal. Burbules and Callister (2000) distinguish between "quality of access" and "quantity of access" and also between "conditions of access" and "criteria of access." Considerations of *how much* need to be counter-balanced by considerations of *how good*. This view is consistent with Connell's (1993, p. 16) account of "distributive justice": in relation to access to technology, it is about not only who gets how much of the technology resources, but also who gets the benefits associated with such resources and how much of them (Comber & Green, 1999).

CONCLUSION

In education policy terms, there are many questions to be asked about our analysis. For instance, are we just telling old "class stories?" What if anything has changed due to continuous introduction of new technologies? Does access to new technologies make a difference in the distribution of educational (dis)advantage?

Some time ago Lipkin wrote of new technologies:

> Them that has, gets . . .. If a particular race, sex or economic group occupies an inferior position in society, you only have to be able to add one and one to see that technology will compound the problem. (Lipkin, cited in Zakariya, 1984, p. 29)

If Lipkin was right in 1984, then the evidence of this paper is that he is still right in 2004. It seems that, for the families in our study, old inequalities have not disappeared in the increasingly networked society; they are neither the same as previously, nor have they simply been added to. All the families in the study have home access to the Internet, so, in the parlance, they are all among of the technology "haves." But when compared to the other three families, the Browns are simply not as well off as the others despite Brad's success in gaining an apprenticeship. And the engagement with technology and the social world of the Rodriguez family, regardless of equal access to ICT, is clearly different to that of the Lawfords and Lakes.

We have attempted to capture and illustrate a portion of the complexity of contemporary social and educational inequalities within and across the lives of a small sample of young people and their families. It does not seem to us that equal access to ICT, without attention to other socio-political aspects of advantage and disadvantage, will do much to close the digital or social divide.

The above conclusion may not be a surprise to policy sociologists who have long been grappling with issues if inequality in schooling and the relationship between disadvantaging and advantaging practices, backgrounds and cultures. However, we hope our conclusion that families and children are not automatically advantaged by having ICT access may act as something of a corrective to the prevailing, indeed ubiquitous, ICT policy discourse that tends to equate ICT access with social and educational advancement. In particular, there is a need to challenge the widespread prominence in schools of ICT policies that are directly related to school marketing policy rather than any educational policy. The marketing message falsely associates ICT with "success" and implies that, if they attend schools with the latest electronic wizardry, children can be securely placed among the technology "haves" who will experience economic and social success. Knowledge of and access to ICT may be important for young people in the twenty-first century, but it is hardly the panacea that will redress other forms of inequality.

ACKNOWLEDGMENTS

We wish to acknowledge that this research was supported by an Australian Research Council grant. We thank Lisa Phillips who worked with us in the early stages of the project.

REFERENCES

Australian Bureau of Statistics (2001). AusStats 8147.0. *Use of the Internet by Householders, Australia, Online*: http://www.abs.gov.au/Ausstats/ABS (accessed 16 August 2002).

Ball, S. J., Davies, J., David, M., & Reay, D. (2002). 'Classification' and 'judgement': Social class and the 'cognitive structures' of choice of higher education. *British Journal of Sociology of Education*, *23*(1), 51–72.

Bell, D. (2001). *An introduction to cybercultures*. London: Routledge.

Bolt, D., & Crawford, R. (2000). *Digital divide: Computers and our children's future*. New York: TV Books.

Bourdieu, P. (1990). *The logic of practice* (R. Nice, Trans.). Stanford: Stanford University Press.

Burbules, N. C., & Callister, T. (2000). *Watch IT: The risks and promises of information technologies for education*. Boulder, Colorado: Westview Press.

Castells, M. (2001). *The internet galaxy: Reflections on the internet, business, and society*. New York: Oxford University Press.

Comber, B., & Green, B. (1999). *Information technology, literacy and educational disadvantage research and development*. Project Report to DETE SA (Vol. 1). Adelaide: University of South Australia.

Companie, B. (2001). *The digital divide: Facing a crisis or creating a myth*? Cambridge, MA: MIT Press.

Connell, R. W. (1993). Schools and social justice. *Our Schools/Our Selves*. Toronto: Education Foundation.

Facer, K., Furlong, J., Furlong, R., & Sutherland, R. (2001). Constructing the child computer user: From public policy to private practices. *British Journal of Sociology of Education*, *22*(1), 91–108.

Fincher, R., & Saunders, P. (Eds) (2001). *Creating unequal futures? Rethinking poverty, inequality and disadvantage*. Sydney: Allen & Unwin.

Foster, S. P. (2000). The digital divide: Some reflections. *International Information and Library Review*, *32*, 437–451.

Garham, N. (2000). 'Information society' as theory or ideology. *Information, Communication and Society*, *3*(2), 139–152.

Gordon, D. (2001). *The digital classroom: How technology is changing the way we teach and learn*. Cambridge, MA: Harvard Education.

Griffin, M. (2000). *Digital divide*. Sydney Morning Herald e-mag, 4 May, 26–30.

Hellman, H. (1996). A toy for the boy's only? Reconsidering the gender effects of video technology. *European Journal of Communication, 11*(1), 5–32.

Holloway, D. (2002). Disparities in internet access: A case study of western Sydney. *Australian Journal of Social Issues, 37*(1), 51–69.

Lacroix, J., & Tremblay, G. (1997). From Fordism to Gatesism. *Current Sociology, 45*(3), 115–125.

Lentz, R. (2000). The e-volution of the digital divide in the U.S.: A mayhem of competing metrics. *Info: The Journal of Policy, Regulation and Strategy for Telecommunications, 2*(4), 355–377.

Livingstone, S. (1999). Personal computers in the home: What do they mean for children? *Intermedia, 27*(2), 4–6.

Negroponte, N. (1996). *Being digital*. London: Routledge.

Nixon, H. (2001). ICT, literacy and disadvantage: An unspeakable topic? In: C. Durrant & C. Beavis (Eds), *P(ICT)ures of English: Teachers, Learners and Technology* (pp. 191–210). Kent Town: Wakefield Press.

Papert, S. (1996). *Mindstorms*. Brighton: Harvester.

Reay, D. (2001). Finding or losing yourself?: Working-class relationships to education. *Journal of Education Policy, 16*(4), 333–346.

Sefton-Green, J. (2001). The 'end of school' or just 'out of school'?: ICT, the home and digital cultures. In: C. Durrant & C. Beavis (Eds), *P(ICT)ures of English: Teachers, Learners and Technology* (pp. 162–175). Kent Town: Wakefield Press.

Selwyn, N. (2000). The national grid for learning: Panacea or panopticon. *British Journal of Sociology of Education, 21*(2), 243–255.

Travers, P., & Richardson, S. (1993). *Living decently: Material well-being in Australia*. Melbourne: Oxford University Press.

U.S. Department of Commerce (1999). *Falling through the net: Defining the digital divide*. http://www.ntia.doc.gov/ntiahome/fttn99/contents.html.

Van Rompaey, V., Roe, K., & Struys, K. (2002). Children's influence on internet access at home. *Information, Communication and Society, 5*(2), 189–206.

Vincent, C., & Martin, J. (2002). Class, culture and agency: Researching parental voice, I, *23*(1), 109–128.

Virtual Communities (2002). Available: http://www.virtualcommunities.com.au [Retrieved, 18 August 2002].

Webb, S. (2001). Avatar culture: Narrative, power and identity in virtual world environments. *Information, Communication and Society, 4*(4), 560–594.

Zakariya, S. (1984). In school (as elsewhere), the rich get computers, the poor get poorer. *American School Board Journal*, March, 29–32.

WRITING INEQUALITIES: LITERACY AND SOCIAL CLASS IN THREE PRIMARY SCHOOLS

Ann Williams and Eve Gregory

INTRODUCTION

Educational statistics in Britain make depressing reading. Recent surveys show that 80% of children from professional families gain university degrees compared with 14% from working class homes:[1] that black children are more likely to leave school with fewer academic qualifications even though they enter the system showing promise: that only a small minority of children from comprehensive schools[2] gain places at Oxbridge although 90% of the population attend such schools: that a mere 4% of medical and dentistry students come from working class backgrounds etc. In spite of John Major's[3] optimistic insistence that Britain has become a classless society, it would appear that class differences in educational performance are not disappearing. On the contrary, a recent OECD[4] survey, based on data gathered from 16,000 people born in 1958 and 1970 shows that the detrimental effects of inequality of opportunity are actually growing and that the opportunities gap between those from different social backgrounds is no better for those born in 1970 than it was for those born a generation earlier in 1958.

One of the first priorities of the new Labour government when it came to power in 1997 was to attempt to address these inequalities: in the words of the then Secretary of State for Education, David Blunkett, "to build up an education system where there is excellence for the many, not just the few." Their first initiative was

Ethnographies of Educational and Cultural Conflicts: Strategies and Resolutions
Studies in Educational Ethnography, Volume 9, 67–82

ISSN: 1529-210X/doi:10.1016/S1529-210X(04)09005-9

to ensure that all pupils have equal access to the same curriculum in school by establishing mandatory daily literacy hours.[5] This was followed a year later by a corresponding numeracy hour. The reduction of class sizes, teacher monitoring and performance-related pay are among additional measures introduced to improve schools' performance.

Despite the new measures however, the league tables of national test results continued to indicate that schools in middle class districts outperform those in less advantaged areas. One explanation for this consistent variation in test scores was offered in the government-commissioned evaluation of the National Literacy Strategy[6] and the National Numeracy Strategy which stated that "Outcomes of schooling are heavily influenced by non-school factors, especially family background. School outcomes have higher correlations with family variables than with any other factor in the school" (Levin, 1999, p. 4). Government attention then turned to parents and to their role in their children's education.

The association between children's early success or failure in school and parents' social and educational background has been well documented, and the home cultures and literacy practices which produce successful middle class children in particular have been the subject of large body of research (Snow & Ninio, 1986; Taylor, 1983; Wells, 1985). In its effort to raise achievement in all sectors of the population, the government set about redefining the relationship between home and school and redistributing the responsibility for education. Their declared aim is to instil a "culture of achievement" in all parents irrespective of social class. David Blunkett stated "We need parents who are prepared to take responsibility for supporting their child's education." A series of initiatives was introduced, directed at improving the environment and increasing opportunities for families whose children were not achieving the same success as most middle class children: SureStart, Education Action Zones, New Deal for Communities and, more recently Excellence in Cities were established in poor areas, including Mountford,[7] the area where one of the project schools is situated. Parenting courses, family learning schemes and adult literacy and numeracy classes were set up, accompanied by a series of government publications and websites offering educational advice.

Parents were advised for example, "to visit their local library, museums and places of interest; to provide a quiet environment and to set aside time to work together on homework projects and to give their children confidence by using praise and encouragement." As Gewirtz points out in her critique of Labour's education policies however, such advice is not directed at middle class parents who already do these things. "In Bourdieuian terms," she writes, "these things are viewed as part of the 'habitus': 'the unspoken habits of mind and daily practices that are routinely assumed and performed almost unconsciously' of the middle classes" (Gewirtz,2001, p. 371). The true aim of the government she suggests, "is the eradication of class differences by reconstructing and transforming working class parents into middle class ones" (Gewirtz, 2001, p. 366). If this is the case, it seems legitimate to ask whether such strategies can succeed in bringing about equality of opportunity or whether they merely play into the hands of the middle classes, permitting them to deploy their already considerable resources to maintain their position at the top of the education ladder.

THE STUDY

In this paper we will consider this question in relation to some of the data gathered in the course of a recent project[8] carried out in London and the south-east of England. The aim of the longitudinal, ethnographic study was to investigate home/school literacies over a period covering the first three years of schooling: Reception, Year 1 and Year 2. The research was sited in three primary schools: Mountford, Tarnside and Rowan.[9] After a term's observation, five children from the Reception[10] classes at Tarnside and Mountford schools and six from Rowan were invited to participate in the project. The aim was to include both boys and girls with a range of abilities, as judged by the teacher and the researcher, from each school. The three schools contrasted sharply in terms of the socio-economic composition of the catchment area, ethnic make-up of the school and the SATs[11] results. Mountford is located in an extensive estate of social housing on the outskirts of a southern town. As part of the plan to reduce social exclusion there have been major programmes to improve the estate which falls within the bottom 5% of English electoral wards on indices of deprivation. Educational Action Zones, SureStart, Playlink, New Deal for Communities projects are already running on the estate. The school population is 97% Anglo, most of the remaining 3% being from the Asian sub-continent. 56% of the pupils are entitled to free school meals. The school's record in SATs has been poor but has recently improved.

In Tarnside, situated in inner London, 72% of the pupils are from minority ethnic backgrounds, the majority from African or African Caribbean families with a small number from the Asian sub-continent. Pupil turnover is high as the school receives many refugee children who are subsequently re-housed. Almost half of the children qualify for free school meals. In spite of the somewhat shifting school population and the high number of bilingual children, the school achieves scores near to the national average in the SATs tests.

Rowan, in complete contrast to the two former schools, is set in the wealthy suburbs of outer London. Most of the children are from middle class, professional backgrounds and a mere 2% qualify for free school meals. There is a very low turnover of children and a long waiting list of hopeful families. In the National Tests, the school outperforms most other schools in the area. It is also a Beacon[12] school.

Data

The data, which was collected over a three year period, comprised:

- a morning's classroom observations (all of which include a literacy session) made on a weekly basis in the first year, and fortnightly for the following two years, in all three schools;
- audio-taped recordings of selected literacy hours;
- notes and recorded interviews with parents made on regular home visits, notes from participant observation in family events and outings;
- interviews with teachers, heads and educational support staff including SENCOs;[13]
- self-recordings made by the children of themselves engaged in literacy events at home;
- recordings of the children reading in school with the researcher.

Analysis

Our aim was to investigate variation in the achievements of the children in the three project schools in the light of the relationship between home and school literacy practices. The perspective we take is that of the New Literacy Studies group (Barton & Hamilton, 1998; Street, 1993), whereby literacy is conceived, not as a single autonomous phenomenon, namely "schooled literacy," but as a social construct, "formed within the context of dynamic social fields and as the cumulative result of participation within a range of discourses and social relationships" (Carrington & Luke, 1997, p. 98). In this sense, individuals participate in multiple literacies which vary according to context. Given the socio-economic and ethnic differences between the three schools, it was anticipated that there would be considerable variation between families in terms of literacy practices. In order to explore these differences and to attempt to relate such practices to children's achievements in school, we began by applying Bourdieu's notion of capital to the resources available to the project families. Bourdieu's framework incorporates both material resources in the form of cash and material goods directly convertible into money, and non-material cultural and social capital.

ECONOMIC CAPITAL

In terms of material or economic capital, there were predictable difference between the families. Rowan parents were the most "comfortably off." Five families had two incomes and were able to afford two cars, one or more holidays per year, and a range educational aids and technology for their children. All lived in well-equipped, expensive houses with large gardens, where the children had plenty of room to play, entertain friends and do their homework in peace. In contrast no Mountford families had two incomes and fathers worked in poorly paid, often short term jobs. Four of the children lived in rented council accommodation in small houses with steeply sloping gardens and limited space for playing and doing homework. All the children shared bedrooms. No mothers had access to a car during the daytime so all trips into town had to be made on foot or via expensive bus journeys. One Mountford family only went on holiday in 2002 – a trip paid for by a local charitable organisation.

In Tarnside where only one family had two incomes, life seemed to be a desperate struggle to survive in inner London, while balancing work, expensive childcare and in two cases, studies. The families lived in a variety of flats and houses, but in only one case could the accommodation be said to be able to provide adequate space to play and do homework in peace. One family left London occasionally – to stay with relatives. Three families had no access to a car at all.

Already we can see stark differences between the opportunities families are able to provide for their children. If we consider the government's tips for parents, it is easy to see which of the three groups of parents would find it easiest to fulfil the directives to take their children on educational trips, provide peaceful surroundings for homework activities, in short to be "good parents." Lack of mobility and funds made it difficult for many of the working class parents to visit museums and other places of interest. Moreover, cramped living conditions, work and studying commitments placed restrictions on the space and time available for homework.

CULTURAL CAPITAL

The material advantages that the Rowan parents were able to offer their children serve to illustrate the interrelationship between economic and cultural capital. The accumulation of economic capital permits families firstly to accrue material (objectified) cultural capital in the form of books, educational technology and cultural artefacts and secondly to obtain educational qualifications or "institutional capital" (Bourdieu & Passeron, 1977). In turn, the possession (or lack of) of material wealth and academic credentials impacts on a family's non-material or "embodied cultural capital," that is the "set of skills, dispositions, practices and knowledges embodied by an individual, . . . and acquired over time through a process of inculcation and assimilation into the individual habitus, through parental and community practices" (Bourdieu cited in Carrington & Luke, 1997, p. 103).

The immediate impact of Rowan parents' ability to afford trips to interesting places and holidays abroad was that they were able to enhance their children's experience of school literacy from the earliest years. In Year 1 for example Rowan children were able to participate in class discussions on an informed basis:

Rowan: *Year 1*

Alice, the teacher, is asking about boats, the topic for the half term.

Charlie: It could be a speed boat

Jack: Or the boat we went in (*they have just had a school trip on a paddle steamer*)

Chris: A paddle steamer

Peter: Or a submarine.

When Alice asks who has been in a boat, most children raise their hands. Several have been on cross channel ferries to France.

Such cultural experiences were rare in the two other schools since many museums charge entrance fees, transport is extremely expensive and the cost of a holiday for a family is prohibitive for many families. Three of the five Mountford children for example had never been on a train. One of the Tarnside children had never been to the seaside and none had ever visited a museum with their families. Difficult financial circumstances prevented the Mountford and Tarnside parents from engaging in the kind of out of school activities many middle class children take for granted. Between them the Rowan children had after-school tuition in violin, piano, ballet, drama, gymnastics, football, tennis and swimming. Several were Beavers or Rainbows.[14] Sunday school was the only out-of-school activity regularly attended by some children in the Mountford group. Tarnside children also attended Sunday schools, Saturday schools and in one case, drama classes.

EDUCATION

It was possibly in the field of education however, that the Rowan parents were able to transmit the most valuable cultural capital to their children. Education was given priority in these homes and during field visits formed the main topic of discussion. In many ways the Rowan parents conformed to the stereotype of parents "prepared to take responsibility for supporting their children's education" described by David Blunkett. They had all acquired considerable institutional capital in the form of degrees and qualifications and were keen for their children to be equally successful.

They were well-informed and active consumers in the education market place, making use of websites, written publications and their extensive social networks to obtain the best education possible. In spite of the excellent SATs results achieved by Rowan for example, these parents were not content to leave the task of teaching to the teachers but complemented school work or in some cases compensated for what they saw as the school's shortcomings. The following extracts are taken from two interviews with Rowan mothers:

Rowan: Year 1: interview with Andrew's mum

Mum: He loves the Funday Times.[15] And we read through and do the exercises and it's often word games and things

AW: He spends a lot of time on so-called literacy then

Mum: Yes we do, we do . . .

AW: Do you buy any of those books.. the sort of National Curriculum books?

Mum: I have got loads of them. They're everywhere and every now and then he'll want to do a page but he might say 'I do it at school and I don't want to do it now' and you can't push it. But sometimes he's quite happy to go through them. I sometimes feel that he needs something like that 'Peter and Jane' or something . . . I did buy the first three . . . 'Here is Pat' . . . or 'This is Pat the dog' . . . . 'Here is Peter and here is Jane' . . . we got through them very fast . . . but they were so repetitive and he felt that he could do it.

Rowan: Year 1: interview with Alison's mum

Mum: Yes it's nice for them to have a reading book choice[16], but they can pick up a book one day that's got two words on a page and the next day another one that's got a whole page of print So I started her on this reading scheme and that was at the end of Year 1 and that's the time when she really went . . .. She got up to Book 5 . . . I had picture cards . . . so we'd read the book and any words that she wasn't sure of we'd take the card out and stick it on her wall and then she'd go through them every night when she went to bed and just go over the words and she got to Book 5 and I thought, 'Well, she knows all the words so we came off the reading scheme and I started her on some easy little Ladybird books.

In spite of their very different backgrounds and difficult financial circumstances, Tarnside parents evinced similar determination in the field of education. Although three of the mothers had been born outside Britain, they worked hard to familiarise themselves with the British education system. Two had embarked on access courses in order to qualify for university. Another, having left school at sixteen, had worked hard to develop a career in catering and "already had a pension and life insurance by the age of eighteen." Lola's mother, a Ugandan woman who worked as a night nurse in order to finance her own studies in computer science was typical of the group. She bought books from the hospital "where they have ones at a very cheap price – affordable," and diligently supervised homework:

Tarnside: Year 1: interview with Lola's mum

Mum: The teacher will 'give them maths and some science on the same sheet . . . but she'll explain it very well on the sheet. So now she (Lola) knows the steps so I just have to check it. She can read the homework and know what it is they want her to do. Normally we do it on a Friday evening.

Kim's mother while working part-time and studying for a degree, made time to work at home with Kim. The following extract is taken from Year 1 field notes:

Tarnside: Year 2: notes on a visit to Kim and his mum

Kim loves maths and is happy to do lots of maths at home. He doesn't like English and mum has trouble getting him to do it.

He has already done quite a bit of 'Maths For Ages Six to Eight' and chooses two exercises – one with additions and a second with subtractions

Mum: Do you know what this sign means? It's a plus sign

K: Does that mean add?

Mum: Yes and this one? It's a minus sign

K: That means take away doesn't it.

Mum: So these are additions and these are subtractions.

In other Tarnside families, mothers bought National Curriculum books from W. H. Smith and in two cases sent their children to Saturday school.

Attitudes were very different in the Mountford community. Parents here were less confident in their own ability to help their children. The following extract is taken from the Year 1 Mountford fieldnotes:

Mountford: Year 1: notes from conversation with Justin's mum

Mrs Parker seems to be in the dark about what to do with the school reading book. Justin tells her that she is supposed to read it to him but she feels that he should try and read it to her. They do it at breakfast time every day. He seems to be able to read the books (Kipper & Chip) she says, but she's not sure whether he's reading or just remembering the books that they've read in school. I ask if she has had any information from school about the home reading book. She hasn't. Apart from the reading book, there is no homework, although she would like him to have a bit.

Mountford parents relied very much on the information disseminated by the school which in many cases proved to be rather sketchy.

Mountford: Year 2: interview with Neil's mum

AW: Do they tell you what to do with the reading book for example.

Mum: They don't tell us about it at all and the only thing I find out is from Neil if he's in the mood to tell me which sometimes he's not. I don't think it would hurt them to let us know exactly what they were doing. They could tell us what they're learning that week. It couldn't hurt. The only time I see his teacher is in the playground and you can't talk to her properly anyway.

In general, the Mountford parents appeared reluctant to intervene in their children's education, believing that "teacher knows best":

Mountford: *Year 2: interview with Natalie's mum and dad*
AW: What does she get for homework now?
Mum: She doesn't always get homework . . .. Sometimes it's spelling isn't it
Dad: Or times tables
AW: Is it the same every week?
Dad: No, it's not regular
Mum: She's not had any for a while has she
Dad: In fact she's started to do her own now, like in her home book . . . where they write all the books they read . . . she's started writing . . .. Because she wants homework, I suppose, she does her own homework.

LINGUISTIC HABITUS

One explanation for the Mountford parents' reluctance to approach teachers may lie in one particular strand of embodied cultural capital namely the language practices and discourses that constitute their linguistic habitus. Language plays a crucial role in constructing power relationships (Fairclough, 1989) and, in U.K. in particular, in social stratification. It is not simply the difference between home and school discourses that make for asymmetrical power relationships, but the structural properties of language itself that are part of a community's social capital. Most of the families living on the Mountford estate are speakers of non-standard English unlike the teachers, all of whom speak standard English. Non standard varieties are widely socially stigmatised in U.K. although of course linguistically they are as complex and rule governed as standard languages (Trudgill, 1999). Local dialects have no part in the National Curriculum, although they are spoken by a majority of the population in Britain (Williams, forthcoming). Thus the language of the Mountford children's homes was not acceptable in school as the following extracts from a Year 2 lesson indicate:

Mountford: *Year 1: classroom observation*
It is the Literacy Hour: the children are sitting on the mat and the supply teacher has opened the big book
1.Teacher: Which page is this? (*pointing to a page*)
Child: The one we was reading yesterday
T: *Were* reading

2.T: Where did we get to yesterday?
Ch: Houseflies
T: So where will I look?

Ch: We *ain't* done houseflies yet
T: Ain't, ain't!! Is there such a word?

3. T: What are these?
Ch: Bullet points*
T: There's a T at the end of bullet.

**The child uses a glottal stop for final T. However, a final T before a following consonant is realised as a glottal stop in RP or BBC English(Wells, 1984).*

Children's and parents' failure to use the "legitimate language" in school gives rise to deficit notions among educators. As long ago as 1969, Labov dismissed the notion of verbal deprivation as part of "the modern mythology of educational psychology" in his paper "The Logic of Non-standard English," and Houston (1970) noted that since language learning is a species universal, disadvantaged children cannot be linguistically deprived: the ability to abstract, generalise and categorise is innate and implicit in the language itself and for this reason much language is impregnable to environmental variation (Tizard et al., 1988). Nevertheless notions of deficit persist. For example in a recent interview with the SENCOs,[17] Peter and Keith at Mountford, the following dialogue was recorded:

Peter: And in fact in reception, if you spend time there, in Maureens's class, you notice it there just in the lack of language. The number of children that are just not speaking.

AW: Just don't say anything? But is that emotional difficulty? Because I remember Kelly didn't say much did she in your class last year and I just wonder whether it's because she was shy and that kind of thing.

Keith: An example – we've been working with two Year 5s* since May last year and they had a set of pictures . . . and they were asked to choose the pictures of eggs and they chose the fried eggs and they totally missed the eggs in the shells and Deidre said 'Well they are eggs' and they didn't connect . . .. And that's Year 5, that's six years on, so we're still picking up on these fundamental things that you take for granted.

AW: What do you attribute this to then? You've worked in other schools in other areas.

Keith: Nobody talks to them.

Peter: I think you know it is hard to separate the emotional difficulties from the technical acquisition of the language but a lot of language is taken on board through modelling isn't it and I think the lack of children talking is not that they're all children like Kelly, but the fact that they live in a very passive environment where they're not engaged.

AW: And you don't think they engage with other children or with their siblings or with children in the street?

Keith: The majority of them . . . and if you listen and watch it's control language which is the language of this community. Nothing is explained. You don't do it. Stop . . . don't . . . you never hear explanations.

*Ten year olds

The danger is that such attitudes colour the judgements of the professionals whose role it is to evaluate children's competence. Speech therapists, carrying out language tests in Mountford nursery, claim that approximately 90% of the children start with serious or moderate language delay. No one challenges the claims: it is simply "common knowledge" in the school and the LEA.[18] Such judgements, in turn, have an impact on school policy. The Reception teacher, a very caring and concerned teacher, reflected that because of language problems, the children in her class would never achieve the targets set for the year – i.e. they should recognise 45 high frequency words and know the name and sound of every letter of the alphabet. She felt that most of them would struggle to learn 30 words and the targets were reduced accordingly. Already in the very first year of school then, these children are being offered a restricted curriculum.

In Rowan very different picture applies. Teachers, parents and children alike are speakers of Standard English. There is no dissonance between home and school merely a continuum. The cultural and linguistic capital these children bring from home is accepted and authorised in school.

SOCIAL CAPITAL

Linguistic practices, a constituent of embodied cultural capital, are deeply embedded in an individual's sense of identity and as such impact on access to social capital. As we have seen above, the linguistic capital of Mountford residents has minimal value in the school context and the deficit view of speakers held by some education staff can lead to asymmetrical relations not only between children and teachers but also between parents and staff. The following extract is from Mountford Reception fieldnotes:

> *Mountford: Reception: notes on a visit to Justin's mum*
>
> Mrs Parker said that Justin had started to stutter when he was in the nursery. The play leader told her to ignore it, but the school doctor told her that she 'should be picking it up'. When she enquired how, the doctor said to a teaching assistant who was present, 'Can't she understand anything?' Mrs Parker says she felt terrible and too upset to respond.

Justin's mother suffered the same humiliation as the mothers in Reay's study for whom "the primary school constituted a field that was least favourable to their linguistic productions and which condemned them to a more or less desperate attempt to be correct or to silence" (Bourdieu, 1992, p. 97; Reay, 1998, p. 166).

Linguistic prejudice is just one of the factors that contribute to social stigmatisation.

In terms of exploitable social capital, families living in social housing are very badly off. All such areas of social disadvantage are stigmatised and the present government's focus on social exclusion and urban deprivation serves to confirm public perceptions. The website of the "New Deal for Communities" for example bristles with superlatives: "Government strategy is to tackle *multiple deprivation* in the *most deprived neighbourhoods* in the country . . . ." As Reay and Lucey point out (Reay & Lucey, 2000, p. 411) "large local authority estates are perceived to be ghettoes of the workless and the hopeless, areas that have become morally, emotionally and spiritually disconnected from the rest of society."

As a consequence, the relationship between schools and families in such areas is often uneasy. Few parents in Mountford attended parents' evenings for example. In spite of strenuous efforts to welcome parents into school, a recent move to prohibit them from bringing their young children into the school building in the morning has increased feelings of alienation:

Mountford: Year 1: conversation with Neil's mum and dad

Mum: The only time I do even get a glance at Neil's classroom is when I take the packed lunch to him and the teacher's not there yet. I can't just stick it down outside the door. But saying that the door's always shut and I don't feel I'm allowed to just go in.

AW: I wonder why it is.

Mum: They reckon it's fire regulations To be honest with you I don't really like that sort of thing. I'd like to be able just to go down with Neil and at least hang his coat up for him . . .

School for these parents is not a social space in which they feel at home. The message conveyed to the families by the media, the authorities and ultimately by the school itself is that there are strong boundaries linguistically, physically, and socially between their home environment and that of the school. What is familiar to them from home is not acceptable in school. Parents are very aware of the asymmetrical power relations and this in turn makes them hesitant to take the initiative on educational issues. They leave education to the professionals, i.e. the teachers.

The situation in Rowan could not be more different. The following extract is taken from the Year 1 fieldnotes:

Rowan: Year 1: 8.45 am

Ten or so parents in the classroom. Some arrive very early. I am always surprised at how relaxed they are in the classroom. Hattie's mum helps herself to a tissue from the box to blow her nose. Ned's mum notices that her baby is crying in his plastic car seat and lifts him up onto the painting table that Alice (teacher) has set out for the day with paper, paints, objects etc. The mums all greet each other and chat for what seems like ages. Annie's mum enquires about Alice's health as she had heard that Dominic (reception teacher) was unwell.

The above extract clearly illustrates the lack of social distance between parents and staff in Rowan. Parents are welcome here and feel quite at ease in this classroom.

They are not intimidated by the teacher with whom they are on first name terms and the classroom is familiar territory – they know where the tissues are kept etc.

For the Rowan parents, school is a social nexus. Class representatives organise dinners, coffee mornings and outings in the holidays. Parents' evenings are fully subscribed and during the school day the corridors are full of mothers (and fathers), helping with reading, maths, computing and handicrafts. In this school however, the perception of parents and of their role is quite different from that in the housing estate. Parents in Rowan are seen as a resource and are regarded as skilled mediators of literacy and other subjects. Rowan parents are articulate and confident in their dealings with school staff and see themselves as working alongside teachers for the benefit of their children. The school has a very powerful and charismatic head but parents feel able to approach her and even challenge her as the following extract from an interview suggests:

Rowan: *Year 1: interview with Alison's mum*

Mum: Mind you Mrs Walker has her opinions and she's very good with words and she's always right and you come out thinking, 'Did I really ask what I meant to?' and 'Did I get an answer or am I totally being fobbed off?' I had a lot of problems with my second daughter – I felt she wasn't getting the support she needed and I really kicked up a big stink.

AW: And did they listen to you?

Mum: Yes, but it's a two way partnership cos I now go into school, I see more what goes on in school, I will approach the teachers more. Until I went into school I didn't actually see what went on in school and you have this picture . . . I mean I know how much I do at home with Jessie and she's tutored but you don't see what goes on in school . . .

Both Rowan and Mountford had unusually homogeneous school populations. Tarnside, situated in an area of mixed housing, has a heterogeneous population both in terms of class and ethnicity. The project parents felt they were welcome in the school and that the school management made efforts to embrace all cultures. The following extract is taken from the Reception class fieldnotes:

Tarnside: Reception class

The nursery and reception classes were having an international day. Some children were dressed in the costumes from their parents' country of origin – Stewart had a Nigerian suit, Sheri had a Ghanaan top and headdress . . .. The children had brought a wonderful array of food – banana fritters, many different kinds of sweet and savoury rice, little noodles, tiny samosas, mangoes, bananas, plantain chips etc The press came and took photos. Sheri's mum was very pleased – she said such an afternoon would have been unheard of during the previous head's regime.

The good relations in Tarnside were in part due to the fact that several members of staff were themselves members of minority ethnic groups and able to act as advocates for families and children. Parents felt they were welcome in school and appreciative of the teachers' work. Lola's mum for example remembered Lola's reception class teacher fondly,

> Mrs Khan helped her a lot. She loves Mrs Khan and misses her terribly. She taught her how to pronounce which was very good.

CONCLUSION

The data we have presented reveal three schools serving very different communities. In a system which prides itself on its commitment to equality of opportunity and social inclusion however, can we say that the children in all three schools have equal opportunities to succeed? While measures have been introduced to ensure that all children have access to the same curriculum in school, the government's enthusiasm for increased parental responsibility in education would seem to result in even greater inequalities. Working class parents as yet have neither the economic nor the social capital to become middle class consumers in the education market place. Moreover, attempts to change parental attitudes towards education can only be successful where both the parents and the schools are involved in the transformation. In Mountford, long held views about social deprivation and deficit would seem to inhibit any cautious attempts at re-socialisation. In Tarnside, mothers strive for educational success in a manner that is typical of many migrant groups for whom individual self- realisation is a necessity if they are to succeed in an alien environment. The Rowan parents meanwhile, with all the benefits that accrue from valuable economic, social and cultural capital and the help of a supportive and successful school, can fulfil all the requirements of being good parents and exploit the system to its full extent. It is not hard to predict which children will be the university graduates of the future.

NOTES

1. NFER Evaluation of Excellence in Cities Programme; April 2002.
2. Non-selective state schools.
3. Conservative Prime Minister, 1989–1992.
4. Organisation for Economic Cooperation and Development.
5. The literacy and numeracy hours are part of the Labour government's National Literacy (NLS) and Numeracy Strategies (NNS) introduced in 1998/9 to improve standards in state schools.
6. See note v.
7. An estate of social housing on the outskirts of the town.

8. *Literacy practices at home and at school: community contexts and interpretations of literacy*. Eve Gregory, Brian Street, Dave Baker & Ann Williams. Leverhulme funded project. 2000–2003.
9. Pseudonyms have been used to preserve anonymity.
10. Children enter the Reception class at age 4.
11. Standard Assessment Tests: national tests in literacy maths and science held at ages 7, 11 and 14.
12. A school which provides a model of good practice for other schools in the area.
13. Special Education Needs Coordinators.
14. Junior divisions of Cub Scouts and Brownies.
15. Children's section of a broadsheet newspaper.
16. The school operates a "real books" reading programme.
17. See endnote xiii.
18. Local education authority.

ACKNOWLEDGMENTS

This research was supported by the Leverhulme Trust.

Grateful thanks are due to all the teachers, head-teachers, families and children who gave so generously of their time and hospitality throughout the three years.

We would also like to thank Brian Street and Dave Baker co-directors of the project: *Literacy practices at home and at school: community contexts and interpretations of literacy*: Leverhulme funded project. 2000–2003, and Diane Reay for her valuable comments on the paper.

REFERENCES

Barton, D., & Hamilton, M. (1998). *Local literacies*. London: Routledge.

Bourdieu, P., & Passeron, J.-C. (1977). *Reproduction in education, society and culture*. London: Sage.

Carrington, V., & Luke, A. (1997). Literacy and Bourdieu's sociological theory: A reframing. *Language and Education, 11*(2), 96–112.

Fairclough, N. (1989). *Language and power*. London: Longman.

Gewirtz, S. (2001). Cloning the Blairs: New Labour's programme for the re-socialisation of the working class. *Journal of Educational Policy, 16*(4).

Houston, S. (1970). A re-examination of some assumptions about the language of the disadvantaged child. *Child Development, 41*, 947–963.

Labov, W. (1969). *The logic of non-standard English*. Georgetown Monograph. Ling. 22.

Levin, B. (1999). *Value for money in the national literacy and numeracy strategies*. OISIE, University of Toronto Press.

Reay, D. (1998). Linguistic capital and home-school relationships: Mothers' interactions with their children's primary school teachers. *Acta Sociologica, 42*, 159–168.

Reay, D., & Lucey, H. (2000). I don't really like it here but I don't want to be anywhere else: Children and inner city council estates. *Antipode, 32*, 410–428.

Snow, C., & Ninio, A. (1986). The contracts of literacy: What children learn from learning to read books. In: W. H. Teale & E. Sulzby (Eds), *Emergent Literacy: Writing and Reading*. Norwood, NL: Ablex.

Street, B. (1993). *Cross-cultural approaches to literacy*. Cambridge: Cambridge University Press.

Taylor, D. (1983). *Family literacy*. London: Heineman.

Tizard, B., Hughes, M., Carmichael, H., & Pinkerton, G. (1988). Language and social class: Is verbal deprivation a myth? In: N. Mercer (Ed.), *Language and Literacy from an Educational Perspective: A Reader*. Milton Keynes: Open University Press.

Trudgill, P. (1999). Standard English: What it isn't. In: T. Bex & R. Watts (Eds), *Standard English: The Widening Debate*. London: Routledge.

Wells, G. (1985). *Language development in the pre-school years*. Cambridge: Cambridge University Press.

Wells, J. C. (1984). *Accents of English 2: The British Isles*. Cambridge: Cambridge University Press.

Williams, A. (forthcoming). Non standard English and education. In: D. Britain (Ed.), *Language in the British Isles* (2nd ed.). Cambridge: Cambridge University Press.

ADDRESSING INEQUITIES: LESSONS IN SYNCRETISM FROM MEXICAN AMERICAN AND PUERTO RICAN CHILDREN AT HOME AND AT SCHOOL

Susi Long and Dinah Volk

> Marcial selects an English picture book from the bookshelf and sits on the floor next to his friends, Juan and Martita. He opens the book and, as he turns the pages, he "reads the pictures" aloud in Spanish. Intermittently, he stops to talk to Juan and Martita who are also turning the pages of English picture books. A few feet away, Kiesha, sits reading the pictures of a book aloud in English. She looks over at Marcial and watches him as he reads in Spanish. Then she goes back to her book. Juan looks up and watches Kiesha for a moment. Kiesha moves next to him and holds her book so that both children are able to see the pages. Then she begins to read to Juan in English. The teacher stops by and praises both Marcial and Kiesha for doing what good readers do – reading the pictures and sharing the reading experience with friends.

These children were five-year-olds in a kindergarten in the southern United States. Marcial, Juan, and Martita entered the classroom four weeks earlier speaking only Spanish. Kiesha spoke only English. Through their interactions, the children constructed syncretic practices, blending and recreating aspects of their home and school cultures in ways that made it possible for them to participate as active and expert members of the class. The teacher celebrated their expertise and, in doing so, she was careful not to create a hierarchy of cultures. She praised all children as

Ethnographies of Educational and Cultural Conflicts: Strategies and Resolutions
Studies in Educational Ethnography, Volume 9, 83–106

ISSN: 1529-210X/doi:10.1016/S1529-210X(04)09006-0

readers but she did not privilege the child who read in English over the child who read in Spanish. She understood that all of the children were informed strategists who skillfully integrated funds of knowledge (Moll, Amanti, Neff & Gonzalez, 1992) from rich and varied experiences.

In a classroom that honors the syncretic nature of children's interactions, expertise is continuously redefined as children move seamlessly in and out of the roles of expert and novice (Rogoff, 1990). In the process, the likelihood of privileging of one culture over another is minimized and all children benefit. Although there is a clear goal of helping developing bilinguals grow to become confident, proficient speakers of English, other languages are not devalued in the process. The English-only students learn that speaking more than one language is a highly coveted ability and the native Spanish speaking children learn that drawing from a range of cultural experiences makes it possible for them to interact expertly in a wider variety of settings.

We argue that teachers who create contexts in which the syncretic nature of child-child and adult-child interactions is valued, also create contexts in which aspects of all cultures are valued and utilized and in which deficit perspectives and inequities are challenged. In such classrooms, children are viewed for what they know and can contribute to the classroom community rather than from a deficit perspective. Skilled teachers understand that creating contexts for syncretic practices in multilingual classrooms generates learning opportunities for all children and multiplies the resources available for learning.

The transformation of classrooms to become places where syncretic interactions are embraced requires transformation in teacher attitude which, in turn, impacts practice. Changes in attitude and practice come with the acquisition of knowledge. Therefore, we believe that, for teachers to understand and appreciate syncretism and its role in broadening and deepening the worlds of all learners, they must understand the nature of syncretism in child-child and adult-child interactions. Toward that end, this chapter presents two ethnographic studies of Latino[1] children in the United States: (a) a study of Puerto Rican kindergartners in a U.S. city in the Midwest; and (b) a study of Mexican-American kindergartners in a U.S. city in the South. The studies illustrate the language and literacy teaching and learning that occur when syncretism is allowed to flourish at home and at school. Findings illustrate the skillful ways that children draw on various cultural experiences to create new contexts for learning. The presentation of these studies is followed by a discussion of implications for teachers – how they might use this knowledge to build equitable practices that maintain the richness of diverse cultures while creating a place for children to interact and learn with and from one another.

THEORETICAL FRAMEWORK

Transformational and Deficit Perspectives

The theoretical framework guiding these studies draws from the work of Paulo Freire (1989) who argues that transformation in schools and in society is possible when teachers value and utilize the diverse cultural schema of every student. Our work is further informed by critiques of the deficit perspective that dominates many school settings (Bartolomé & Balderrama, 2001; Garcia, 2001) in the United States. According to this perspective, the documented lack of school success of many children of color, of many children whose first language is not English, and of poor children in general is attributed to deficits in the children themselves, their families, and cultures. Most often, parents are cited for not reading to their children, not emphasizing the importance of education, not disciplining their children, not speaking English to their children, and/or for their own "dysfunctions" which interfere with their children's learning.

Discussions of the deficit perspective and the inequities it both reproduces and springs from include exposés contrasting the schools that children attend and the conditions in which they live. Educators such as Kozol (1991) and Ladson-Billings (2000) locate the cause of some children's school problems in these "savage inequalities" of schools and society that are often internalized as limits to effort and self esteem. While recognizing the hardships in many families' lives, we present data to counter the over-simplified cause-and-effect arguments of the deficit perspective. We argue that differences in child rearing practices, for example, must be recognized as integral to other cultures and valued in their own right, not as deficits because they do not conform to a "standard" model. We would go even farther and argue that different practices must be made visible before they can be valued.

In contrast to work informed by a deficit perspective, our research is guided by studies – many of them ethnographies – that illuminate the rich cultural practices that exist in diverse communities (Gregory & Williams, 2000; Guerra, 1998; Heath, 1983) and studies that focus on the importance of using that knowledge to transform pedagogy (Delpit, 2002; Hull & Schultz, 2002; Nieto, 1999). This work has provided evidence to counter the deficit perspective and to suggest that many children and their families have an array of resources that are relevant to school learning.

Syncretism

We use the term syncretism to describe the reinvention of cultural practices (Apter, 1991; Shaw & Stewart, 1994). Syncretism is more than a mixing of existing cultural forms but is, instead, a creative process in which people transform culture as they draw on diverse resources, both familiar and new. Syncretism is an inherent feature of cross cultural encounters. Duranti and Ochs (1997), writing about syncretic literacy in the homes and communities of Samoan Americans "extend syncretism to include hybrid cultural constructions of speech acts and speech activities that constitute literacy" (p. 173). This work illustrates the ways in which families at home and teachers in community schools draw on practices and tools from both Samoan and North American cultures as they construct new forms of literacy.

More recently, researchers have investigated the ways children and teachers appropriate practices and knowledge from other contexts in children's lives as resources for school learning (Dyson, 1999; Gutiérrez, Baquedano-López, Tejeda & Rivera, 1999; Solsken, Willett & Wilson-Keenan, 2000). Such work explicitly explores the learning potential of newly created practices and the processes from which they emerge.

Many of these studies are rooted in the work of Bakhtin (1981). They use his term *hybridity* to refer to the different voices that can coexist within an utterance and to the "laminated, overlapped, and interwoven nature" (Gutiérrez et al., 1999, p. 2) of the practices created. In this chapter, we prefer the term *syncretism* because of its use to describe the creation of new forms, not just complex blended ones. We acknowledge that the definitions of syncretism and hybridity in the literature lack clarity and that both terms emphasize the problematic and creative nature of cultural practices in contact.

Literacy as a Sociocultural Process

From a neo-Vygotskian perspective (Rogoff, 1990), children's learning is embedded in a sociocultural process in which children, as cultural novices, experience patterns of thinking and communicating in interactions with more expert members of their cultures. This process has been called guided participation, emphasizing the active roles of the expert and novice as well as the creation of something new rather than just the replication of the old.

Consistent with socio-cultural theory, the studies presented here are grounded in a conception of literacy as a social and cultural process (Baynham, 1995). Literacy is understood as a collaborative process that exists in multiple forms that vary within and across settings.

If literacy can vary by context, then the question of what literacy practices are valued in any context becomes relevant. In industrialized societies, these valued practices are the ways of reading and writing emphasized in school (Street, 1999).

Consequently, teachers may expect parents to replicate school-identified ways of interacting with print such as storybook reading and, when these do not occur or when they occur in different forms, may assume that no parental support is provided and that children will lag in literacy development. The literacy practices constructed in the homes and communities of children from diverse backgrounds remain invisible to many teachers.

Literacy and Learning in Homes

The educational literature focuses on learning in school and much less attention has been given to how children learn at home. Our work builds on studies (Goelman, Oberg & Smith, 1984) that describe learning at home as primarily embedded in activities that serve other purposes. This literature is consistent in suggesting that children participate in meaningful learning and literacy experiences at home. The literacies constructed there may be similar in some ways to the literacies that count in school and different in others.

Educational and literacy beliefs and practices in Latino families are described in studies of working class or poor Puerto Rican and Mexican-American families (Hidalgo, 2000; Soto, 1997; Valdés, 1996). Patterns emerge from this work, with many practices attributed to both cultural groups and some discussion of variations among families.

The literature (Delgado-Gaitan, 1994; Soto, 1990; Valdés, 1996; Volk, 1999; Volk & de Acosta, 2001) reports wide variation in the ways and the frequency with which Latino parents support at home their children's academic work in school. Some studies suggest that Latino parents rarely or never engage in deliberate teaching, while others describe formal and informal lessons. Some studies conclude that most literacy activities in Latino homes are related to homework. Others observe that when Latino parents help their children, they stress accurate word and letter recognition at the expense of meaning, as their own teachers did. Still other work describes a range of literacy experiences, some deliberate instruction, some embedded in other activities, both balancing a focus on letters with an interest in meaning, often tied to family contexts.

The work of Moll et al. (1992) on Latino families' funds of knowledge challenges the stereotype of Latino families as lacking in resources relevant to education. Arguing that families and communities possess knowledge about a variety of topics and many related skills, Moll and his colleagues have worked with teachers to discover what families know, to recognize its value, and to use it as the basis for developing curriculum in schools that draws on these resources.

Summary

This literature in combination with our own work suggests that, by looking closely at the language and literacy interactions of children in homes and in schools, lessons can be learned that have the potential to inform pedagogy in classrooms and thereby address issues of inequity. The discussion of our findings highlights the multiple strategies used by children, parents, and teachers at home and at school to support language and literacy learning while using home and community knowledge. Implications are drawn for the construction of more equitable and supportive classroom contexts.

LATINOS AND INEQUITY

> Latinos [in the United States], as a work force, are disproportionately concentrated in low-wage jobs with few benefits . . . Married Hispanics with children continue to have higher poverty rates than comparable African American or Anglo families. The nation's 31 million Latinos are often under-educated, a factor that portends little improvement in their economic plight. (Valverde, 2000, p. 2)

Issues of inequity constitute reality for a range of Latino cultures across the United States. While in this article we focus on similarities in the educational inequities and multiple resources of Mexican-American and Puerto Ricans, these two groups have cultural practices, histories, and political relationships to the United States that are similar in some ways and quite distinct in others. Moreover, when reviewing our analyses, it is important to note that cultures should not be seen as monolithic and static; the Latinos described here create their culture as they are shaped by it.

According to the 2000 census, there were 32.8 million Latinos living in the U.S., representing 12% of the total population (Therrien & Ramirez, 2001). Of those, about 66% were Mexican-Americans and 9% were Puerto Ricans. The following points illustrate the educational status of Latinos as a group in this country (Garcia, 2001; *The condition of education*, 2001):

- Latino children make up the fastest growing ethnic group in U.S. public schools. In 1976, nonwhite and Latino enrollment represented 23% of the total children in public schools; this group is projected to represent 70% of the total or 45 million students in 2026.
- In 1990, of all 16–24 year olds, only 67% of Latinos had a high school diploma or its equivalent compared to 86% of African Americans and 88% of whites.

- In 1997, 30% of all 13 year olds were one grade level below the norm on standardized achievement levels. This was true for 27% of white students, 40% of Latino students, and 46% of African American students.
- In 1999, school dropout rates for 16–24 year olds were 28% for Latinos, 12% for African Americans, 8% for whites, and 11% for all people in that group.
- The National Assessment of Educational Progress for 1996 reports that 98.5% of white 17 year olds, 94.8% of Latino 17 year olds, and 94% of African Americans 17 year olds have reached at least a *beginning* level of skills and understanding in reading. At the next level – *moderately complex* procedures and reasoning – are 45.1% of whites, 20% of Latinos, and 18% of African Americans.

STUDY #1: PUERTO RICAN KINDERGARTNERS AND FAMILY SUPPORT FOR LITERACY LEARNING

The data shared here are from a broader study of literacy events (Volk & de Acosta, 2001) in the homes, bilingual kindergarten, churches, and Sunday schools of three Puerto Rican children. The following sections outline the study's method, provide information about the participants and their families, and describe and analyze the syncretic nature of literacy practices observed in their homes.

Method

Fieldwork was initiated in the kindergarten at the beginning of the school year; the researchers attended parent meetings and conducted participant observations during weekly, day-long visits. The focal children were selected during this time in consultation with the teacher, using information from observations and reading assessments. The group of three Spanish dominant children included: two girls and one boy; one an accomplished beginning reader, one making average progress, and one struggling; all three with older siblings.

The data collected included reading and writing activities and both oral and written texts. From January through June, observations and audiotapings were conducted in the classroom twice a month for the first four hours of the day when most literacy events occurred. Observations and tapings were conducted in each home once a month for between two and four hours at a time. Observations and interviews were also conducted in the families' churches. Copies were collected of the children's journals, written work completed at school and at home, spring report cards, and fall and spring assessments.

In March interviews, parents helped the researchers draw network maps detailing the people who interacted with the children in literacy-related interactions. These maps were used to select literacy events for observation and taping during the subsequent three months. Semi-structured interviews in June with the parents and the teacher explored their literacy histories and their descriptions of how and why they supported the children's developing literacy. To further understand the participants' perspectives, the researchers also worked with two Puerto Rican cultural insiders.

In developing an understanding of literacy across settings, the literacy event was used as a unit of analysis. Literacy events were defined as "activities where literacy has a role . . . observable episodes which arise from [literacy] practices and are shaped by them" (Barton & Hamilton, 1998, p. 7). Literacy events were understood as situated interactions, occurring in specific contexts. Within literacy events, literacy practices, "what people do with literacy" (Barton & Hamilton, 1998, p. 6) as well as the ways in which people understand and value literacy, were analyzed.

Central to the analysis of syncretism were the concepts of intertextuality and intercontextuality. The former is the juxtaposition of two or more texts, either oral or written (Bloome & Egan-Robertson, 1993) and the links people create among them. Intercontextuality (Floriani, 1994) locates the construction of a text within the wider process of constructing a context. Prior and present texts and contexts, when recognized and acknowledged, become potential resources for present and future literacy events (Putney, Green, Dixon, Durán & Yeager, 2000).

Using these conceptual tools, the data analysis began with the identification of literacy events and the use of a multilayered approach to understand the construction of these events (Gregory, 1998). Ethnographic techniques were used to situate literacy events in the immediate and wider social contexts (outer layer) including the literacy histories and practices of the homes, community, and classroom. The components of the literacy events (middle layer) including the participants and their literacy practices were then identified, drawing on the analysis of the outer layer. The analysis of syncretism through intertextuality and intercontextuality took place within that middle layer as texts and contexts were identified and references explored within and across events. The analysis then moved turn-by-turn through the events, identifying patterns as well as textual and contextual referents. Literacy events selected for discussion are representative examples, illustrative of the distinctive patterns of syncretism in the literacy events in all three homes (Solsken et al., 2000).

Participants

The three children, Julializ Torres, Manuel Huerta, and Fidelia Ugarte, attended the same bilingual kindergarten. Their school and homes were located in two adjacent working class neighborhoods with substantial Puerto Rican populations in a large Midwestern city on the U.S. mainland. The children were all five-year-olds who turned six the year of the study and all lived within extended family networks. These networks included parents, siblings, aunts, uncles, cousins, and grandparents as well as "hermanos y hermanas de la iglesia" [church brothers and sisters]. (Fidelia lived with her aunt, uncle, and cousin though she referred to them as her mother, father, and sister.)

All the parents had attended school in Puerto Rico and had received their high school diplomas or the equivalent. Even though all the parents worked, the three children were eligible for the free lunch in school provided for low-income families. The three families had lived in Puerto Rico and elsewhere before coming to this city to join relatives. All three attended Protestant Latino churches.[2] The families spoke primarily Spanish though the three children were learning English and spoke it occasionally at school and primarily with siblings and friends at home.

Findings

Syncretic Literacy Practices with Parents and Siblings at Home

In the following pages, representative examples from the data are used to illustrate the syncretic nature of children's interactions with parents and siblings in literacy events at home. Many of these events were based on the experiences of the adults and children in school, in the United States and in Puerto Rico. Children often did homework with parents and siblings, reviewed school work with them, used workbooks purchased at the grocery store, played school, and sang songs and rhymes from school. But these were hardly the only type of literacy interaction. The children read books-their own and others from the library or school, listened to stories read to them, used coloring books, wrote greeting cards, played cards games, played with a minicomputer, and recited poems, some traditional to Puerto Rican culture and some of their own creation. Religious literacy events in the homes were also regular and significant events in the homes. The children memorized psalms to recite in church and participated in Bible readings with their families almost daily.

Most of the literacy events that were observed or described by participants were social interactions with text rather than individual ones. That is, participants usually used texts in the public spaces of their homes and/or used them in interaction with others. For example, on one occasion, Julializ and her 6- and 3-year-old cousins played a Nintendo game that included print on the television screen while, in the same room, her mother helped her 9 year old brother study his spelling words and a young man, a church brother, helped her 12 year old brother with his homework in the kitchen. Almost all religious literacy events were also social as children and adults sat together in a circle, reading, discussing, and praying.

Manuel and his mother review school worksheets. The first representative example of a syncretic literacy event illustrates the ways that the parents and children used and made references to school texts and contexts. The event was co-constructed by Manuel (MN) and his mother, Sra. Huerta (DH), and began when she asked to see his school backpack. Manuel then mentioned that his father was in Puerto Rico, substituting an L sound for the first R, a common practice in rural Puerto Rico and among those with less schooling. Sra. Huerta corrected his pronunciation, modeling the text identified with educated speakers. As Manuel practiced these sounds, his mother took two completed worksheets out of his backpack. The first had pictures of items; only those beginning with R were to be circled. The second was about the letter F. The following excerpt begins at that point.

(1) DH: ((looks at worksheet)) Vamos a ver . . . [Let's see . . .]
(2) MN: Es de esta letra. [It's about this letter.]
(3) DH: Ajá, y ¿cómo se pronuncia esta letra? . . . [Aha, and how do you pronounce this letter? . . .]
(4) MN: R. ((uses name of letter R in Spanish))
(5) DH: . . . Rrrrrr rrrrana. Rrrastrillo. Rey, ruedo, reloj y rosa. (. . . Fffff fffrog. Rrrrrake. King, circle, watch and rose.)
(6) MN: Y columpio. [And swing.]
(7) DH: Sí, pero columpio no se dice con R. Yo te dije, las que se dicen con R ¿Viste? . . . [Yes, but swing doesn't begin with R. I told you those that begin with R. See? . . .]
(8) MN: Ma yo quiero //pintar ()//. [Mom I want //to color ()//.]
(9) DH: //Tú tienes que// pintar más que la F. ¿Verdad? Los mismos colores y la pintaste de colores. [//You have to// color more than the letter F. Right? The same colors and you colored it.]
(10) MN: O no. [Oh no.]
(11) DH: Oh sí, para saber que es la F, ¡mira! Yo te voy a hacer la F en un papel y tú verás que te vas a dar cuenta. Que si tú pintas éstos del mismo color tú vas a darte cuenta que es una F. Pero ahora tú no te das cuenta. [Oh, yes, to know that it's the letter F, look! I'll make an F on a piece of paper and you'll see that you get it. That if you color these the same color you'll get that's an F. But now you're not getting it.]
(12) MN: ¡Ajá! ¡Yo me dí cuenta! [Aha! I got it!]
(13) DH: . . . Es, ¿que ésta la que? [. . . It's, what is this?]

(14) MN: La. [The.]
(15) DH: ¿La qué? La F ¿qué? [The what? The F what?]
(16) MN: Aaaa grande. [Aaaa big.]
(17) DH: ¿Cómo se dice? //Ah ha.// [How do you say it? Uh huh.]
(18) MN: ((laughing)) //Mayúscula.// [Upper case.]
(19) DH: Mayúscula, ¿y ésta? [Upper case, and this one?]
(20) MN: Minúscula. [Lower case.]
(21) DH: Es exactamente. [Exactly.]

Sra. Huerta marked the beginning of the worksheet review with "Vamos a ver" (turn #1). This marker was similar to the one regularly used by the classroom teacher to begin instructional interactions. Throughout the event, Sra. Huerta continued to use an oral lesson text similar to the teacher's that is referred to in the literature (Mehan, 1979) as the IRE sequence and identified as typical of teacher talk in U.S. schools. Thus, she asked known information questions (#3, #13, #17, #19), used unfinished declaratives (#15), and confirmed Manuel's use of the "school" words for upper and lower case letters with a positive evaluation (#21). In addition, she modeled the pronunciation of the R sound in Spanish and provided examples of R words. At the end of the event, she assigned Manuel homework since the teacher had not done so.

Manuel participated in the construction of this school text and context by responding to his mother's questions (#4, #14, #16, #18, #20) and challenging some of her assertions (#10, #12). He also challenged the school text and context – though not the focus on literacy – when he interrupted his mother to ask for another coloring book, a literacy text acknowledged elsewhere by his mother as one of his favorite (#8). Only when Sra. Huerta had assigned homework was Manuel successful in establishing coloring books as a topic of discussion.

In these ways, Manuel and his mother together transformed the school text and context. While this event was initiated in reaction to materials brought from school, their purposeful appropriation of school-related resources in this instance of deliberate instruction contrasts with the description in some other studies of learning activities in Latino homes as merely reactive to initiatives from school (Delgado-Gaitan, 1994; Valdés, 1996). Using the worksheets and identifiable elements of school talk and behaviors, they co-created a literacy lesson that also drew on the culture of their home by referring to family members, using Spanish, and by making reference to the island and correct ways of speaking there.

Julializ and her mother read the Bible. The second representative literacy event was constructed in Julializ's (JU) home. As excerpted below, this syncretic Bible reading/ reading lesson was part of an almost daily ritual of Bible study. It began with Sra. Torres (MT) and Julializ, each with Bibles in front of them, sitting together at the dining room table. Following her mother's direction, Julializ located a psalm. Then, like Sra. Huerta, Sra. Torres used elements of the teacher text including known information questions, a confirmation, a question used as an indirect imperative, and reminders about appropriate literacy behaviors. She then prompted Julializ to recite a prayer before reading "la Palabra" [the Word; for Pentecostals the literal Word of God]. Every family member was mentioned and the assistance of God and His angels was invoked for this religious literacy task. Thus, as they together set the scene for reading, Julializ and her mother syncretized the sacred texts, practices, and contexts with instructional and family ones.

(1) MT: Ok vamos a leer. [Ok let's read.]
(2) JU: Vamos a leer. // // [Let's read.]
(3) MT: // // El 138 mami aquí mira. Sigueme con el dedo, ¿ok? Ay si tú me cambiaste la pagina. Mira aquí. Y aquí. 138. Y ala//baré.// [138 dear here look. Follow me with your finger, ok? Hey you changed the page on me. Look here. And here. 138. And I will praise.]
(4) JU: //Alabaré. // [I will praise.]
((Sra. Torres and Julializ read, turns overlapping, Julializ a beat behind her mother))
(5/6) MT & JU: //Con todo mi corazón. Delante de los dioses, te cantaré salmos.//
[With all my heart. Before the gods, I will sing psalms to you.]
(7) MT: //Me pos//traré. [I will bow down.]
(8) JU: //Me pos.// ¿Aquí ma? [I wi. Here ma?]
(9) MT: Sí en la dos, allí mismo. [Yes in the two, right there.]
(10) MT & JU: //Me postraré hacia Tu santo templo.// [I will bow down toward Your holy temple.]
(11) MT & JU: //Y alabaré.// [And I will praise.]
(12/13) MT & JU: //Tu nombre// por Tu misericordia y Tu fidelidad. Porque has engrandecido Tu nombre y Tu palabra sobre todas las cosas. El día que clamé, me respondiste. Me fortaleciste con vigor en mi alma.// [Your name for Your compassion and Your faithfulness. For you have exalted Your name and Your word over all things. The day that I called You, You answered me. You made me strong and bold in my soul.]
(14) MT: Te alabarán. [They praise you.]
(15) JU: No hagas rápido mami. [Don't go fast mommy.]
(16) MT: Oh ok. I'm sorry.
(17) MT: Mami por la cuatro. Aquí. Te. [Dear on the fourth. Here. You.]

(18) JU: Te. [You.]
((Sra. Torres provides text, Julializ echoes))
(19/20) MT, then JU: Alabarán. [They will praise.]
(21/22) MT, then JU: O Jehová. [Oh Jehovah.]
(23) JU: ¿Dónde? [Where?]
(24) MT: Aquí. Porque han oído. [Here. Because they have heard.]
(25) JU: Porque han oído. [Because they have heard.]
((echo reading continues, then JU reads independently with prompts from MT))

Sra. Torres began this excerpt with a verbal marker, "Ok vamos a leer," just as Manuel's mother and the classroom teacher had, to make reference to an imminent instructional context and text. Then the lesson proceeded with Sra. Torres repeating reminders about literacy behaviors and using three strategies for literacy instruction. The first was the neurological impress method in which she sat behind Julializ and read with her, but a beat ahead (turns 5–#13). Then, in response to Julializ's request for her to slow down (#15), Sra.Torres provided more scaffolding with echo reading in which she read small segments of the text for Julializ to repeat (begins #19). Later, Sra. Torres provided only occasional prompts and several positive evaluations as Julializ read enthusiastically on her own.

In turns 15 and #23, Julializ, like Manuel, interrupted her mother's reading. This was uncharacteristic behavior for school. Neither child ever interrupted the teacher or initiated questions, requested clarification, or challenged what she had said. But this appeared to be characteristic of parent-child talk in the homes, even during lessons such as these. The parents provided some opportunities for the children to participate and the children took others.

Fidelia reads with her cousin's help. The third representative example illustrates syncretism created in child-child interactions and took place in Fidelia's home during the interview with her parents. When we asked them how they helped support Fidelia's learning in school, 6 year old Felicidad drew a worksheet in her school notebook, reproducing the worksheet text typical in school. Simple words were aligned with pictures to aid the beginning reader in her efforts to read them. But there was an important difference. Instead of a picture of a mother matched with the word "mamá" [mom], Felicidad had matched it with the name of the girls' mother, Eva. She had transformed the generic worksheet into a meaningful text charged with affect for these two girls, both separated from their birth mothers, Felicidad adopted by the Ugartes and Fidelia living with them temporarily.

Julializ reads English with her cousin's help. In this example of a child-child interaction, Julializ (JU) and her cousin Zoila (ZO) who was a year older, syncretized Spanish and English. This occurred as Zoila helped Julializ read a list of English words that had been provided by the Julializ's teacher.

(1) ZO: La O (ō) es U (ō ō). [The O is U.]
(2) JU: To. Go.
(3) ZO: P. A (ā). //P.//
(4) JU: //P//lay.
(5) ZO: La O (ō) es. A (ŏ). [The O is. A.]
(6) JU: Nnnn ot. Not.
(7) ZO: U (ŭ). I-U (Ĕ-ŭ). Ruuuuuun.
(8) JU: Run.
(9) ZO: Oo (oo). Ll ook.
(10) JU: Look.
((joint reading continues with JU reading more words on her own))

Throughout the event, Zoila allowed Julializ to read the words that she could read and, when she hesitated, provided cues for the vowel sounds and demonstrations of how to sound out letters to create a word. Though the list of words was in English, the girls spoke Spanish and Zoila's cues and demonstrations were in Spanish. For example, in turn #1, Zoila provided a cue for the O sound in *to* using the sound of U in Spanish. Julializ then read *go* correctly on her own, using a different O sound, though one that was the same as the Spanish O. In line #5, Zoila provided a cue for another English O, this time using the Spanish A sound.

This event illustrates the syncretic use of oral and written Spanish and English as observed in all three homes. Texts in Spanish, such as the Bible, were most often read and discussed in that language. However, other texts, such as children's books, were in English and these were sometimes read in English, sometimes in Spanish translation, and sometimes with cues in Spanish provided so the target child could read in English. That is, with the English texts, Spanish was used as a resource and cues to both the sounds of the letters, as above, or to the meaning of the words was provided.

STUDY #2: SYNCRETIC SUPPORT FOR LANGUAGE AND LITERACY LEARNING: MEXICAN-AMERICAN KINDERGARTNERS

The data presented in this section are drawn from a six-month study of six Mexican-American kindergartners in an English-dominant school in the southern United

States. The purpose of the study was to better understand literacy practices used by peers as they interact informally at school. Findings are presented here to illuminate the syncretic nature of literacy practices engaged in by peers at school in support of the language and literacy use of three children from that study.

Method

Data were collected in the kindergarten from September through March. Using field notes, video tape, and audio tape, data were gathered at school and at home. School data included video tape and field notes taken during formal and informal activities throughout the school day including: formal lessons and whole class read-alouds, activity times when the children self-selected from a range of possible activities alone or with other children, independent reading and writing periods, 1–1 teacher-child interactions, transitions from the classroom to other classes, lunchtime, and outdoor recess. School data also included interviews with the children conducted in English and in Spanish. Representative samples of the children's writing and drawing were collected as documental data. Home data included parent interviews conducted in the homes of each of the three children at the end of the study. The classroom teacher, a native-English speaker who spoke some Spanish, and the classroom teaching assistant, a native-Spanish speaker provided translations.

Data were analyzed by three researchers – the university professor, the classroom teacher, and a graduate assistant – during multiple analysis sessions in which transcribed and documental data were scrutinized for emergent patterns. Those patterns were named and coded as categories and considered in terms of frequency and quality of evidence. Each researcher further scrutinized data sets related to specific categories. Interpretations were shared across the research team as a form of triangulation through which interpretations were confirmed or disconfirmed.

Participants

The three primary participants this study – Marcial, Martita, Juan – were students in the school district's ESL (English as a Second Language) kindergarten meaning that the teacher had some background in working with second language learners and all ESL kindergartners in the district were assigned to her classroom. The school also drew from English-only populations, primarily African American. In a class of 23 children, the teacher had 16 non-native English-speakers representing five different language backgrounds.

The three children who are the focus of this study began their kindergarten year as monolingual Spanish-speakers. At the beginning of the school year, when asked if they could read, all three children said that they could read "only in Spanish." Juan explained (in Spanish), "[I can read in Spanish] because I know Spanish and a lot of Spanish but not English." The children seemed confident that they would learn English at school. During the second month of school, Juan said, "Now I am in school, English is easy."

The focus children in this study came from two-parent homes in which the fathers worked and the mothers stayed at home with younger children. The fathers spoke both English and Spanish. The mothers were monolingual Spanish-speakers. All participants lived in the same low socioeconomic community and were bused to the school. The dominant view across families was that they were in the United States to create a "better life" than they had in Mexico. All three fathers came to the U.S. without their families. The mothers and children followed later after homes and incomes had been established. The mothers interacted predominantly with their families and with other native-Spanish speaking women in the neighborhood.

Findings

Findings include a range of practices or strategies and artifacts that were used by peers and by the teacher to scaffold the language and literacy use of the primary participants. Representative data excerpts are presented to illustrate how these scaffolded events allowed the children to draw syncretically from diverse funds of cultural knowledge to make sense of new experiences and to be able to participate successfully.

Syncretic Practices Used by Children at School

Engaging participants in side-by-side reading. A strong pattern that emerged across the data and that illustrates syncretic interaction was the engagement of the three primary participants in regular side-by-side reading episodes. This typically happened as the children were coming in the classroom at the beginning of the day and during the "free activity" times scheduled each morning and afternoon. Both monolingual and bilingual peers frequently engaged Martita, Marcial, and/or Juan in reading books together. The event described at the opening of this paper, is one representative example. All children participated successfully as readers because they were able to draw on a range of cultural experiences to create a new experience.

Translating and clarifying. Often, the bilingual Spanish/English-speaking children provided support for Juan, Martita, and Marcial by translating from English to Spanish and by clarifying adults' meaning/intentions. One example occurred in late September when the teaching assistant was reading an English picture book to a small group of native Spanish-speaking children including Marcial, who was then just beginning to learn a few English words, and Dolores, a Spanish/English bilingual. At one point, the teaching assistant stopped reading and asked the children, in English, to describe an illustration.

Assistant: Tell me what you see here?
Marcial: (Looks closely at the illustration).
Assistant: What do you see here?
Marcial: (Looks confused).
Dolores: (Repeats Ms. Diaz's question but turns to Marcial and translates it into Spanish).
Assistant: Tell me about the picture.
Dolores: He is looking.
Assistant: Marcial, what do you see here?
Marcial: (Describes what he sees in Spanish).

In this episode, Dolores provided support by clarifying and translating for the teaching assistant and for Marcial. For Marcial, she translated the teaching assistant's English question, "What do you see here?" into Spanish. It is interesting that Dolores, knowing that the teaching assistant spoke both English and Spanish, made the decision to translate for Marcial. When Marcial did not respond immediately, Dolores seemed to know that he needed time to study the picture and to formulate a response. She then clarified his behavior for the teaching assistant by explaining, "He is looking." Dolores became the mediator who understood and was able to respond in ways that were supportive, using strategies that the teaching assistant did not use. In a true blending of culture and language, by translating and clarifying, Dolores created a situation in which Marcial could comprehend and participate with success.

Providing demonstrations of appropriate behavior. Often unintentionally, the bilingual or English-only children provided demonstrations of appropriate classroom behavior that were observed and adopted by Martita, Juan, and Marcial. By observing and mimicking behavior, they learned what to do and say in the various cultural settings of this American school – in the classroom, the lunchroom and on the playground. This occurred consistently during the first months of the school year when Martita, Juan, or Marcial paid particularly close attention to the bilingual Spanish/English speaking children and copied their behaviors. Drawing on their own culturally-crafted notions of how to act and react, in combination with learning through observation, a syncretized form of understanding resulted.

This is illustrated in an incident that occurred in early September. The music teacher stood in front of the class and the children sat in chairs arranged in a semicircle. The class was singing a song that required them to repeat lines after teacher.

While the other children were singing, Juan looked around the room, waved to the researcher, and played with his chair. When Rocio, a bilingual Spanish/English speaker, began to participate by singing and mimicking the teachers movements, Juan looked at Rocio and began to sing and move.

As the year progressed, Martita, Juan, and Marcial looked more and more to the monolingual English-speaking children for demonstrations of appropriate behavior. In the beginning of the year, however, they typically looked to their bilingual Spanish/English speaking peers for guidance through demonstration – they watched and followed what the bilingual Spanish/English speaking children said and did. This provides an example of an interesting shift in the blending of cultures – first a subtle blending as Martita, Juan, and Marcial seemed more comfortable patterning their behavior after children who were also from their Mexican-American neighborhood and later, as they more confidently took the lead from the native English-speaking children in the room.

Enacting cultural roles through sociodramatic play. During free activity time, many of the children in the classroom often enacted the roles of adults in their cultural worlds, usually adults from their school experiences. This provided opportunities for Martita, Juan, and Marcial to engage in "school play" in ways that helped them better understand the structures, language, and routines of the school day. The following illustration provides an example of the way the children involved themselves in the enactment of cultural roles through play and thereby reinforced their understanding of those roles in real life. This "school play" episode took place late in the year (March) after Martita, Juan, and Marical had developed some competence with English. It took place during activity time as Martita led a "reading lesson" for a small group of children who each held a copy of the same book. Because teaching reading was a particular strength of the classroom teacher, many of the children were enthusiastic users of literacy strategies that the teacher demonstrated many times every day. In this example, Martita emulates the teacher's demonstration of the use of specific literacy strategies. She begins by giving "teacherly" advice as she helps the children read the sentence, "This tiger lives at the zig zag zoo":

Martita: Okay, like this (she points to the words in the book as she reads). This tiger.

Other Children: (Reading with Martita) This tiger (they stop at the word, 'lives,' because they don't recognize it).

Martita: Something. Say 'something.' Skip it. (she is using the "skip it and go on" strategy that the teacher has taught them to use; using the word, 'something' as a placemarker, Martita skips the word and leads her group to continue reading). This tiger *something* at the zigzag.

Martita & Juan: Zigzag.

Children: Zig zag zoo.
Martita: This tiger l-l-l-l-l- (beginning to sound out 'lives').
Teacher: (Walks up to join the group) What makes sense? What else can we do?
Martita: Stretch it out.
Children: L-l-l-l –iv.
Juan: Lives!
Teacher: Way to go!
Martita: This tiger lives at the zigzag zoo.

Throughout this episode, Martita enacted the role of teacher by using precisely the same reading strategies that the teacher demonstrates as she engages the whole class in shared reading experiences. Given the opportunity to "play teacher," Martita was able to practice and thereby better understand the cultural roles of teacher as well as student. At the same time, she was able to act as "expert" by supporting the language and literacy learning of the other children in the group. Syncretically, she merged prior knowledge with the current setting (the opportunity to play sociodramatically) to construct an experience that supported her understanding of "schoolness."

Emulating strategies used by the teacher. Many of the strategies that the children used syncretically, were those that had been demonstrated by the teacher and that the children later emulated. For example, Ms. Bell celebrated the use of both Spanish and English and the children picked up on those demonstrations and began to honor multilingual abilities in similar ways. An illustration of this comes from an episode in which the teacher was leading the class in reading the Morning Message (a message to the class that she has written on the board) aloud. She asked for volunteers to come to the board and circle words they recognized:

Teacher: Juan, what word do you know?
Juan: (Walks to the board and points to the word, 'October') October.
Teacher: That's a big word.
Juan: (Circles the word, 'October" with a marker)
Rocio: He is learning a lot of English.
Teacher: He is. He is learning a lot of English.
Rocio: He knows a lot of Spanish too.
Teacher: Yes!

Another practice that the children emulated was soliciting help from the developing bilinguals in using Spanish. For example, one day in October, the teacher was reading an English book about a scarecrow to the class. She pointed to the picture of the scarecrow and looked at the children asking if anyone could help her say that word in Spanish. Juan provided the Spanish word for "scarecrow" and the teacher repeated it. Juan corrected her pronunciation and she thanked him. The children were frequently observed emulating this practice in their interactions with one another as they asked, "How do you say that in Spanish?"

Other strategies that were demonstrated by the teacher and emulated by the children included: using English supported by demonstration, gesture, and change in tone of voice; accepting and celebrating children's approximations as they attempted to use both Spanish and English; expecting success rather than anticipating failure; and engaging in activities using repetitive texts and supportive artifacts.

WHAT DOES THIS MEAN IN TERMS OF CHALLENGING INEQUITIES?

How might we use findings from these studies to help teachers understand the power of syncretic practices in multilingual classrooms; to encourage teachers to challenge inequities and to let go of commonly-held deficit perspectives? How can findings from these studies help teachers value non-mainstream contributions, so that they will understand the need for constructing contexts where children are able to draw on a range of cultural experiences for the benefit of every child? What suggestions might we provide to help them see real possibilities for transformation in the day-to-day life of their classrooms? And, what does this mean in terms of helping teachers build the knowledge base necessary to begin to question existing practices and affect change?

First, it is important to consider the finding that the children in these studies were able to engage in literacy events largely because they were able to draw on diverse cultural experiences to provide the combination of understandings that made participation possible. Over and over again, data from our studies demonstrate the ease with which children become active and expert when they and their interlocutors are able to draw on diverse funds of knowledge.

Second, we must look closely at the characteristics of the contexts in which syncretic interactions occurred. In both studies, children and adults drew efficiently and effectively from a range of cultural experiences when: (a) the atmosphere was one of comfort and risk-free; in other words, participants felt comfortable enough to risk drawing on non-mainstream cultural information/skills/knowledge/experience; (b) the events were social in nature; there were opportunities to interact purposefully with supportive partners; (c) the participants felt at ease using either Spanish or English and code switching as necessary; (d) the children were treated as fully competent learners; (e) children had extended opportunities to observe others and to synthesize that learning in their own time; and (f) children were able to play central roles as mediators of learning for other children. Given these conditions, children and adults were able to draw on aspects of their cultural worlds to help them create new worlds thereby creating new opportunities for learning.

Third, in order for teachers to see real possibilities for transformation in their own classrooms, it may be helpful to glimpse the specific ways that the teachers in these studies provided opportunities for syncretic interactions to take place. The following examples are a few of the activities they created and the clear demonstrations they provided that encouraged children to draw on diverse cultural funds of knowledge:

- Both teachers used Spanish either as the primary medium of instruction (in Study #1) or as needed to facilitate learning and to celebrate multilingualism for all children (in Study #2).
- Ms. Martin, the teacher in the Midwest, used traditional children's chants from Latin America to teach literacy concepts including rhyming and letter sounds.
- Ms. Martin organized a period of Sustained Silent Reading (SSR) when the children read quietly to themselves. This soon became what Mrs. Martin called Sustained Outloud Cooperative Reading, when the children looked at books and talked about them together. Given this opportunity, the children had apparently drawn on their experiences at home with literacy as a social event, rather than one based on individual interactions with text.
- Ms. Bell, the teacher in the South, consistently used Spanish not only to communicate with the native-Spanish speaking children, but also to broaden an appreciation of multiple languages for the monolingual English-speaking children.
- Ms. Bell utilized the resources of the Spanish-speaking children by soliciting their help in using Spanish and by praising their expertise (and the expertise of the other language users in the classroom) in using two languages.
- Ms. Bell used environmental print from home and community worlds and the children's names to demonstrate that every child was literate and to provide a familiar graphophonemic basis from which children could make analogies as readers and writers.

Finally, it is important to understand that these syncretic activities were rooted in the teachers' deep appreciation for children's expertise in utilizing varied cultural resources as learners. We know that this level of understanding is more likely to evolve as teachers engage in ongoing professional study that encourages them to examine existing practices and to envision new practices (Long, 2002). Therefore, if we are to counter a deficit perspective and truly challenge inequities, programs of teacher education and professional development must focus on long-term experiences that help teachers: see and value practices, languages, and people that are both similar to and different from their own; appreciate the complexity with which we all draw from diverse funds of knowledge as we make sense of new experiences; understand that, by drawing from diverse funds of knowledge, we create new contexts that support us as learners in important ways; and use these understandings to create environments and engagements that encourage learners to draw syncretically on knowledge constructed in homes, communities, and schools.

CONCLUSION

In the United States, schools are most often understood as places where children of color, children whose first language is not English, and poor children should be taught to conform to a monolingual, English-only, middle class standard and where their deficiencies and those of their families can be addressed. This deficit perspective is pervasive and powerful; it prevents teachers from seeing or understanding the potential of resources such as those described here, and it creates inequities that limit the learning potential for all students.

To continue to build a solid foundation for transforming practice in ways that challenge inequity, we believe there is a need for more studies such as ours that identify ways in which children draw on a range of cultural experiences to create new ways to participate successfully. There is also a need for other studies that analyze the pedagogy and practices of teachers like Ms. Martin and Ms. Bell who value syncretic practices and create contexts for them to flourish. And, we need to know more about the opportunities that educators have (or do not have) to be involved in the ongoing study of the sociocultural and syncretic nature of learning, issues of social justice, and the pedagogical implications of both. Possibilities that grow out of such careful examinations of equity and practice have the potential to enrich learning for all children, create more equitable educational experiences, and provide more support for teachers as they work to move beyond a status quo that continues to marginalize non-mainstream populations.

NOTES

1. Whereas "Hispanic" is the official designation for this group, those who self-identify as "Latinos" tend to adopt a more progressive identity. The debate over which label to use in highly charged at all levels.

2. The evangelical movement within the Protestant tradition emphasizes the Bible as the word of God, personal salvation, and evangelism. Pentecostal churches are a part of the evangelical movement and emphasize feelings of connectedness to God and the personal experience of enlightenment, personal communication, A. G. Miller, April 6, 1998). Evangelical Protestantism has become increasingly widespread in recent years among Latinos in the U.S. (Espinosa, Elizondo & Miranda, 2003).

REFERENCES

Apter, A. (1991). Herskovits's heritage: Rethinking syncretism in the African diaspora. *Diaspora, 1*(3), 235–260.

Bakhtin, M. M. (1981). *The dialogic imagination: Four essays*. Austin, TX: University of Texas.

Bartolomé, L. I., & Balderrama, M. V. (2001). The need for educators with political and ideological clarity. In: M. de la Luz Reyes & J. J. Halcón (Eds), *The Best for Our Children: Critical Perspectives on Literacy for Latino Students*. NY: Teachers College.

Barton, D., & Hamilton, M. (1998). *Local literacies: Reading and writing in one community*. London: Routledge.

Baynham, M. (1995). *Literacy practices: Investigating literacy in social contexts*. London: Longman.

Bloome, D., & Egan-Robertson, A. (1993). The social construction of intertextuality in classroom reading and writing lessons. *Reading Research Quarterly, 28*(4), 305–333.

Delgado-Gaitan, C. (1994). Socializing young children in Mexican-American families. In: P. M. Greenfield & R. B. Cocking (Eds), *Cross-Cultural Toors of Minority Child Development* (pp. 55–86). Hillsdale, NJ: Lawrence Erlbaum.

Delpit, L. (2002). The skin that we speak: Thoughts on language and culture in the classroom. New York, NY: New Press.

Duranti, A., & Ochs, E. (1997). Syncretic literacy in a Samoan American family. In: L. B. Resnick, R. Saljo, C. Pontecorvo & B. Burge (Eds), *Discourse, Tools, and Reasoning: Essays on Situated Cognition* (pp. 169–202). Berlin: Springer-Verlag.

Dyson, A. H. (1999). Coach Bombay's kids learn to write: Children's appropriation of media material for school literacy. *Research in the Teaching of English, 33*(4), 367–402.

Espinosa, G., Elizondo, V., & Miranda, J. (2003). *Hispanic churches in American public life: Summary of findings*. Notre Dame: Institute for Latino Studies, University of Notre Dame. Retrieved from www.nd.edu/~latino.

Floriani, A. (1994). Negotiating what counts: Roles and relationships, texts and contexts, content and meaning. *Linguistics and Education, 5*, 241–274.

Freire, P. (1989). *Education for critical consciousness*. NY: Continuum.

Garcia, E. E. (2001). *Hispanic education in the U.S.: Raíces y alas*. Lanham, MD: Rowman & Littlefield.

Goelman, H., Oberg, A., & Smith, F. (1984). *Awakening to literacy*. Portsmouth, NH: Heinemann.

Gregory, E. (1998). Siblings as mediators of literacy in linguistic minority communities. *Language and Education, 12*(1), 33–54.

Gregory, E., & Williams, A. (2000). *City literacies: Learning to read across generations and cultures*. London: Routledge.

Guerra, J. C. (1998). *Close to home: Oral and literate practices in a transnational Mexicano community*. NY: Teacher College.

Gutiérrez, K. D., Baquedano-López, P., Tejeda, C., & Rivera, A. (1999). Hybridity as a tool for understanding literacy learning: Building on a syncretic approach. Paper presented at the meeting of the American Educational Research Association, Montreal, Canada.

Heath, S. B. (1983). *Ways with words: Language, life, and work in communities and classrooms*. Cambridge: Cambridge University.

Hidalgo, N. M. (2000). Puerto Rican mothering strategies: The roles of mothers and grandmothers in promoting school success. In: S. Nieto (Ed.), *Puerto Rican Students in U.S. Schools* (pp. 167–196). Mahwah, NJ: Lawrence Erlbaum.

Hull, G., & Schultz, K. (Eds) (2002). *School's out: Bridging out-of-school literacies with classroom practice*. New York, NY: Teacher College.

Kozol, J. (1991). *Savage inequalities: Children in America's schools*. NY: Harper.

Ladson-Billings, G. (2000). Reading between the lines and beyond the pages: A culturally relevant approach to literacy teacing. In: M. A. Gallego & S. Hollingsworth (Eds), *What Counts as Literacy: Challenging the School Standard*. NY: Teachers College.

Long, S. (2002). Reflections: What made the difference? *Primary Voices, 10*(6).

Mehan, H. (1979). *Learning lessons: Social organization in the classroom*. Cambridge, MA: Harvard University Press.

Moll, L. C., Amanti, C., Neff, D., & Gonzalez, N. (1992). Funds of knowledge for teaching: Using a qualitative approach to connect homes and classrooms. *Theory into Practice, 31*, 132–141.

Nieto, S. (1999). *The light in their eyes: Creating multicultural learning communities*. NY: Teachers College.

Putney, L. G., Green, J., Dixon, C., Durán, R., & Yeager, B. (2000). Exploring collective-individual development in a bilingual classroom. In: C. D. Lee & P. Smagorinsky (Eds), *Vygotskian Perspectives on Literacy Research: Constructing Meaning Through Collaborative Inquiry* (pp. 86–126). Cambridge: Cambridge University.

Rogoff, B. (1990). *Apprenticeship in thinking: Cognitive development in social contexts*. Oxford: Oxford University.

Shaw, R., & Stewart, C. (1994). Introduction: Problematizing syncretism. In: C. Stewart & R. Shaw (Eds), *Syncretism/Anti-Syncretism: The Politics of Synthesis* (pp. 1–26). London: Routledge.

Solsken, J., Willet, J., & Wilson-Keenan, J. (2000). Cultivating hybrid texts in multicultural classrooms: Promise and challenge. *Research in the Teaching of English, 35*(2), 179–212.

Soto, L. D. (1997). *Language, culture, and power: Bilingual families and the struggle for quality education*. NY: SUNY.

Street, B. V. (1999). *Multiple literacies and multi-lingual society*. London: NALDIC Literacy Papers: National Association for Language Development in the Curriculum.

The condition of education 2001: In brief. (2001). Washington, DC: National Center for Education Statistics, U.S. Department of Education (NCES 2001–125).

Therrien, M., & Ramirez, R. R. (2001). The Hispanic population in the U.S., March 2000. *Current Population Reports*. Washington, DC: U.S. Census Bureau, Dept. of Commerce.

Valdés, G. (1996). Con respeto: Bridging the distance between culturally diverse families and schools. NY: Teachers College.

Valverde, A. (2000). Executive director's corner. *Adelante: The Hispanic Border Leadership Institute Newsletter, 2*(3), Arizona State University.

Volk, D. (1999). The teaching and the enjoyment and being together . . .: Sibling teaching in the family of a Puerto Rican kindergartner. *Early Childhood Research Quarterly, 14*, 5–34.

Volk, D., & de Acosta, M. (2001). Many differing ladders, many ways to climb . . .: Literacy events in the bilingual classroom, homes, and community of three Puerto Rican kindergartners. *Journal of Early Childhood Literacy, 1*, 193–224.

"I DON'T THINK SHE KNEW I COULDN'T DO IT": BANGLADESHI PUPILS AND ACHIEVEMENT IN THE EARLY YEARS OF SCHOOLING

Sue Walters

INTRODUCTION

There has been a great deal of quantitative, survey research produced in the last thirty years which states that there is underachievement amongst ethnic minority children in English schools. This quantitative research reveals an increasingly complex picture of ethnic minority achievement and underachievement. Early work tended to simply demonstrate that ethnic minority children were underachieving in school (Little, 1972; Mabey, 1981; Mabey, 1986), this then shifted (as research became more sophisticated, gender and class were introduced as variables and pupils ceased to be simply categorised as black or white) to the identified achievement of some groups and the underachievement of others (e.g. Brent, 1994; Craft & Craft, 1983; DfES, 2003a, b; Drew & Gray, 1990; ILEA, 1990; Kysel, 1988; Sammons, 1995).

The picture that emerged on reading these research reports was complex and not always consistent, especially when different categorisations of ethnic groups were utilized. Bangladeshi children were often included, with Pakistani and Indian children, in the category "Asian" for example and sometimes categorised separately. Sometimes the category "East African Asian" was used to distinguish Asian children whose families had last lived in East Africa and at other times

Ethnographies of Educational and Cultural Conflicts: Strategies and Resolutions
Studies in Educational Ethnography, Volume 9, 107–127

ISSN: 1529-210X/doi:10.1016/S1529-210X(04)09007-2

they were included under the category "Indian" or "Asian." However, nearly every survey report in the 1980s and 1990s which looked at Bangladeshi children as a category found that there were worrying levels of underachievement amongst Bangladeshi pupils (ILEA, 1987; Kysel, 1988; McIntyre, Bhatti & Fuller, 1993; Newham, 1995; Ofsted, 1999; Richardson & Wood, 2000; Wiles, 1999). Although exceptions to this picture were later to be found both in the report of Gillborn and Mirza (2000) (who showed that Bangladeshi attainment was improving and that it was better than White attainment measured in GCSE scores as early as 1991 in Tower Hamlets) and in statistics from Islington and Manchester (personal communication), statistics from Camden (Amin et al., 1997), the Policy Studies Institute (Modood & Berthoud, 1997), the Youth Cohort Study (Pathak, 2000) and Demack et al. (2000) continued at the end of the nineties to show worrying levels of underachievement amongst Bangladeshi pupils.

Such quantitative, survey research was not without its problems and limitations. Tanna (1990) critiqued much of it for being too sketchy, leaving too much unexplained and for relying on imperfect samples and Tanna (1990), Haque (1999) and Harris (2001) have claimed that the surveys made little reference to social class or socio-economic status. However, despite such criticisms, as a result of these surveys the underachievement of Bangladeshi pupils came to be established as an accepted reality in many circles (particularly in the DfEE, Ofsted and the Home Office) by the early 1990s.

Why were certain ethnic minority groups underachieving? Researchers and statisticians attempted to establish the reasons for underachievement by exploring, amongst other things, length of stay in the U.K. or late arrival for schooling in the U.K. (House of Commons HAC, 1987; Kysel, 1988; Little, 1972; Swann, 1985), lack of fluency in English (House of Commons HAC, 1987; Gillborn & Gipps, 1996; Kysel, 1988; Sammons, 1995; Swann, 1985), teacher behaviour, attitudes and resources (House of Commons HAC, 1987; Kysel, 1988; Mcintyre et al., 1993 & Kivi, 1991; Murshid, 1990), poor reading attainment (Little, 1972; Mabey, 1986; Phillips, 1979; Sammons, 1995), poor home-school relationships or under-resourced home background (Kysel, 1988; Murshid, 1990; Sammons, 1995) and, despite the critique of Tanna, Haque and Harris, socio-economic factors, including poverty, unemployment and class location (Drew & Gray, 1990; Kysel, 1988; Mabey, 1981; Murshid, 1990; Sammons, 1995).

With the exception of a consideration of teacher behaviour and attitudes, all of the above are what Meehan (1979) terms out of school "input factors." He critiques such studies for only being able to focus on the input variables that affect educational outcome (output) rather than what actually happens inside schools. Schools are treated as a "black box" in between input and output factors. He claims that "students" careers, school achievement and teacher quality . . . are worked out in the interaction among educators, parents, students and others on a practical basis in everyday contexts'. Statistical studies are unable to capture the processes of education and therefore cannot explain academic achievement (Meehan, 1979, p. 6). Merriam (1986) argues that reality is holistic, multidimensional and ever changing, not a single, fixed objective phenomena waiting to be discovered, observed and measured. The studies referred to above treat "underachievement" as something single and fixed that happens at the end of schooling. The ability to consider processes and experiences, to look at what happens over a period of time, is the province of ethnographic research. Ethnography places an emphasis on understanding phenomena and processes within their particular social, historical and spatial contexts. It allows for a richness of detail rather than the "forgetting" that is involved in statistical research (Keith, 1993). Rather than considering outcomes, ethnography places an emphasis on understanding and identifying particular social processes and practices (Connolly & Troyna, 1998; Emerson, Fretz & Shaw, 1995). Ethnography can give some account of "the values, practices, relationships and identifications" of people and ask of a situation "What is going on here? How does this work? How do people do this?" (Massey & Walford, 1998, p. 5). It suspends premature judgement on what should be selected as data. Rather than start with pregiven categories to be investigated or rely on a preconceived framework for analysing data, analytical frameworks can be created from interactions with informants and theories can be modified and developed and new questions and avenues can be explored. An ethnography can look at a situation from many perspectives by gathering data from a range of sources and in a variety of forms (Massey & Walford, 1998, pp. 5–9).

Not suprisingly, a body of ethnographic work focusing on ethnic minority pupils and schooling began to emerge in the 1980s and 1990s (e.g. Connolly, 1998; Foster, 1990; Gillborn, 1990; Sewell, 1997; Wright, 1992). This ethnographic research focused on "racism" present within schools manifest in the interactions between teacher and pupils, and in some research also between pupil and pupil (Connolly, 1998; Gillborn, 1990; Wright, 1992), on pupils' differing experiences of school according to their ethnicity and on debates concerning the implementation of multicultural and anti-racist policy in LEAs and schools.[1] Taken together these studies focused attention on how teacher judgements, based on negative views of pupil's behaviour, led to low set-allocation for Afro-Caribbean pupils. This research focused almost exclusively on the Afro-Caribbean child (usually boys) with some mention of South Asian pupils in some research (usually as a contrast to the Afro-Caribbean child although Bhatti (1999) and Anderton (1992) are exception to this) but with no specific focus on Bangladeshi pupils and their experiences of school or their attainment in school. Thus published qualitative work added little to a specific understanding of the processes of Bangladeshi underachievement.[2]

Bangladeshi children have been studied by (Gregory, 1994, 1996b, 1998, 2001; Gregory et al., 1996; Gregory & Williams, 1998a, b, 2000; Rashid & Gregory, 1997). Her ethnographic and ethnomethodological work has specifically focused on emergent bilingual children learning to read (Gregory, 1992a, 1993a, b, 1994, 1996a, 1996) and many of the children studied have been Bangladeshi. Her ethnographic research has drawn attention to the importance of home literacy practices for children's success in learning to read in school. Shared reading practices (common to school and home whether initiated in home or school) appeared to be the basis of early reading success. If teachers became aware of and used some of the literacy practices of the home in the classroom (Gregory & Williams, 1998a, 2000) or if children were able to initiate and participate in the special kind of dialogue and pattern of turn taking with the teacher that constitutes learning to read in the classroom (Gregory, 1992a, b, 1993b, 1994) then reading success was possible. Gregory's work demonstrates what ethnography can bring to an understanding of the complexities of learning in the classroom and in the home, however, her studies do not link her findings about how emergent bilingual children successfully learn to read with their actual achievement in school (however measured), nor provide us with evidence that the children are, or go on to be, successful, independent readers. I will return to discuss this issue in relation to my own research and findings.

Thus little research has been conducted which focuses on Bangladeshi children and their perceived underachievement. It is also the case that most research conducted into ethnic minority underachievement has considered children who go to school in inner-city or metropolitan areas where there is a large ethnic minority population.

THE STUDY

The central aim of the study was to examine the experiences Bangladeshi children, the processes of their daily life in school, in relation to achievement. Ethnography provided a way of doing this. What was happening in the classroom? How were the children "doing" school and doing in school? How did their teacher perceive them and assess them? Did the Bangladeshi pupils constitute a distinct group with distinct needs? There was an openess in the research to understanding the research children as active agents in "doing school" rather than simply passive "vessels" molded by school culture and knowledge. As Woods states.

> pupils are not empty vessels to be filled, nor pieces of clay to be pressed into shape. They are, rather, complex individuals in their own right, with developed characters and infused with rich cultural forms, within which they interact as full contributory participants.
>
> (Woods, 1980, p. 9)

The research was conducted in line with Pollard and Filer's view that there is a need for studies of "the activity of children" as they negotiate within the opportunities and constraints afforded by the "social conditions, institutional arrangements, expectations, conceptualisations, forms of discourse and positioning" that surround them (Pollard & Filer, 1999, p. 7). The notion of "doing school" is chosen deliberately to signal that, firstly, the children are considered as active agents and secondly, that what constitutes "school," "learning," "being a pupil," "reading successfully" are products of (dynamic) classrooms and discourses that are socially, historically and politically located.[3]

The research was conducted between September 2000 and July 2001 in three First Schools (Reception Year through to Year 3) in a predominantly white LEA and focused on six Year 3 Bangladeshi pupils. The decision to focus on pupils in Year 3 was taken as professional experience suggested that this was the point at which many children began to struggle in school, especially in relation to literacy and the demands of being able to read to "get by" in the classroom. It also meant that the children would have enough English to be able to self-report. A predominantly white, monolingual, rural LEA was chosen as research studies had not looked at isolated pupils in relation to experiences of schooling and achievement. There are also important differences between urban and rural delivery and support for policy makers, LEAs and headteachers. A final reason was that previous work for the LEA provided a background knowledge of the area, the schools and many of the families subsequently involved in the research. This made access informed and straightforward.

Data was collected through observation, interview and school documents. The case study pupils, parents, siblings, headteachers, classroom assistants, EAL teachers, student teachers and teachers from previous years in the school were included in the interviews and observations. Six other (white monolingual) children in each classroom were also included in the research observations and interviews. A year was spent as a participant observer conducting the fieldwork.

This paper will report on some of the initial findings about learning to read and taking part in classroom lessons with regard to two of the case study pupils and one sibling in the study. The pupils are all English as a Second Language pupils and started school with either no English or very little English.

DOING SCHOOL

I think a lot of things I knew from memory at Greenhill. The teachers would read books and you were allowed to take them home. I would choose books that were easy, lots of pictures and books the teachers had read in class and when I'd bring it home I'd get my brother to read it to

> me and I'd pick up words that I didn't know and just memorize it so that I could read the whole book although I would not know which words I was saying and at school I read it to the teacher and this was from memory and the teacher was very happy 'Salima's really getting along'. Then she would spot my finger wasn't following the words so I would let the teacher hold my finger and I would just say it and she would turn the page as well. Then I think she realised that I wasn't really reading it, she noticed I was looking at the pictures and she asked me 'are you reading from memory?' I think I was doing it for quite some time and I was borrowing the same books.
>
> (Salima 29/3/02)

Salima is the sister of one of the case study children in the study. She is now sixteen and has just finished her Secondary schooling. In this account of reading at Greenhill (the first school she attended between the ages of five and eight) Salima shows us something of how she went about "doing school." As Gregory showed in her research, early reading in school is about reading with the teacher and being a successful reader is about joining in the interaction patterns initiated by the teacher. Salima, in her account, demonstrates that she was very aware of the interaction pattern required and what the teacher wanted to hear and see her do to demonstrate that she could "read." Salima calls on many strategies to be able to produce the desired performance of reading. She chose reading books the teacher had read to the class so that she was familiar with their content and the correct intonation for reading them, she also chose books that were easy and had lots of pictures. She took the books home and got her older brother to read them to her so she could pick up the words she didn't know and memorize them so she could read the whole book to the teacher. She herself recognises that this kind of "reading" was not the kind of "reading" that other children or other adults might do at school ("I would not know which words I was saying and at school I read it to the teacher and this was from memory"). Yet the strategies she used were successful for the young Salima "the teacher was very happy 'Salima's really getting along.' " This "getting along," is what made her teacher happy and it would appear from this account that young Salima wanted to please the teacher. The use of plurals in Salima's account "the teachers would read books" "I would choose books that were easy" suggests that Salima did this on more than one occasion and other comments in the interview ("I think I was doing it for quite some time and I was borrowing the same books") would suggest that this was so. The teacher herself contributes to the performance of "reading." Salima had developed a way of reading by commiting a story, word by word, to memory so she was not able to point to the words on the page as she "read" them. This is part of the interaction pattern that the teacher required and at first, according to Salima's account, the teacher compensated for this lack by holding and guiding Salima's finger for her and by turning the page for her as they "read." The teacher becomes suspicious of Salima's reading only when she realises that Salima is "looking at the pictures" and using them as a guide to what to "read" on each page of the book rather than looking at the text. The teacher finally asks "are you reading from memory?"

What is interesting is that when asked what happened as a result of her teacher recognising how she was going about "reading," Salima replied, "The teacher was amazed that I could do it all from memory. She let me carry on." When asked her how she finally made the shift from "reading" by using her memory to "reading" using the text in a book. "You realise the letters are making the same sound like 'L – ION.' You see the pattern."

> I used to come home at lunchtimes so I used to have cartoons and Sesame Street.... After watching Sesame Street I learnt about decoding things it was all in Sesame Street. For example, 'mat' take the 'm' away. A lot of repetition and seeing the same words over and over again. And also in school there was a teacher who broke words into bits and I used to put them together and I think that really helped me. Also looking at words round you. Wherever you look there are English words all around and I used to copy them down. And I used to say to my brother 'I know this'.
>
> (Salima, 29/3/02)

Even though Salima's teacher recognised Salima's strategy for reading was to commit the whole story to memory (a home literacy practice – a point that will be discussed later) she, according to Salima, allowed her to carry on and seems not to have helped her find new strategies. Another teacher in the school, perhaps at the direction of the class teacher, did help Salima find a different strategy by breaking "words into bits" otherwise Salima finds her own way, by calling on other resources at home – watching TV, copying words down and using her brother – to familiarise herself with how print works.

Salima described other memories of First School. One of her ways of learning and fitting in at school was "to copy any work I could find, other children's work I could see, the children on either side of me. Then the teacher would put ticks and I don't think she knew I couldn't do it" (29/3/00). She would also put her hand up "like other children" when the teacher asked a question. She claimed that it was the other children in her class who helped her learn "because they wanted me to be part of their group, they were really nice." "When the teacher used to set tasks I just used to go and ask my friends and they would tell me the answers..." Salima also used her home and her family members to help her with the things she felt she needed for school. "I had help from my brothers and my dad." Telling me to learn the alphabet, how to pronounce things properly like "cornflakes," "cup of tea." However, these strategies (ways of going about taking part in the work of the classroom)[4] weren't always successful for Salima. "When the teacher was asking questions and all the other children put their hands up I put my hand up and then the teacher would ask me and I wouldn't know." When her friends helped her by telling her the answers "I would get my targets and they would think I was making progress but I wasn't. I used to feel I was cheating myself" (29/3/02).

According to Salima's account, by the time she was a Middle School pupil (aged 8 years to 11 years) her "strategies" for learning and taking part in school ceased to work for her. She lost the support and help of the other children in her class (and was bullied and this lead to her being frequently absent from school), her understanding was still limited and this increasingly prevented her from taking part in classroom life and lead to a great deal of boredom and isolation in school and her brothers could not help her at home because their way of doing maths was different to the way it was done in school (Cline and Abreu also found this to be the case in their research on the relationship between ethnic minority parents and their children's schools – Cline & Abreu, 2001). She was left behind and felt left out and this carried over into High School (age 12 years onwards) where she fell further behind and where she was placed in the lower or bottom sets. Salima found it hard to learn in these sets because of the poor behaviour of the other pupils. Even though she repeated Year 10 she failed to be entered for her GCSEs at the level she wished.

Salima's account, briefly represented above, gives us some idea of how she tried to "do school" in the beginning, how she used various ways of joining in and being like the other children and pleasing the teacher but how these strategies gradually let her down in the sense that she "did" school but her ways of doing it didn't allow her to "join in" or to "achieve" in the way she would have liked or in the way considered as achievement by the educational system. She ended up an isolated, underachieving student. The strategies she used on starting school she worked out for herself and took from her world.

Salima's efforts to "do" school, to learn and fit in (and what subsequently happened to her) seemed a useful framework with which to consider the six case study children. I had become aware already of how the six were going about "learning" in school, how they were taking part in classroom life and how their teachers viewed them and that key assessments were made of them in the light of this. I was aware of how their ways of taking part were creating identities and assessments of their abilities. They were all considered to be "doing well" by their teachers. Salima's account of her schooling, which came half way through the fieldwork focused me on thinking about how the case study children were "doing school," attempting to learn and take part. Were they doing similar things to Salima? Were they approaching school differently? What kind of resources and help were they calling on and using in school and how successful were they (and how successful were they likely to be)? In the discussion below I focus on two of the case study children and say something about this in relation to just two aspects of their school life: learning to read and taking part in maths/numeracy.

THE CASE STUDY CHILDREN

Tumi, the first case study child I am going to discuss here, is considered to be a bright student and a good reader in Year 3, "She's an able little girl. She reads beautifully . . .." (Classroom Assistant 21/5/01). "I think she's really quite bright . . ." (Class teacher 7/11/00). Tumi is Salima's younger sister and she uses some of her sister's strategies for "doing school." My field observations show that she looks at other children's work in class when she is stuck and that she looks to see whether other children have put their hands up in class to answer a teacher's question. What is of interest is though is the way Tumi has come up with her own way of taking part in reading and developing her identity as a "good reader," an identity that has status in her classroom amongst her peers and which has very positive implications for how she is assessed by the adults in the classroom.

All three adults in the classroom during the course of the year, reported that Tumi read very fast and missed out words when she read. Various explanations were put forward for this but none of the adults doubted that Tumi was an able reader. Her sometimes poor "performance" in discussing what she had read was put down to the fact that she rushed the reading and hadn't taken in the meaning. One day, after taking part in a reading activity with me and as we were preparing to read a book together, ("The Lion, the Witch and the Wardrobe" a particularly difficult book, with many chapters in, for a Year 3 child) chosen by Tumi, Tumi started talking about how she "read."

Sue: Are you going to read?
Tumi: (pause) No
Sue: Why not?
Tumi: Cos I'm nervous.
Sue: Why do you feel nervous?
Tumi: Well sometimes I cheat.
Sue: Sometimes you cheat. What do you mean sometimes you cheat? What do you do?
Tumi: First I read this bit (opening the book at the last page)
Sue: What the end?
Tumi: Yeah and then I read this bit and I read it all at one page. All one page by one page I just look at the pictures (she turns the pages quickly starting at the back of the book moving forward, stopping or slowing when she reaches a page with a picture).
Sue: Yeah
Tumi: But I don't read it
Sue: you don't
Tumi: yeah, but when there's some words like this I don't even read it I just . . .
Sue: So how do you know what is happening?
Tumi: Well I look at the pictures and it looks like something is happening but sometimes I read the words too, easy words. Like "the Queen of" and "impress of loan island", "the eye safe conduct to come and speak with you."
Sue: that's very interesting.

(The classroom assistant comes into the room).
Sue: So have you been doing that for a long time?
Tumi: yeah
(I laugh)
Sue: How many people know that you do that?
Tumi: Well nobody

(27/3/01)

Tumi had her own way of appearing to read and of being able to consume books. Reading harder books that had chapters in them rather than the easy readers, with no chapters, that beginner readers read, and reading fast gave her a high status amongst the other children. However, her way of reading meant that she was not able to "read for meaning" in the way that pupils are conventionally meant to be able to "take meaning" from what they read. Her fast reading and leaving out words when taking part in a reading-aloud interaction with another adult (who was hearing her read) was a clever way of covering that she was not reading in the conventional sense, nor able to. Tumi "read" by taking clues and cues from the text she was "reading" (she had an excellent knowledge of how story books worked and pointed out a few things to me during the course of the year that I was not aware of) and from these "props" and her experience of stories from home (her sister read to her nearly every day and Tumi had a large collection of Walt Disney videos and other children's films at home) she created her own versions of the stories. Many of the reading activities I undertook with Tumi and my observations of Tumi in class confirmed that this was how she went about "reading."

Her teachers did not know that she was doing this to the extent that she was,[5] they were puzzled by her reading-out-loud style and the guidance she was offered throughout the year (in terms of reading instruction) was to "slow down." (According to her reading record book and my observations and conversations with her teachers, no other kind of reading activity, other than reading-out-loud to an adult, was used). Tumi used certain other strategies which helped her successfully take part in reading-out-loud interactions with the teacher. She read with a lot of expression for the voices of characters in the books she was "reading." Even when the words spoken by the character were rushed out and the ends of the sentences left out, the way Tumi began the "speaking" and the range of voices she could call on (old and crabby for an old woman, booming for a King) convincingly suggested that she was reading with understanding of what was happening. She used an adult, teacher-like vocabulary to talk about books, "it was very interesting" (12/9/00) and she was good at distracting the adult by talking about something she liked in the story when she was stuck with an answer for a "what is happening?" question. Tumi was also able, just like her sister, to call on her memory of a story that had been read to the class to demonstrate that she could engage with the text in front of her.

How successful is Tumi with her strategies for taking part in reading? Her teachers are puzzled but are convinced that she is a good reader. She is not placed in the bottom sets and she retains her high status as a reader amongst her peers. Tumi's knowledge of how texts and stories work, her imagination and her knowledge of story worlds and language from home mean that she can convince others that she is an able reader.

However, what she hides in the classroom and in the reading-aloud-interaction with the teacher, in an effort to take part successfully and have a high status, are the things that she gets stuck with when she engages with text. What is hidden from her teachers and her peers is the fact that she struggles with a lot of vocabulary in the story books she reads. This impedes her understanding to a far greater degree than any of the teaching staff recognise because she hides this so well when she reads to them. An early indication that Tumi had problems understanding vocabulary (that would not present a problem to the monolingual children in the class) was during a Literacy Hour group work session when the children were writing answers to questions about a text they had on a worksheet in front of them. In my fieldnotes I recorded,

> She is working in her group, she is not interacting with anyone. She has only underlined one adjective and has done one question. She is stuck with the second question. She could find the place in the text that gave the answer to the question but she didn't know what to do with it. It was a question about lorries. It turned out that she didn't know what 'lanes' and 'leftovers' were or what 'narrow' meant. This meant that she didn't understand the sentence that she needed to understand in order to answer the question.
>
> (12/9/00)

During the rest of the year of reading together, Tumi did not like being asked if there were any words or phrases that she wanted to know the meaning of although there were words and phrases that she did struggle with. For example, in a session on 12/6/01 she rather resentfully asked about "moaning" and "gleaming" both key words in understanding what was happening in the story.

Like her sister, Tumi also engages in "I don't think she knew I couldn't do it" behaviour. However, in comparison with her sister, Salima, Tumi had a far more sophisticated way of engaging in reading in the school context and a range of strategies that may take her as an able reader through Middle School. Like her sister, Tumi gets help from her home but this time Tumi receives help from her sister who is familiar with Tumi's school having attended it herself and Salima is thus able to help Tumi by explaining things the way the school does them. This was especially evident in relation to Maths during Year 3. Tumi had problems taking part in Numeracy Hour because of the language demands of the subject. Tumi reported at the end of the year that her increasing ability to take part successfully in Numeracy Hour was due to her sister explaining things to her at home. Tumi also puts her hand up for everything in the classroom (except in Numeracy) and spends a lot of her time engaging with the adults. She uses adult language, charms the teachers and uses her quite good general knowledge of the world to take part in whole class talk time. All of these "behaviours" result in Tumi as being seen as an able, bright girl. She has an identity as "able" and "charming" and "delightful" who "will do extremely well at her Middle School."

The second case study child, Attar, also has a high status as a reader. His teacher tells me during my first visit to the classroom that he is "an excellent reader" and this is a status that has come through school with him from his Reception Year classroom. At the end of his first term in Year 3 his teacher reports to me that "his reading is phenomenal. Its absolutely um . . . he can read Harry Potter brilliantly" (6/11/00). Like Tumi, Attar has chosen a very high status book as his reading book. The teacher had started reading this book to the class at the beginning of the year (but had not been able to find the time to continue) and Harry Potter was a chapter book (all the children in each of the Year 3 classrooms aspired to reading "chapter books"). Like Tumi, when Attar was reading the book in a reading-out-loud interaction with an adult, he used great expression and gave each of the characters different voices. On more than one occasion in the classroom, the teacher had spoken to the class about how important it was to read with expression.

> What we are going to start tomorrow is 'Perseus the Dragon Slayer'. Why it's a good book to read is it's got a fantastic story, you'll like it a lot and it's a book we can read with more expression. I'm finding that when I'm hearing lots of you read we are getting the same sort of voice all the while and when something exciting is happening in the book or we have characters that are speaking we are not getting different voices . . .. So when we start reading Perseus tomorrow we are going to liven up our voices, we are going to have different voices for different characters' (15/1/01)

And Attar is very good at providing this kind of reading for the teacher.

However, over the course of the first term, as I heard Attar read and asked him to take part in some other kinds of reading activities with me, it became clear that Attar was also finding it extrememely difficult to "take meaning" from what he was reading in a way expected by school and unlike Tumi he did not have the imaginative link with fairy and fantasy stories to draw on, nor knowledge of the world depicted in his reading books, to make his own stories as he read. These are my notes about a reading session I had with Attar at the start of the second term (after his teacher has described his reading as "phenomenal") with the dialogue transcribed from a tape of the session. The book he is reading is not a particularly difficult book, especially when compared with Harry Potter, and one that would have been read by the top third of the readers in the class with reasonable understanding:

I ask what book he is reading.

Attar: The Guard Dog.
Sue: Why did you chose this book?
Attar: Cos the dog is a guard dog.
Sue: Do you know what a guard dog is?
Attar: Um
Sue: What it means?
Attar: Yeah. Uhh . . . it . . . I forgot.

I explain to him what a guard dog is.

He has read some of the story already. I ask him what has been happening in the story and who is in the story (as I don't know the book at all).

Attar: Attar: um that fat girl. First it starts with the dogs. There were six puppies in the window and then the petshop.

He is turning the pages and then he alights on a piece of text and he just reads the piece of text to me. He asks me to explain "inhabitant" to him (a word in the bit of text he has just read out loud) which I do. He then picks out words in the section he has already read and asks me what they mean: eg. "racket", "loathing", "dislike", "vulgar". After we have sorted out what lots of the words mean he asks me if he can read now.

He reads with great expression, he starts reading with a real "reader" style ie a projected voice. He loses some fluency when he has to work out how to say words like "hullabaloo". I stop him after a page or two to see if he understands what is happening. He can say who is talking to who (the kennelmaid to the manager). I have to explain to him what a manager and a dog's home are (the setting for the story). What is happening in the story is lost on him really as there are so many words he needs to know the meaning of and he is not familiar with the idea of a dog's home etc.

(15/1/01)

Some of the problems that Attar had with reading were recognised by his Year 2 teacher.

He could read anything. He could work things out but he didn't always take in what he was reading and the comprehension wasn't always there. He got a 2B. His expression got better, worked really hard at it. But he wasn't taking in what a story was about, he improved and started to use expression but it was still mechanical.

(16/10/00)

His Year 3 teacher also recognised some of his problems.

He, the words he struggles on are the unfamiliar English words, for example, 'craning', when – I can't remember what Dudley's mum's called, Mrs Dursely or Petunia, she was craning and he said 'cranning' (*like tanning*) cos that is exactly how you would say it but with the English language being the way it is it's actually not like that . . . his writing is sort of quite specific that's why we're doing the work, he knows all of his List 1 and List 2 he can spell all of them. Fantastic speller. So we're working him on using a thesaurus to expand his vocabulary.

(6/11/00)

What is interesting here is that although both teachers recognise some of the difficulties Attar has, both focus on his reading-out-loud performance as a way of either understanding the difficulty or of assessing the difficulty (for the Year 3 teacher, Attar's problems are to do with pronounciation, for the Year 2 teacher Attar's performance of reading would indicate how much he was understanding).

Attar also has a very high status and identity as "good at maths." Again this is something he has brought with him from his Year 1 and Year 2 classrooms. His interactions with the teacher in Year 3 maths and the enthusiasm he displays by putting his hand up for many of the questions during "carpet time" at the beginning and end of Numeracy Hour confirm this identity for the teacher.

> As a pupil on a good day he is brilliant, gives you the answers you need, he's always thinking at a higher level than the majority of the rest of the class. He's very inquisitive you know, he'll ask questions that help the others understand and sometimes make you think about what you teach as well which I really like and you know on a good day he works really hard, gets the work done very, very quickly, very neat, top standard . . .
>
> (6/11/00)

As suggested by this teacher's repetition of "on a good day," Attar is not always seen in such a positive light in the classroom. This is how she continues the above account of him.

> . . . but on a bad day, and the good days and the bad days relate to how he has been with me, he'll just do nothing and be completely lazy and not make any effort and just write nonsense cos he thinks he can get away with it so that's what he's like.
>
> (6/11/00)

An incident at the beginning of the school year had convinced the teacher that Attar had deliberately pretended not to understand very much English in the classroom and used this as an excuse for not completing work or presenting her with poor, sloppy work. She had "caught him out" (the teachers' words) talking to a group of the children in the class and heard him using a lot of English. "He didn't know I was there . . .. He was chatting away. Then I lent over and said 'Attar, don't ever pretend you don't understand me again' " (11/10/00). She tries out, in the course of talking to me on a number of occasions, many explanations for why Attar should do this, including that he sees her as a new teacher who he can "try out." However, in the end the teacher returns to explaining Attar's "pretending" in terms of his "culture" and his "religion"; he plays her up and tests her because she is a woman, she cannot speak to his parents and because he is a muslim boy.

Whatever the rights and wrongs of Attar pretending not to understand, the incident meant that the teacher was adamant that Attar did understand everything and that his poor work on "bad days" was due to how he related to her as a female teacher. Attar's difficulties with language and vocabulary were thus hidden which had consequences for Attar. Here are some more fieldnotes from a reading session.

> Before we start reading together we discuss maths (he had just spent the playtime preceeding this reading session kept in the classroom because he had not finished his maths work). Attar says he didn't understand the word 'investigate'. I ask him what he had to do. He replied 'I had to say which coin made £1.25, £1.06 and £2.20'. He then read me question three and said 'this is what Lauren help me with'. 'Question 3: Mark was offered 2 silver coins to pay for a 17p toy. Investigate how much change he got'. Attar could read the question out but he couldn't do it. He didn't understand 'offered' and 'investigate'. Once he understood 'offered' (I explained it) he could tell me that Mark had two silver coins to pay. I then explained 'investigate'. He liked my explanation that investigate just meant to find out and he substituted this in Question 4 and read out 'Find out ways of using silver coins to pay 50p'. He hadn't been able to do this question either because he didn't understand what the question was asking. He had done Questions 1 and 2 but got stuck with 3 and 4 because he didn't understand the language. I asked him if he asked the other children for help. 'No'. Did he ask the teacher? 'Yes'. Then he changed his answer to 'No'. I asked him about staying in at break. 'The teacher thought I wasn't working but I was thinking. I wasn't messying about'. In the reading that we do next it becomes clear that there are many words that Attar doesn't know the meaning of.
>
> (30/10/00)

It is worth noting that Attar, because he does not have a close friend in the class or belong to a supportive friendship group, does not have other children in the class to call on as a resource to help him as Salima did. In addition, he spent most of the year, playing on his own in the playground and playmates that he did find, as in previous years in the school, tended to be "naughty boys" and Attar had spent most of Year 1 and Year 2 in trouble for his playground behaviour.

Attar's "bright" status meant that he was in the top group for Literacy and Numeracy but this status was always in tension with his "naughty boy behaviour" and his "attitude" to the teacher which threatened his standing. His achievement in school was considered to be high but, as with Salima and Tumi, certain things were hidden from the teacher that affected the ability of Attar to complete school work and "do well." His needs in terms of being an English as Additional Language pupil (vocabulary and language) were hidden from the teacher partly by Attar himself in a bid to keep his high status as a reader and high flyer in Maths and partly by the teacher's explanation and response to his "pretending."

THE USE OF HOME LITERACY PRACTICES AND "ACHIEVING ACHIEVEMENT"

Gregory's work on the importance of home literacy practices in learning to read for Bangladeshi pupils (and other ethnic minority pupils) has successfully challenged notions of children caught between the clash of home and school and notions of the "deficit home" as a reason for poor achievement in reading. My findings echo hers in the sense that the three pupils discussed above did bring to their learning to read practices that they were familiar with from their home and "community" life. Using one's memory, listening and then producing a performance or recitation using a copied rhythm and intonation, using cues/text to produce an oral performance, gaining status and the identity of "clever" through progressing through work more quickly than others are practices the children were familiar with from their Koran school classroom and were ways of learning that would be familiar to all family members. However, my findings also suggest that such ways of going about learning to read or taking part in the classroom are not always necessarily successful for the children concerned and whether they are successful or not depends on a variety of rather complex factors (e.g. support at home, relationship with the teacher, the knowledge of teacher concerning the needs of EAL pupils, the child's pre-school experience, peer support in the classroom, the child's experience of books and stories, knowledge of the world referred to in school and so on) and on whether schools and teachers are explicit about what reading is in school.

The three children referred to put a lot of effort into their taking part in school and appearing as achieving pupils. They worked hard at "achieving achievement." However, the "hiding" that went on meant that their needs were not seen and were not acted on in terms of provision. Their teachers lack of knowledge about the needs of English as Additional Language pupils[6] compound this problem. Whether the two case study children will continue to "achieve" in reading and in their other school learning is an open question.

CONCLUSIONS: LANGUAGE AND ETHNICITY

In the accounts above, language is not seen as an issue for the three pupils as they are socially fluent and because they hide what they can't do to protect their status and self-esteem. Their teachers equate their social fluency with "academic" or "classroom work" fluency in Engish but it is clear that both pupils have real language needs that need addressing in some way for them to be able to take a full part in classroom life and have access to the curriculum, especially as they progress through school and "reading independently" and taking from the text (rather than the oral pronouncements of the teacher) becomes the more dominant mode of accessing information (and finding out what tasks are to be completed) in the classroom. Explanations and concerns for these pupils' difficulties are always related to their home life and their (cultural) background by their teachers. This is not surprising as the children do such a good job of covering up their language difficulties and teachers are not aware of the needs of English as Additional Language pupils. In effect the children are seen as Bangladeshi pupils rather than as English as Additional Language pupils. Is being seen as "Bangladeshi" useful? A focus on ethnicity works against these children in a key way. Their language needs are ignored (language needs, the research indicated, they share with other non-Bangladeshi children) and the reasons for their behaviour and attitudes are found in their ethnic identity. Language should be central to policy and provision rather than ethnicity.

NOTES

1. And subsequently found itself caught up in a debate about the validity, reliablity and generalisability of research evidence, about what constituted racism and about the role of "the partisan" in sociological research (Troyna, 1984, 1991, 1992, 1993, 1995; Troyna & Carrington, 1989; Gomm, 1993, 1995; Gillborn, 1995; Hammersley, 1995; Foster, Gomm & Hammersley, 1996).

2. Bangladeshi children, as a distinct group, have been studied by Haque who combined qualitative and quantitative research methods to study Bangladeshi underachievment. Her analysis concluded that it was difficult to identify variables that were directly linked to achievement, "Certainly, there were some similarities in students' experiences but none were identical; each of the factors appeared to influence individuals differently" (Haque, 1999, p. 128).

3. The term "doing school" also signals a connection with ethnomethodological work which seeks to show the methods or methodology that people use in taken-for-granted ways to accomplish day-to-day living (Payne & Cuff, 1982, p. 3). In this case the focus is on the methods the research children use to accomplish (or not accomplish) taking part in school, being a member of the class, being a successful reader, being a pupil and so on and how successful they are, or are allowed to be, in these endeavours.

4. I am not using the term strategies in the same way it is used by Pollard (1994) and Wood (1980) ie. in terms of pupils "coping," or negotiating with the constraints imposed on them by structural features such as govn policy, teachers, the curriculum etc., nor in the way Pollard and Filer's deploy the term in their concept of "dimensions of strategic action" (Pollard & Filer, 1999. This is because I do not interprete the research data in terms of the case study children "coping," it seems to me that something much more dynamic, fluid and complex is taking place which I have attempted to suggest through the concept of "doing school." As to the "dynamics of strategic action" typifications Pollard and Filer use, these seem to me to muddle intention with outcome ie they assume that what a pupil intends by a certain action or strategy is what the teacher understands and responds to. Although this is certainly the case with some of the actions of the case study children referred to here, there were many occasions when a child intended one thing and the teacher understood their action or behaviour to denote something entirely different.

5. And despite my priviledged access to the children and the amount of time I spent with them, it took two terms of puzzlement and undertaking different reading activities with Tumi before I could begin to see and understand what she was doing as she "read" and why she always "read" at such speed and left words out.

6. It was not a requirement of Teacher Training Institutes to include anything about providing for EAL pupils or ethnic minority pupils in the classroom as part of their PGCE courses before September 2002. I asked all of the teachers I interviewed whether they had had any training or professional development in the Language Needs of EAL pupils either when they were training or since they became teachers. While some said they had received no training at all others said that they had received some "in-service" training which had focused on multiculturalism or how to settle a new beginner-bilingual into the classroom. None of the teachers had received any professional development or in-service training which focused on Second Language Acquisition or the specific language needs of EAL pupils.

ACKNOWLEDGMENT

The research was funded by an ESRC studentship.

REFERENCES

Amin, K., Drew, D., Fosam Gillborn, D., & Demack, S. (1997). *Black and ethnic minority young people and educational disadvantage.* London: Runnymede Trust.

Anderton, E. (1992). *Bangladeshi pupils' experience of secondary schooling: A case study of an inner city comprehensive school.* Unpublished M.Ed Thesis, University of East Anglia.

Bhatti, G. (1999). *Asian children at home and at school: An ethnographic study.* London: Routledge.

Brent (1994). *Report summarising the analysis of the 1993 GCSE results.* London: London Borough of Brent.

Cline, T., & Abreu, G. (2001). The relationship between home mathematics and school mathematics in multi-ethnic primary schools. *Naldic Conference 'Improving The Mathematics Achievement of Children Learning English as an Additional Language'*. Luton.

Connolly, P. (1998). *Racism, gender identities and young children: Social relations in a multi-ethnic, inner-city primary school.* London: Routledge.

Connolly, P., & Troyna, B. (1998). *Researching racism in education: Politics, theory and practice.* Buckingham: Open University Press.

Craft, M., & Craft, A. (1983). The participation of ethnic minority pupils in further and higher education. *Educational Research, 25,* 10–19.

Demack, S., Drew, D., & Grimsley, M. (2000). Minding the gap: Ethnic, gender and social class differences in attainment at 16, 1988–1995. *Race, Ethnicity and Education, 3,* 117–143.

DfES (2003a). *Youth cohort study: Activities and experiences of 16 year olds – England and Wales 2002.* DfES Website: www.dfes.gov.uk/statistics.

DfES (2003b). *Pupil level annual schools' Census 2003.* DfES Website: www.dfes.gov.uk/statistics.

Drew, D., & Gray, J. (1990). The fifth year examination achievements of black young people in England and Wales. *Educational Research, 32,* 107–116.

Emerson, R., Fretz, R., & Shaw, L. (1995). *Writing ethnographic fieldnotes.* Chicago: University of Chicago Press.

Foster, P. (1990). *Policy and practice in multicultural and anti-racist education: A case study of a multi-ethnic comprehensive.* London: Routledge.

Foster, P., Gomm, R., & Hammersley, M. (1996). *Constructing Educational Inequality.* London: Falmer.

Gillborn, D. (1990). *'Race', ethnicity and education: Teaching and learning in multi-ethnic schools*. London: Unwin Hyman.

Gillborn, D. (1995). *Racism and antiracism in real schools*. Milton Keynes: Open University Press.

Gillborn, D., & Gipps, C. (1996). *Recent research on the achievement of ethnic minority pupils*. London: HMSO.

Gillborn, D., & Mirza, H. (2000). *Educational inequality: Mapping race, class and gender*. London: Ofsted.

Gomm, R. (1993). Figuring out ethnic equity: A response to Troyna. *British Educational Research Journal, 19*, 147–163.

Gomm, R. (1995). Strong claims, weak evidence: A response to Troyna's 'ethnicity and the organisation of learning groups'. *Educational Research, 37*, 79–86.

Gregory, E. (1992a). *The nature and significance of boundary negotiation between teachers and children from 'non-school-orientated' backgrounds in early reading lessons*. Unpublished PhD Thesis, Institute of Education.

Gregory, E. (1992b). Learning codes and contexts, In: K. Kimberley, M. Meek & T. Miller (Eds), *New Readings: Contributions to an Understanding of Literacy*. London: Black.

Gregory, E. (1993a). What counts as reading in an infant classroom? *British Journal of Educational Psychology, 63*, 214–230.

Gregory, E. (1993b). Sweet and sour: Learning to read in a British and Chinese school. *English in Education, 27*, 54–59.

Gregory, E. (1994). Negotiation as a critical factor in learning to read in a second language. In: D. Graddol, J. Maybin & B. Stierer (Eds), *Researching Language and Literacy in Social Context*. Clevedon: Multilingual Matters.

Gregory, E. (1996a). *Making sense of a new world: Learning to read in a second language*. London: Paul Chapman.

Gregory, E. (1996b). Learning from the community: A family literacy project with Bangladeshi-origin children in London. In: S. Wolfendale & K. Topping (Eds), *Family Involvement in Literacy: Effective Partnerships in Education*. London: Cassell.

Gregory, E. (1998). Siblings as mediators of literacy in linguistic minority communities. *Language and Education, 12*, 33–54.

Gregory, E. (2001). Work or play: Unofficial literacies in the lives of two East End London communities. In: M. Martin-Jones & K. Jones (Eds), *Multilingual Literacies: Reading and Writing in Different Worlds*. Amsterdam: Benjamins.

Gregory, E., Mace, J., Rashid, N., & Williams, A. (1996). *Family literacy history and children's learning strategies at home and at school: Perspectives from ethnography and ethnomethodology*. Final Report of ESRC Project R000 221186. London: ESRC.

Gregory, E., & Williams, A. (1998a). London literacies: Home and school reading practices in London. In: C. Leung & A. Tosi (Eds), *Rethinking Language Education*. London: Cilt.

Gregory, E., & Williams, A. (1998b). Family literacy history and children's learning strategies. In: G. Walford & A. Massey (Eds), *Children Learning in Context*. London: JAI Press.

Gregory, E., & Williams, A. (2000). *City literacies: Learning to read across generations and cultures*. London and New York: Routledge.

Hammersley, M. (1995). *The politics of social research*. London: Sage.

Haque, Z. (1999). *Exploring the validity and possible causes of the apparently poor performances of bangladeshi students in British secondary schools*. Unpublished PhD Thesis, University of Cambridge.

Harris, R. (2001). Keynote Speech, Naldic General Council Meeting, 7th July.

House of Commons, H. A. C. (1987). *Bangladeshis in Britain: Session 1986–1987, first report*. London: HMSO.

ILEA, Department of Research and Statistics (1987). *Ethnic background and examination results 1985 and 1986*. London: RS 1120/87.

ILEA, Department of Research and Statistics (1990). *Differences in examination performances*. London: RS.

Keith (1993). *Race, riots and policing: Lore and disorder in a multi-racist society*. London: UCL Press.

Kivi, M. (1991). Lies, damn lies and GCSE results. *Education, 177*, 401.

Kysel, F. (1988). Ethnic background and examination results. *Educational Research, 30*(2), 83–89.

Little, A. (1972). Performance of children from ethnic minority backgrounds in primary school. *Oxford Review of Education, 1*, 117–135.

Mabey, C. (1981). Black British literacy: A study of the reading attainment of London black children from 8–15 years. *Educational Research, 23*, 83–95.

Mabey, C. (1986). Black pupils' achievement in Inner London. *Educational Research, 28*, 163–173.

Massey, A., & Walford, G., (1998). Children learning: Ethnographers learning. In: G. Walford & A. Massey (Eds), *Children Learning in Context Studies in Educational Ethnography* (Vol. 1). London: JAI Press.

Mcintyre, D., Bhatti, G., & Fuller, M. (1993). *Educational experiences of ethnic minority students in the city of Oxford*. Oxford: Oxford University Department of Educational Studies.

Meehan, H. (1979). *Learning lessons: Social organisation in the classroom*. Cambridge, MA: Harvard University Press.

Merriam (1986). *Case study research in education: A qualitative approach*. San Francisco: Jossey-Bass.

Modood, T., & Berthoud, R., (1997). *Ethnic minorities in Britain: Diversity and disadvantage*. London: Policy Studies Institute.

Murshid, T. (1990). Needs, perceptions and provisions: The problem of achievement among Bengali (Sylheti) pupils. *Multicultural Teaching, 8*, 12–15.

Newham, London Borough of (1995). ELS GCSE Monitoring Report. London.

Ofsted (1999). *Raising the attainment of minority ethnic pupils: School and LEA responses*. London: Ofsted.

Pathak, S. (2000). *Research topic paper: Ethnicity in education, training and the labour market*. London: Dee.

Payne, G., & Cuff, E. (1982). *Doing teaching: The practical management of classrooms*. London: Batsford.

Phillips, C. (1979). Educational underachievement and different ethnic groups. *Educational Research, 21*, 116–130.

Pollard, A. (1994). Towards a sociology of learning in primary schools. In: A. Pollard & J. Bourne (Eds), *Teaching and Learning in the Primary School*. Buckingham: Open University Press.

Pollard, A., & Filer, A. (1999). *The social world of pupil career: Strategic biographies through primary school*. London: Cassell.

Rashid, N., & Gregory, E. (1997). Learning to read, reading to learn: The importance of siblings in the language development of young bilingual children. In: E. Gregory (Ed.), *One Child, Many Worlds: Early Learning in Multicultural Communities*. London: David Fulton.

Richardson, R., & Wood, A. (2000). *Inclusive schools, inclusive society: Race and identity on the agenda*. Stoke-on-Trent: Trentham.

Sammons, P. (1995). Gender. *ethnic and socio-economic differences in attainment and progress: A longitudinal analysis of student achievement over nine years. British Educational Research Journal, 21*, 465–485.

Sewell, T. (1997). *Black masculinities and schooling: How black boys survive modern schooling*. Stoke On Trent: Trentham.

Swann (1985). The Swann report (Education for all: The report of the committee of inquiry into the education of children from ethnic minority groups). London: HMSO.

Tanna, K. (1990). Excellence, equality and educational reform: The myth of South Asian achievement levels. *New Community*, *16*, 349–368.

Troyna, B. (1984). Fact or artefact? *British Journal of Sociology of Education*, 153–166.

Troyna, B. (1991). Underachievers or underrated? The experience of pupils of South Asian origin in secondary schools. *British Educational Research Journal*, *17*, 361–376.

Troyna, B. (1992). Ethnicity and the organisation of teaching groups. *Educational Research*, *34*, 45–55.

Troyna, B. (1993). Underachievers or misunderstood? A reply to Roger Gomm. *British Educational Research Journal*, *19*, 167–174.

Troyna, B. (1995). Beyond reasonable doubt? Researching 'race' in educational settings. *Oxford Review of Education*, *21*, 395–408.

Troyna, B., & Carrington, B. (1989). Whose side are we on? Ethical dilemmas in research on 'race' and education. In: Burgess (Ed.), *The Ethics of Educational Research*. London: Falmer.

Wiles, S. (1999). Report to conference. Naldic Conference, Leicester, 20th November.

Woods, P. (1980). *Pupil strategies: Explorations in the sociology of the school*. London: Croom Helm.

Wright, C. (1992). *Race relations in the primary school*. London: David Fulton.

MAKING IT: CARIBBEAN CHILDREN TRANSGRESSING BARRIERS AND INEQUALITY TO ACHIEVE SUCCESS

Colton Paul

INTRODUCTION

The research on Black underachievement is well documented. But the explanations posited as causes for this failure are problematic. They are reductive and fail to explain adequately the reasons for Black children's underperformance. The wealth of research into Black underachievement is not matched by research into Black achievement, and explanations for this are equally flawed, as are policies designed to curtail underperformance. I argue in this paper that underachievement is the product of social and cultural forces, and success is dependent on all concerned in the educational development of the child, including the child, overcoming those forces and accommodating each other in order to provide the knowledge and skills necessary for success.

SETTING THE SCENE: PREVIOUS RESEARCH AND LIMITATIONS

The profusion of research on Black underachievement dates from the 1960s. This extensive body of work includes major studies by the ILEA (Inner London

Ethnographies of Educational and Cultural Conflicts: Strategies and Resolutions
Studies in Educational Ethnography, Volume 9, 129–170

ISSN: 1529-210X/doi:10.1016/S1529-210X(04)09008-4

Education Authority) between 1966 and 1975 (summarized in Little, 1978; Tomlinson, 1981), and a landmark study by Coard (1971). Evidence of underachievement was likewise provided by the Rampton Report (1981), Taylor (1981), the Swann Report (1985), by Fitzgerald et al. (2000), and by Gilborn and Mirza (2000). What is more the Gilborn and Mirza report revealed that the performance of African Caribbean pupils declined as they progressed through the school system, a trend identified by previous research, notably the ILEA studies.

THE EXPLANATIONS

In the 1960s explanations for Black underachievement were based on a deficit model. Black children, it was felt, were handicapped by an inferior culture, "innate" low intelligence, and "behavioural disorders," being more "deviant," "restless," "destructive" and "quarrelsome" than their peers (Nehaul, 1996; Ogbu, 1978). In the 1970s and 1980s Nehaul (1996) argues, the "unintentional" and "intentional" racism of teachers were proposed as key factors affecting the performance of Black children. Other theories focussed not on ethnicity but on class and language. In our current multicultural climate the focus has shifted once again from the school to the child. Sewell (2000), for example, argues that racism does not play any significant role in the underachievement of children of Caribbean heritage. Black children underachieve because of their adherence to a counter-culture that is anti-school, anti-education, and fed by a popular culture with a consumerist philosophy.

THE POLICY RESPONSES

In the 1970s and 1980s official responses to Black underachievement shifted from the assimilationist and cultural eradication philosophy of the 1960s to policies designed to combat racism and promote inclusiveness. Focus was placed on providing a multicultural education through a curriculum with a multicultural perspective and philosophy, which would promote achievement amongst Black and other ethnic minority pupils (Gilborn, 1990; Willey, 1984). Yet despite this African Caribbean children continue to fail, as the numerous research highlighted above demonstrate.

PROBLEMS AND LIMITATIONS

The explanations for Black underachievement are problematic. The deficit model mythologised, or "problematized," the child and his race by defining his failure as something that is inherent (Nehaul, 1996; Ogbu, 1978). In locating the problem within the child this theoretical model ignored other factors that are responsible for his/her failure and manufactured an innocent White subject justified in its marginalization and exclusion of the Black child. The later theories, Nehaul (1996) argues are just as flawed. Neither the theory of language, racism, or class explain why children of Caribbean heritage underachieve. The racism model of the 1970s and 1980s problematized the school and teachers, whilst fashioning an innocent Black subject. The Black child and his community are constructed as victims and denied any responsibility in the underachievement of the Black child (Sewell, 2000). The theory of language fails to explain why Asian children and other minority groups, who are bilingual surpass African Caribbean children in academic performance, a fact that is apparent in the numerous studies identified above. What is more, a focus on language as the principle determinant in the underachievement of the Black child, diverts attention from "institutional factors" that contribute to low academic attainment among Black children, by locating the blame, again solely in the child (Edwards, 1983; Labov, 1977). The theory of class, which academics like Sewell subscribe to, fail to account for the fact that African Caribbean children fail so dramatically in comparison with Whites and Asians of the same class (Gilborn & Mirza, 2000; Little, 1978). I subscribe to Gilroy's (1992) analysis that race and class are interrelated. It is erroneous to suggest that black children underachieve because of class, whilst omitting the most significant element- race, from the equation, which Kincheoloe and Steinberg (1997) identified as being of importance in thinking about social and educational inequalities. With the "critical antiracism" model adopted by Sewell (2000) there is a return to the model of the 1960s. In this paradigm an innocent White subject is created exonerated from responsibility in the problematization of interpersonal relations between teacher and child and in the prejudicial practices directed against the Black child. In failing to satisfactorily explain the causes for Black underachievement these theoretical models fail to explain adequately the reasons for Black achievement, a fact Bhikhu Parekh (1988) was acutely conscious of and commented on. In fact, the implicit myth in all these theoretical models is that children of Caribbean heritage do not succeed at all.

EXPLAINING SUCCESS AND FAILURE: A CRITICAL MULTICULTURAL APPROACH

In order to arrive at a deeper understanding of the causes of Black underachievement and success it is necessary to adopt a multidimensional approach, which takes into account historical processes. Such an approach is advocated by Ogbu (1978),

McCarthy (1990) and Kincheoloe and Steinberg (1997). In Ogbu's view it is vital to take into account the "cumulative effects" of history in institutions as diverse as school and employment sites on the academic performance of the Black child. Of fundamental importance in the analysis of Black performance is the need to ask crucial questions about knowledge and power in their historical and contemporary setting and manifestations: what has been, and is, the nature, function and purpose of knowledge and power in the educational development of the Black child? Ngugi (1986) argues that of the two forces operating to oppress the Black child, physical force and knowledge, knowledge is the most insidious and destructive. This is precisely the perspective adopted by Kincheoloe and Steinberg (1997) in their discourse on Critical Multiculturalism, and the philosophy which underpins my thinking. To understand underachievement and social injustice amongst Black and other minority groups, Kincheoloe and Steinberg (1997) argue, it is important to assess the nature and operation of knowledge in the public and private sphere, its association with power, and the ways these interact to affect and transform human perception, identity, interpersonal relationships and human performance in arenas as diverse as schools, the workplace and the home. In adopting this approach I do not deny the genetic component of behaviour. But I believe, like Sewell (2000), that it is entirely possible to talk about the effects of internal psychological states on behaviour and performance without reverting to pseudo- Darwinian theories. I agree with the views expressed by Kincheoloe and Steinberg (1997) and Bruner (1996) that Culture is a powerful and pervasive force and a significant determiner of behaviour and performance. The nature of knowledge and power in the public and private spheres, which shape identity and define interpersonal relations are significant forces in the underachievement of Black children. White mythologies and their association with power and prestige and Black mythologies and their affiliation with powerlessness, work separately and in tandem to deny the Black child the knowledge and skills necessary for success. Black children succeed when mythologies are transgressed, when power is used benevolently and co-operatively and when application becomes the governing principle in the task of teaching and learning.

MYTHOLOGIES AND POWER

Mythologies and power take on a range of guises and wear a variety of masks. They are multifaceted processes. Mythologies are defined by Barthes (1973) as popular forms of culture, "a system of communication . . . a message," or a "type of speech," which incorporate verbal and non-verbal forms of communication, and which transforms the subject into an unnatural, yet naturalized object.

Mythologies for the French anthropologist Claude Levi-Strauss are analogous to Barthes description of myths. In Levi-Strauss's (1993) view mythologies are forms of expression, a system of communication and a feature of speech. But as Kirk (1988) point out, for Levi-Strauss mythologies are psychological processes before they are manifest practices. Mythologies, in Levi-Strauss's analysis, are the product of the internal structures of the mind. Mythologies, from these theoretical perspectives, are reciprocal processes. The interdependent nature of mythologies is manifest in the interplay between the external manifest mythologies and the internal processes of the mind, one influencing the other. Mythologies transform the subject for specific intents, which are usually to create conformity, induce passivity, disarm and depoliticize the intended audience. That is why Barthes has defined mythologies as "depoliticize speech." But mythologies induce more than docility in the audience. Mythical language can arouse passion and mobilise the audience to act politically. But the audience is transformed ultimately into docile or political subjects in order to attack or marginalize the "other," eradicate difference, or maintain and justify social inequalities and injustice. Mythologies are indistinguishable from knowledge and power. Power is defined by Barthes as bourgeois in nature, which shapes mythologies and determine the character of society. In his analysis of power, however, Barthes creates a passive subject. A more concrete definition of power is provided by Foucault (1991), for whom power and knowledge are innately interwoven, one producing the other. What is more power is both macro and micro in character. Power exists from the level of the state to the individual, which makes revolutionary change from the grassroots a distinct possibility.

WHITE MYTHOLOGIES

Historically knowledge about Black people in White culture has been characterized by absence and stereotype. The stereotypical images conveyed by the media were reinforced in the curriculum, textbooks, and by teachers, and resulted in the perpetuation of racist attitudes and inequalities among the White populace. What is more they impacted on the Black child's psyche and disrupted their self-image and their performance (Coard, 1971; Hicks, 1981; Pearse, 1986; Worrall, 1981). Stone (1981) and Fuller (1981) contradict any notion of a negative Black self-image. However, Fuller may have confused bravado for confidence, and failed to recognize that the children she described may have been acting out of a sense of deep insecurity, rather than any inherent notions of self- worth. As Argyle (1994) suggests what may appear as confidence may be the product of a deep sense of anxiety, or even inferiority. Stone on the other hand does not acknowledge the extent to which the very knowledge she recommends that African Caribbean children learn may undermine the poor self-esteem and self-image that she claims they do not possess.

Contemporaneous cultural forms of knowledge about Black people in the media and other mediums of cultural productions have changed at a surface level, but at the core they remain unchanged (Gilroy, 2000; Hooks, 1992; Kincheoloe & Steinberg, 1997; Pieterse, 1992). The "cultural imperialism" identified by Worrall as being at the centre of the curriculum with its attending philosophy of assimilation and integration, and an Arnoldian concept of knowledge and culture still forms the centre of the knowledge base assimilated by Black children in schools (Kincheoloe & Steinberg, 1997; Gilborn, 1990). The response of the Black child to this continuing barrage of misrepresentation is not to join the Rastafarian movement. Rastafarianism as a "source of power and dignity" has declined in the world-view of Black children, according to Sewell (2000). The "Rasta Heads" identified by Mac an Ghaill (1988), for whom the symbol of Rastafarianism was a source of resistance has given way to a different form of counter-culture, one based around the philosophy of rap culture, and fuelled by a consumerist philosophy Sewell (2000), argues.

The knowledge base that underpinned cultural productions about Black people formed the basis of perceptions of Black children within the education profession. In the 1960s and 1970s this philosophy played a central role in the problematization of the space and interpersonal relationship between children and their teacher, in the misdiagnosis of Black children on an academic and behaviour level, and in their marginalization and exclusion. In the 1960s and 1970s children of Caribbean heritage formed the majority in schools for children with learning difficulties (Coard, 1971; Edwards, 1979; Taylor, 1981). In studies of the relationship between teachers and their Black students in Midland comprehensives, Driver (1981) and Gilborn (1990) argued that teachers frequently misdiagnosed and misrepresented Black children and placed them in the lower stream, which in turn negatively influenced the nature of the interpersonal relationship between pupils and their teachers. In the Gilborn study children of Caribbean heritage were misrepresented, misdiagnosed, and downgraded more significantly their Asian peers. Decades later children of Caribbean heritage still form the majority of the children excluded from school, and who fail to achieve the necessary academic qualifications (Fitzgerald et al., 2000); Gilborn and Mirza (2000).

BLACK MYTHOLOGIES

Black mythologies are characterised by the privileging, referencing, assimilation, personalization and reproduction of White mythologies in Black cultural productions such as television programmes, music videos, and film and in the social practices and forms of behaviour within the home and other socializing agencies. Such processes and customs serve not only to reinforce these mythologies, but the forms of behaviour and cultural practices generated play to deny Black children the support and skills necessary for success. What is more the appropriation and integration of Black mythologies to construct an identity by African Caribbean youths lead to ways of seeing in which education is trivialized and culminate in the display of patterns of behaviour that bring them in conflict with white mythologies and power within the school setting, and other institutions of power which ultimately inhibit the Black child's ability to fulfil his potential.

The collusion of Black cultural productions with the White culture industry are central themes in Gilroy's (2000) and Sewell's (2000) analysis of multiculturalism. According to Gilroy (2000) The "uncritical" collusion of Black cultural productions with the culture industry produces stereotypical images of Black people, which are the conditions imposed by the White culture industry for the acceptance of Black culture into the mainstream. The implication of Gilroy's argument is that acceptance is based on the depoliticization of Black culture and on conforming to the received notion of what it means to be Black, a role that the Black culture industry is only too willing to comply with. Sewell (2000), does not deviate from Gilroy's thesis, arguing that Black culture has become the archetypical cool image, with mass appeal and the "billboard" for the mass consumer market. But its elevation to that status has been accomplished through the unreflective connivance with the very corporations that exploits it, an uncritical complicity from which emerges the devaluation of Black cultural life through images of Blackness that are depoliticized, apolitical, and non threatening, and which conform to "racist types."

In Black cultural productions the street and its attendant myths are elevated to mythical status as are the body and sexuality of the Black male and female. The hyper-masculine and hyper-sexualized Black male with his accompanying mythical symbols and the defeminized, yet hyper-sexualized Black female, are standard images in rap and dancehall. These images Gilroy (2000) argue play comfortably into the myth of the all body no mind image. Sewell (2000) concurs, but levels his criticism specifically at the Black male, ignoring the fact that these images of the defeminized, but supersexualized Black female conform equally well to preconceived and mythic notions of Black femininity. Gilroy (2000) goes on to suggests that the elevation of Black flesh to a symbolic, mythological level is falsely constructed as a form of empowerment, which impacts on both Black and White consumers.

The appropriation of the cultural productions and accompanying belief systems, by Black youths to construct an identity as a means of empowerment leads to the development of a false sense of masculinity and femininity, and constitutes,

Sewell (2000) argues, the most dominant reason for the underachievement of Black youths. Such an affiliation leads to the mythologisation or transformation of school and learning as trivial, conflict with teachers and peers, and to exclusion through Black-on-Black violence. What is more those who subscribe to the philosophy of the counter-culture will often pressurize those who do not to conform. For those who acquiesce the outcome is a loss of the desired academic success. Sewell's argument is supported by Phoenix (2000), who argues that the pressures to conform to a hegemonic male ideal lead many studious students to develop an anti-learning attitude. The anti-school mentality of Black youths also forms a central feature of Ogbu's thesis. According to Ogbu (1998) many Black students are coerced into a peer group culture which is anti-intellectual and in which learning is constructed as "acting white."

Black girls are not immune to the counter-productive forms of behaviour assigned to Black boys. Studies conducted by Fuller (1981), Driver (1981) and Mac an Ghaill (1988) of comprehensive pupils showed that Black girls did not adhere to the counter-culture traditional to Black males, but nonetheless played up to the bad girl image often associated with Black girls and produced patterns of behaviour that were on the surface as counter-productive as those of their male peers. According to Driver, Black girls produced patterns of behaviour that were often more problematic than the Black boys. The girls in Fuller's study did not think that school was "irrelevant," but certainly felt that it was "boring" and "trivial." Despite their behaviour, however, the girls in all these studies performed better than the boys. This was in part due to the girls' attitude to the work and their response to conflict situations. The girls tended to do the work set and attempted to mitigate conflict situations, whilst the boys were keen on neither.

The desire for acceptance by the dominant culture and its psychological and cultural consequences, are significant factors fuelling Black youths affiliation with the counter-productive aspects of rap, dancehall and other negative forms of behaviour. The counter-culture is the school where they gain self-definition. According to Gilroy (2000) in order to gain some sense of security in the face of Black powerlessness and the devaluation and dehumanizing of Black cultural life, the counter-culture with its mythologising of the Black body, and the construction of this mythologisation as natural and empowering has become the altar of worship for the young. In the sexual politics of rap and their "sexual play and recreation," and "black sporting excellence" Black powerlessness and fragmentation find expression and unity.

The Black nationalist movement of the 1960s and its contemporary form was, and is, a response to White racism as well as a reaction to Black mythologies and the social and psychological fragmentation within the Black community, Sewell (2000) argues. However, Sewell postulates, in order to oppose Black and White mythologies and their effects a counter mythology was produced which employed the language of the far right of the dominant culture. The mythologisation of White society and the anti-White rhetoric is integrated with an anti-White establishment rhetoric, and this finds expression in the philosophy and counter culture espoused by the young and identified by Sewell and Ogbu, that learning and education are counterproductive in a White society.

MAKING IT

Becoming successful from the perspective of the research model of the 1960s meant compliance with, and acceptance of, the cultural eradication and assimilationist philosophy. Success from the anti-racist perspective meant a denial of Black selfhood and agency, as Sewell (2000) has suggested, coupled with little understanding of the on-the-ground realities of Black students, which Ogbu (1978) has pointed out. Sewell's critical anti-racist model is essentially a return to the assimilationist model of the 1960s, where no requirements are placed on teachers or the school. All children have to do is accommodate their peers and success will be theirs. The barriers to success that Black children are likely to encounter within and outside school are ignored. According to Sewell becoming successful means the Black child resisting peer pressure that constructs learning as bad, obey school rules, and focus on the task of achieving. The child must learn to do what Ogbu describes as "accommodation without assimilation." Sewell provides two examples of children who have successfully accommodated without assimilating, Kelvin and Samantha. What is both implicit and explicit in Samantha's and Kelvin's narrative are more than students who have successfully learnt to accommodate, but the degree to which the students and Black forms of behaviour are stigmatized by teachers. The racism that Sewell denies exists is both implicit and explicit in these narratives. Sewell himself recognizes and admits this. What is essentially an innocent form of behaviour, bopping, is denounced as bad, whilst the girls and boys seen together constitute a threat. Having recognized and admitted to this "institutional racism" Sewell brushes it aside. What is significant for him is the "accommodation without assimilation" practiced by the students in relation to their peers and to the teacher, which is instrumental in their quest for success. There is much that is commendable in Sewell's argument, and in part I subscribe to it. But becoming successful does not simply involve accommodation on the part of the students. Becoming successful with the teachers' attitude intact does not necessarily guarantee the child success, but maybe a source of frustration and conflict.

Achieving success in the model I propose involves the symbols of power in the education of the child, as well as the child, overcoming their mythologies in whatever form it takes, and embracing the philosophy of accommodation in order to negotiate positive interpersonal relations and apply themselves to the task of nurturing and developing the skills necessary for success. There can be no accommodation without the will to overcome negative perceptions and forms of behaviour. The knowledge and skills necessary to critically evaluate mythologies without assimilating them into one's mental structure is a central part of this process of overcoming and accommodation. Of equal importance in this process of making it is the need to examine and overhaul institutions and structures of power and knowledge that mythologise and exclude the Black child.

METHODOLOGY

The study was carried out in a primary school in east London using a multifaceted, multidimensional, ethnographic approach. This multifarious methodological strategy included interviews with parents, teachers and children, and classroom observations using a proxemic method. Proxemics is concerned with spatial relations and the processes involved in the creation of such interactions. This strategy was, in this study, undertaken for a PhD thesis, entirely experimental. The focus of the research was African Caribbean boys, their parents and teachers.

THE SCHOOL

The research was conducted is a primary school in Forest Gate, in the London Borough of Newham. The school serves a diverse multi-ethnic community, with approximately 358 pupils on its register. White children of U.K. heritage formed the majority (23.7%), with a small percentage (1.1%) of white pupils from other European countries. The school roll also included children of African and African-Caribbean heritage (8.1 and 10.3% respectively), children of Indian (11.7%), Pakistani (7.8%), Bangladeshi (8.9%), and Chinese (0.6%) backgrounds. There was a small percentage of children from refugee communities within the school. But this figure continually fluctuated as children and their families are rehoused, and move away. The school therefore experienced a high level of pupil mobility. At least 27 different languages were spoken by the children in the school, representing a range of 21 countries. Thirty-eight percent of the school children receive free school meals. However, 10% of the school population is from an area of higher social class or status than the majority. The school is served by one of the local infant schools.

THE CHILDREN, THE TEACHERS, AND THE PARENTS

The significant actors in the study were children of Caribbean heritage, their parents and teachers. The parents are Clara, Esther, Leona and Mary. Clara and Leona are single parents. The parents all work, with the exception of Mary. Esther is a part time shop assistant. Both Clara and Leona are secretaries and both work as temps. Mary was doing a university degree, but at the commencement of the research had taken leave of her studies to have, and care, for her newborn baby. All the parents were in their thirties, with the exception of Mary who was in her late twenties when the study began.

The children were all boys, and were 4 in number. At the commencement of the study these children were in year 4 and 5 respectively and at different stages of performance. Beres and Tyrese were in year 5. Beres was performing as well as his peers in the highest group. Beres lived with his mother alone. Beres's younger sibling was sent to Jamaica because his mother felt he would receive a better education in Jamaica. The only reason Beres was not sent to Jamaica was because he refused to go. Beres is extremely reserved. Tyrese was average in terms of performance, according to the teacher, although it was believed, with a little application on Tyrese's part, he would gain level 4 in his English SATs. Tyrese, like Beres, lived with his mother alone. Tyrese was an only child. Tyrese was also very quiet. My observations never revealed him to be anything but extremely quiet, polite and respectful. This perspective was both confirmed and disavowed by Tyrese's mum, Clara, and his teacher, Emily, who was also the deputy head. Their view was that, whilst Tyrese's behaviour was as I have described it, he could be problematic. This was due to the fact that Tyrese liked being part of the crowd.

Gabriel and Jamal in year 4 were also at different stages in their performance. Gabriel was performing as well as his peers in the top group, while Jamal was in the bottom group. Gabriel lived with his mother and older sister. He shared similarities in personality with Beres. Observations showed him to be restrained, reticent. Jamal lived with his mother, her boyfriend, and newborn brother. Jamal was animated and prone to engage in unhelpful behaviour.

In the course of the study the children's teachers were Emily, as indicated above, a white teacher in year 5, and Sylvia, a black teacher from the Caribbean island of Montserrat. With Sylvia's departure, Rebecca, from New Zealand taught the children for the remainder of the term, before leaving for pastures new. In their final year Tyrese and Beres were no longer in the same class. In agreement with Tyrese's mum, he was placed in a different class from Beres to keep him away from the peers who were distracting him so that he could concentrate on his work.

METHOD OF DATA COLLECTION

The method adopted for data collection was multidimensional in nature. One of the techniques employed for the gathering of information was the proxemics method. The other principle methods of data collection were interviews with parents, children and their teachers. A minor projectionist exercise, the analysis of children's work and school documents, such as test results, were other key methods used for amassing data. In its simplest form, proxemics is concerned with interpreting and assessing culturally determined patterns of behaviour, and with the organisation of space at the physical and interpersonal level (Hall, 1963; Watson, 1970). The key objects that formed the focus of my attention and needed to be notated were central to Hall's and Watson's thesis. However, a certain degree of modification was necessary before the system was employed. This took account of my own needs and the nature of the classroom. Apart from obvious factors such as the sex and ethnicity of the actors in the study, I was concerned with posture, "kinaesthetic factors" such as the inclination to "strike, hold, caress, or groom," language and voice loudness, eye contact, and movement. The proxemic approach that I used was experimental in nature. Their use, as Argyle (1994) has suggested has been limited to controlled situations, and have not to my knowledge been used in the hectic and unpredictable location of the classroom. I shall not enter into any detail about proxemics here or elsewhere in this thesis. It is sufficient to say that when perfected for the unpredictable and spontaneous situation of the classroom, the proxemic method can become an extremely useful tool for the systematic observation of classroom behaviour and interactions. The interviews were formal and informal, structured and semi- structured. Interviews were conducted in the school and within the home. Children, parents and teachers, were interviewed separately. Permission for the interviews with the children was granted by parents in a formal letter, and with the consent of the pupils themselves and their teachers before interviews were conducted.

THE PARENTS' STORY

None of the parents interviewed achieved their academic and career goals. They obtained grades that were below the national average. Their low academic attainment and issues of race and gender placed limitations on the career options available to them. The parents assigned responsibility for their underachievement to teachers. But they did not exclude their own parents or themselves from responsibility in their poor performance. Whatever success they achieved parents ascribe to themselves and to their siblings who provided them with much needed support in their early learning experiences. Parents' home/school experiences had a significant impact on how they related to their own children both in educational terms and on a personal level. As a result of their home/school experiences the parents strived to better themselves, nurtured more positive spatial relations between themselves and their children than they themselves were used to, and attempted to provide the necessary support structures within the home for their children to succeed. In other words, they attempted to empower themselves to empower their children.

EDUCATION AND CAREER ATTAINMENT AND DISILLUSIONMENT

The parents expressed deep sadness and frustration at the fact that they had not fulfilled their academic potential or achieved their career goals. They all felt that they could have accomplished much more, both within school and outside in terms of employment opportunities. Their distress and regret are palpable.

CP: How successful were you at school?
Leona: I came out of school with my Pitmans 1, maths, English and secretary science.
CP: Is that CSES or . . .?
Leona: Yes, it was CSEs at that time.
CP: Which grades?
Leona: I got grade 1 for English, which I was shocked, and 2 for maths, and a grade 3 for secretary science and my Pitman's 1 certificate.
CP: How happy were you about your performance in school?
Leona: Well I suppose I could have done a bit better . . .
CP: So Leona would you say that you were motivated? You said you could have done better?
Leona: yeah, I could have done. I think I could have done. I mean my-when I got my results, even though I got a grade 2 for maths I was expected to get a grade 1 in maths. I thought I would get 2 in English. I mean English, I was shocked cause I never thought I'd get-cause I couldn't spell to save my life, so I never thought I would have got a grade 1. But when I got my maths, I was upset about that, because I said no. I should be getting a 1 in maths because I can do maths. I am good at maths, you know.
CP: what did you do after that? Did you go to college?
Leona: I went on to YTS, youth training. I said cause I want- at the end of the day my brother was saying to me that it's not the qualifications, it's experience

that they-everyone's looking for, so I thought how you're gonna get experience in college, so I'm gonna go on a YTS.

CP: and what is your occupation now?

Leona: secretary

CP: where is it that you work?

Leona: Well I do temporary work at the moment. But I have been doing it for quite a few years

CP: and, well obviously that's what you wanted. Was that what you wanted when you were at school?

Leona: well I knew I wanted to do office work. I said "do you know what?", to my mum. "One day," I said, "you know what? I'm gonna do office work cause I want to do a job where I don't get my hands dirty. I don't want to get my hands dirty. I don't want to get my hands dirty. I don't want to get my nails dirty. I don't' want to be in all grease and cooking and –I mean, you know, I want to be in a office. I want to, you know, go to work in a suit and, you know, in them high powered jobs. I want one of them."

CP: And you feel you have achieved your goal?

Leona: not fully, no. Not fully. No.

CP: Is there anything about yourself that you would change Leona?

Leona: I think if I had my time over again, I would have spent more years in College getting more education. I would have done more, more courses, cause I mean at the time, them times, it was free as well. So I would have done all the courses, and achieved as much education as I can, cause the more I know, the better of I would be. And that's the only thing I would change. I mean I've tried to get on to like am, legal secretary courses, but they are so hard to get on. They are really hard. I've tried twice, and twice I didn't get in.

Clara's and Esther's stories mirror Leona's narrative

CP: How did you perform in these schools? Did you get any qualifications?

Clara: Ahhh, no. My qu-well my qualifications, I think for English, I got a 3 average. I got average English, maths, history and social studies, and typing, which is my main feature.

CP: How did you feel about that?

Clara: ahhhh, well after-cause I stayed on to sixth form, but after that, I think I got my job. I felt like I should have done more. I think everyone sort of think like that, am . . . but yeah, I did feel- when I'm on my own, I do think well I wish I had done some, like something else, as well as what . . .

CP: So do you feel you wasted your time in school?

Clara: Well I wouldn't say- well I wouldn't say wasted. But I think if the ah, teachers took more of a, am . . . effort- made more of an effort with us, then I think yeah, some kids could have gone really far. But am . . . it, it did, did- when I left school, it did make me think that I could have done something else, as well as- I mean my aim was to, to be able to type, and I, I can do that very good. But I wish I had done, thought of something else, you know, like a- as I say, like a back up. Am . . . but yeah . . . am . . . you know, I think, the-I'd say I did enjoy school very much, am, and believe that saying is true, the best life is your school days, and that's what I've been trying to tell Tyrese, so enjoy it, you know, while you can.

CP: what is you occupation now?

Clara: Am, I am a secretary. I work for an insurance company. I've been there for two years now. But prior to that I was with the BBC for nine and a half years, again secretary, so I got to move around. And that's what I miss, is the option to move around, cause where I'm now there's not that option. So I want to try and get back.

CP: Am Esther what qualifications did you leave school with? if you don't mind me asking

Esther: Am . . . I had am . . . one GCE In English literature and CSEs, average. That's the grade I'm talking. I got all my CSEs. It's the average that's . . . The highest grade I got was for social studies, and that was a 2, cause I was going in- I was going to be a social worker. I really wanted to be a social worker and am . . . help am, delinquent kids who are-disadvantaged children, that was my am . . . dream when I was a kid. My dream job.

CP: Yes

Esther: But I had family problems and that, and then, I left home early, so I couldn't follow those through.

CP: Yes

Esther: wasn't in that position any more, so . . . that just went down the pan.

CP: Are there any . . . did you go to further education or anything like that?

Esther: The thing is later, yeah, I did a college course. But it was purely, like, to get work really. It was what we needed to do. It just seem like, when I looked in the paper for a job, those were the majority of jobs going at the time, so that's why I took the course.

CP: Would you say Esther that-would you say that you were successful at school? When you left school did you say "yeah!"?

Esther: No

CP: You were disappointed?

Esther: Yeah, because I could have achieved a lot more, as I said, had I been given directions.

LIMITED FUTURE GOALS

The career opportunities chosen by the parents reflect the limited career options and future goals available to them as women in general, and as black women in particular. The fact that Leona and Clara placed such a high premium on their secretarial skills and secretarial work as the archetypal career choice without thought of what else may exist out there for them demonstrates the extent of their aspirations and the limitations of the careers they felt competent to perform. Esther was compelled to follow the same career path as Leona and Clara because of the impediments placed in her path, narrowing her vision and aspiration, and forcing her to settle for something other than what she desired. Limited future goals and career opportunities Ogbu (1978) argues accounts for the significant levels of underachievement evident amongst black children. Children with limited or no career opportunities, such as those that confront the black child, lead to poor performance, Ogbu suggests. The black child is therefore caught in a double bind. Limited or no career choices culminate in poor academic performance. Poor academic performance further curtailed the career opportunities available to the black child.

THE CAUSE OF UNDERACHIEVEMENT

Teachers are assigned the greater blame by parents for their failure and frustrations. Parents, however, do not exclude themselves or their own parents from taking responsibility for their unfulfilled dreams and ambitions. The parents' role in their own failure is both explicit and implicit. The role of teachers in their underperformance has already been touched on by Clara and Esther, above. The parents felt that teachers' prejudices and assumptions inhibited them from providing the necessary support for success. Leona suggests that her teachers were prejudiced, discriminated against her in favour of Asian pupils, and failed to provide the support needed to achieve her full potential. Leona's experience of prejudice is reflected in Clara's narrative. Whilst Esther pointed out that she did not experience racism from teachers, what was true for Clara and Leona was equally applicable to her. She did not receive the assistance necessary to succeed.

CP: Leona can you explain to me, where did you go to school?

Leona: My primary school was Elmhurst School. And then I did go to Stratford school. But in the third year I left cause when I picked my options, I didn't get them. I found that they gave the options-cause they were trying to be moral prejudiced, they gave them to all the Asians.

CP: Really?

Leona: Yeah.

CP: So your options were not granted?

Leona: I didn't get-out of all my options I picked, I got one. I felt that Stratford School, because they're trying to be-they were trying to be non-prejudiced, they'd give preference to the Indian-the Asian people over everybody else. And so I left. I went to Eastlea school. I got all my options besides one. They said because if I got- I can't do cookery and computer studies and biology. So I have to pick two out of them. So I took secretary science for the final cause I didn't want to dissect frogs.

CP: How happy were you about your performance in school?

Leona: Well, I., well I suppose, I could have done a bit better. I mean, am, I must admit in the science class we used to take the piss. We did.

CP: Why was that?

Leona: We used to mess about. I mean fair enough, it was a class of thirty. But only six people used to turn up, three girls and three boys, that's me and two friends and these other three guys. Like base, we'd say, well teach, we're going loopy. Can't we go out on a school trip? Can't you even organize a trip and-I mean, I mean, when he set the work, one thing I always did, I always did my work, and then I'll mess about. But I always done my work first.

CP: Leona am, you felt that- just kind a recap. Did you feel school let you down?

Leona: Yeah. It could have done more. I think when I was at school, if you didn't want to learn, you wouldn't learn, and that was the end of the story. They just wouldn't push you. They wouldn't push you. If you didn't want to learn, you wouldn't learn. And they knew which ones wanted to learn and which ones didn't. I mean, even computer studies, I mean I'd go in the classroom. The man would tell me to get out straight away, cause me and the man, we just didn't get on. We did not get on. And he'd tell me to, to-I mean even when I was in Stratford school, I never used to go Friday afternoons.

CP: Really?

Leona: No I didn't, because it was secondary. I had R.E and history, and me and my history teacher clashed every time. Every time. And then he told me not to come back to his class again. So I said fine. So I never went back to school. I never went to school Friday afternoons. It's only like when I had some trouble my mum had to come down there, and they said to me-my mum. They told my mum that she's in school everyday. But she's never in school on Friday afternoons. I said "well the teacher told me not to come back to his class. I'm not going back to his class." And they said, no you have to. And the first day I went back me and the man clashed. The first day. And I just didn't go back to school. And that was it. Friday afternoons I was never in school. And my mum said to me, rather than walk the street come home, so I know where you are. And whereas when I was at Stratford school-it's at the top of the road from where we lived-and Friday afternoons, I just go home, go shopping with my mum. And I said to my mum, at the end of the day, history and religious education, those ain't gonna help me do nothing.

TEACHING METHODS AND THE PROBLEMATIZATION OF SPATIAL RELATION

What is apparent from Leona's narrative is that the teachers were not motivated to teach the children. Lessons were uninspiring. One of the consequences of this was that Leona and her peers played around and did not turn up for lessons. The nature of the methods employed to teach Mary were key factors in her underachievement. Mary's inability to read, and her lack of confidence, were exacerbated by the approach used to teach her. Mary's illiteracy and low self esteem culminated in her misbehaving and problematizing spatial relations to compensate. Her poor literacy skills and lack of confidence haunted her well into her adult life.

CP: You said you didn't like reading, why?

Mary: I'm not sure. I think I found it hard myself, with the reading, especially back from infant and junior school. We used to get like special English, whatever, and I didn't like the way they forced me, not force, but-I didn't come away with what I suppose other children must have come away with from there. And am . . . so to me even though people might have realised it, inside I weren't very confident. I weren't confident in literacy, writing, and the story writing and things like that . . . and am . . . so obviously it's just carried with me.

CP: I found what you're saying very interesting . . . only cause I think you were a particular way in primary school and you felt nobody noticed that . . .

Mary: Well I did. I had special English. What I'm trying to say is . . . am . . . yeah, they probably didn't because I used to -from my whole school, my main priority was to talk and enjoy myself because I found, like I said, the literacy quite hard to deal with.

CP: Mary that's going back, is that because of your childhood experiences would you say?

Mary: Am . . . well I know that I wasn't confident as a child in that area, and I know that am . . . I feel that maybe under different circumstances, I feel that even if I went to school in this era, it might have been a different thing altogether, because they do . . . I think they pick up on children more, and I think they-it depended on the school, but I do think they do, whereas then-it wasn't that long, but it is long enough, and they didn't. I mean you're right, you've got special English but that was it. That was like, you know, read, read, read, some spelling.

CP: What is special English?

Mary: when I went . . . when . . . when I was at school we used to do all that . . . am . . . read . . . read words with this teacher . . . I don't know, at lunch time, or whatever time it was. One, I probably didn't like to at lunch time anyway. Found it very hard, and they couldn't understand why. And for quite a few years I used to think maybe I was dyslexic when I was getting older. I don't think it is. I just think it's probably just the learning. I don't know, cause I know dyslexic is quite a . . . but I used to think so.

METHOD, CAUSE AND EFFECT

The principle of cause and effect is a very dominant theme in the above narratives. The strategies employed to teach the children, which was underpinned by a particular theory and belief system, demotivated the children and undermined their self-esteem and confidence. The children's response was to get frustrated, rebel and play around. The teachers' response was to become more entrenched in their beliefs and perhaps more confrontational, which in turn aggravated the children's reaction, resulting in a roller coaster ride of no return, where the children are excluded or voluntarily exclude themselves from class in the case of Leona and her peers.

PUPIL AGENCY AND THE PROBLEMATIZATION OF SPATIAL RELATIONS

The responsibility for the breakdown of co-operative patterns of behaviour between teacher and pupil cannot simply be assigned to the teachers. The pupils themselves must be assigned some responsibility for their own behaviour and for the responses of the teachers. The pupils' role in their teacher's behaviour and their agency in their own underperformance is implicit in Leona's narrative. It is not too difficult to conclude that some of Leona's peers found school a trivial and boring affair, which was as much a product of the nature of the lessons and the teachers' attitude as the children own particular perception of school. Such conceptions of schooling culminated in unproductive forms of behaviour characterised by resistance to the teaching and learning process. Leona always ensured that her work was completed, implying that she wished to learn. But she may have done so in the firm knowledge that it would get her nowhere. With little else to occupy her and her peers, and with teachers that seem uncaring, their desire for play overrode every other considerations.

The pattern of behaviour displayed by Leona in particular formed the focal point of the study conducted by Fuller (1981), discussed in the previous section. Whilst the girls in Fuller's study did their work, like Leona, they nonetheless found school both boring and trivial, and displayed patterns of behaviour that were unhelpful and unproductive. It is this trivialization of school and the pattern of behaviour that it generates that Sewell discusses in his thesis in relation to Caribbean males. What Sewell fails to acknowledge, however, is the role of teachers and the wider White society in the formation of these adverse ideas about schooling and learning and the resulting negative patterns of behaviour they produce What Leona and her peers needed to do was to produce a different response, a fact that is also implicit in Leona's story. But for some children there is little point in curbing their behaviour with the teachers' behaviour intact, or with few rewards in terms of employment at the end of their school career. For some children for whom school has become a meaningless past time behaving badly is entirely acceptable. These children may have even less incentive to curtail negative forms of behaviour.

A CLASH OF MYTHOLOGIES AND POWER, EXCLUSION AND MARGINALZATION

What is manifest in the crisis, and in the breakdown of cooperative patterns of behaviour between pupils and their teacher, is a clash of mythologies and power. The mythologies and power of the teacher collide with, and is opposed by the mythologies and power (lessness) of the children. The more overt and explicit the teacher's mythologies and their unjust use of power the greater the assertion of the pupils' mythologies and power to save face and maintain their dignity. With such combating and competing myths and power it becomes apparent that the teacher's ability to control and manage the situation becomes an impossible task. In such circumstances children are forcibly expelled or voluntarily leave the school to walk the streets. In Leona's case her confrontational language and show of strength means essentially that she has disinvested the teacher with the power and respect that she has been denied. The teacher has effectively lost control of the situation and his ability to bring order to their relationship is undermined. The teacher's mythologies and power wins the day and Leona's powerlessness confronts her when she forced to leave voluntarily and to wander the streets. These competing and combating mythologies and power relations between teachers and their Caribbean pupils are precisely the phenomena and their dire repercussions for the Black child described by Gilborn (1990), Driver (1981), Fuller (1981), Stone (1981).

The clash of mythologies and power were an important component in Clara's school life as it was in Leona's and Mary's school experiences. The mythologisation of black pupils was a central feature of Clara's experience of school. Whilst Clara encountered no direct racism from teachers it is clear from her comments that the mythologisation of pupils was manifest in teachers' interaction with them. They made assumptions about black children, were strict and unapproachable. This mythologisation problematized spatial relations between teachers and pupils, and prevented teachers from providing pupils with the support necessary for success. Pupils, however, played an important role in the teachers' response to them, and in the problematization of interpersonal relations, and therefore in their own lack of success. They, like the pupils in Leona's class, placed a high premium on play and exacerbated the conflict between them and their teachers, and in the process defined the way the other more studious pupils were constructed and dealt with. The behaviour of a minority of children led to all children being labelled as problematic. This therefore affected the degree to which teachers were willing to support them. This argument undermines Sewell's thesis that mere "accommodation without assimilation" will lead to success. The children who have accommodated, and who are studious and well behaved are judged with their peers as difficult and unmanageable, and denied the support necessary for success. This in turn gives the children who are studious very little incentive to behave well.

CP: Teachers . . . what were they like? do you feel that they got the best out of you?

Clara: No. No. I don't' think they did. I think they . . . I think they could have tried a bit more, but because, I don't-I get this impression that it was because they-with the black children it was . . . with the black children I felt that they couldn't be bothered with us because- I'm not saying all of us, but some of us just was there to cause trouble, and am . . . to me, it came across

> as they assumed that every black child was like that. So therefore, it just seem like the white, am, kids were getting more attention than the black children were.

Esther's experience of school was less dramatic and more positive than Leona's and Clara's. But like Leona and Clara, she felt that teachers did not provide her with the support necessary for success. They denied her the guidance and scaffolding she needed to achieve her goals.

CP: What about am . . . teachers? What was your relationship like with teachers?

Esther: In general . . . am . . . I got on really well with, with the majority of my teachers. Am there was only one teacher that I didn't get on with, am . . . I went to a catholic school. Her name was sister Esther, am . . . For some reason we clashed. She just didn't like me. I don't know why. But she took every opportunity to . . . to pick on me and attack me, for whatever reason. We just didn't get along. But in general am, I always got along with teachers.

CP: Did that am . . . relationship with that teacher affect your schooling in any way?

Esther: No. No, not really.

CP: So overall would you say school was positive?

Esther: Am . . . from my point of view, maybe not from others'. But as I say from my own experience, I never had any negative experiences in schools. Not from the teachers anyway.

CP: And how did you your school experience help you in terms of performance, in terms of career prospects?

Esther: it didn't

CP: It didn't help?

Esther: No. Not in that respect. I never . . . I never got the am . . . the direction that I felt I should have had. Had I got the direction that I needed, for the talents that I had then am . . . yeah I could have done wonderful things.

CP: You felt you had certain things to contribute . . . to offer?

Esther: Yeah, but I never knew how to

CP: And no one was able to . . . ?

Esther: to direct me, and put me on the right road, so to speak, so consequently, am . . . am . . . I left school after I took my exams at sixteen. I left home at the same time. I started working from when I was sixteen.

CP: You were disappointed?

Esther: Yeah, because I could have achieved a lot more. As I said, had I been given directions.

BLACK MYTHOLOGIES AND ACADEMIC ACHIEVEMENTS

Within the home interpersonal relations between parents and child were problematized. The effect was that the children were denied the support and encouragement that are the prerequisite for success. In all cases the children were located on the periphery of this problematized and seemingly concrete and unbridgeable space, refused access to practical support. Clara was provided with some support from her mother, and in this respect her role was greater in the educational development of the children than the father. But the support she provided was verbal rather than practical. Practical support came from Clara's siblings. This was as true for Clara as it was for the other parents interviewed.

CP: Describe your own relationship with your parents in relation to reading.

Clara: Am . . . our parents didn't really help us, if you see what I mean. It was like you went to school, am . . . and then we came home. We done the home-how I remember it, we did our homework . . . am, I was always going to my brothers for help. So I was ok on that part. Am . . . but ah . . . I think . . . my dad wasn't too-it was always my mum we was always depending on, my mum more than my dad. I think you always do anyway and am . . . I . . . I always remember the background. Mum always wanted us to do well and always drummed in, you have to do certain things. Don't muck about, straight to school, come home, and that's still been my-in the back of my memory, saying the same thing to Tyrese, especially they're all-they're really wild now. So I've always said to Tyrese, you know, you go to school to learn, you have to have an education, even if you want to be a footballer, you still have to know, you have to have some sort of education, am, and you know, I will keep drumming this into him, cause I say to him, it may not make sense now, but it's later on you'll know mum was right.

CP: Your mum's words ring in your ears and that has influenced you with Tyrese?

Clara: Mmm. Yeah, very much. Yeah, very much. Yeah. and it was in our-in our house it was my mum more than my dad. My dad was there, but . . . he was kinda in the back-background. But it was always mum . . . to turn to. My mum-but even though my dad was there, I could never attend to my dad, and same thing for my brothers. They was always- cause I had another sister, but she, she didn't live with us. She lived in the States. So it's difficult. I never had a sister . . . in theory, so I could talk to or you know, get help in that way. . . . . But am . . . yeah, in, in school then-and then I had like my friends and that, and they would help us and that. But I always remember

> it was like . . . go to school, do the work and come home. Homework first, then your-you know do it after. But I remember homework was always first.

Like Clara, spatial relations between Esther and her father were problematic. This led to the marginalization of Esther and to her location on the border, and in so doing denied her the practical scaffolding that are important for academic attainment. Esther has blamed this on the pressures of work and economic factors. But Esther's father was, like Clara's father, a strict disciplinarian, who did not know how to relate to his children except through imposing his harsh authority and power over them and in the process relegated himself and her to the borders of the problematized space between them, and the edge of their respective consciousness.

CP: Were- I think we've spoken about that. Were books read to you when you were younger?

Esther: Nobody really had time. My dad worked everyday. My brothers who were a lot older than me-my younger brother is four years older than me, so obviously they were at different stages at different times. They never really had time for-to do those sorts of things with me.

CP: Am, and your parents, did they encourage you to read?

Esther: No. Never had that kind of influence. Never had that kind of encouragement. I suppose . . . am . . . my dad was . . . cause he worked, he worked all, all the time, so he never really had time to give that kind of input. So am, all he ever asked of us was that we did our best. That's all he ever asked.

CP: So he did encourage you in some ways?

Esther: in some way . . . in a background kind of way. He wasn't like . . . like I am with the kids. I'm on the case . . . am . . . follow up things and that. He never did that sort of thing.

CP: Ok, you are directly involved with the children, but your . . . your dad wasn't directly involved with you?

Esther: Not where my education was concerned. Family oriented. If we were like . . . as a group together, whenever we had those rare moments when we were all together, then yeah that was . . . that was quality time. So you know, that school thing nev- couldn't intrude on that because it would like . . . it would take away from that quality time, if you understand what I'm saying. And that was very important, because we knew . . . because he worked so hard, it was rare for us to have that time together. So, you know, we made the most of it, especially like family functions and things like that.

Whilst Mary's mother was neither tyrannical nor authoritarian, the nature of the spatial relationship between her and Mary was deeply troublesome. Her detached attitude and lack of involvement with Mary fragmented their relationship. The bitter relationship between Mary and her mother, as it was with Clara and Esther and their father, meant that Mary could not receive the support that would have enabled her to succeed. What is more Mary's mother's detachment and lack of involvement in conjunction with the methods employed to teach Mary in school, induced in Mary an aversion to reading and books that remained with her throughout her adult life. Mary's father was as marginal a figure in her educational development as her mother.

Mary: My Mum . . . she's also another one that isn't . . . she is with my last sister, but she wasn't very am, pushy in that area of homework, read a book every night, and things like that. The confidence never really came until adulthood for me, you see, so I find it very . . . I do . . . I would like to enjoy reading but find it very hard to sit down and to read through a long length of time.

CP: ok, I asked you the question earlier, who taught you to read?

Mary: probably at school and am . . . well it must be school. I can't . . . and mum probably encouraged us a bit, but I don't think- I w . . . I was like Jamal, I didn't really wanna know.

CP: what about your dad?

Mary: am . . . dad, I didn't really live with my d- well I didn't live with my dad. But am, and I didn't really grow up with him as such. I just see him from time to time, when he passed through. But as for my dad, I've never seen a book . . . he's brought us a couple of black books over the years, when he's passing with it.

CP: would you say your mum played a central role in your education?

Mary: am . . . positively?

CP: Yes

Mary: probably not positive. I know she really doesn't realise it, cause my mum used to be . . . I remember doing homework sometimes and saying to my mum "mum, I can't spell this word, can you help me?" and she would say to me, am "well I don't know Mary, get a dictionary." She does- you see the thing with my mum is that she wants you to try, but what- Jamal's like that as well, if you just leave him, and say to him, "Jamal, you try." You have to do it with him. You must do it with him, whether it means you do some and do it like that. The minute you tell him go and get a dictionary and do it himself, he's not doing it at all. And I was like that, but it's mum . . . I knew my mum could spell it. But she's telling me to get the dictionary. I have to get frustrated, get annoyed and just stop doing it altogether. And am . . . she couldn't understand. But I used to say "because I want you to help me," and she'd say "yeah, but you know, you need to." Her idea and my idea as a child was different and she obviously felt that her making me do it independently, that would make me come. But in fact it didn't because I didn't want to do it independently, so I didn't do it at all.

CP: So you rebelled, more or less

Mary: yeah

A FRAGMENTED RELATIONSHIP AND AN AVERSION TO READING

Mary's mother was an avid reader. But the fragmented nature of her relationship with Mary was perhaps a key factor in Mary's nurturing of an aversion to reading and to books. Mary's mother's remoteness and want of emotional concern and interest fuelled Mary's resentment for her mother and for reading. The use of reading as punishment for poor behaviour, a strategy employed by her grandfather, was another key factor in developing Mary's dislike for reading.

CP: Mary, am, you spoke about your mum, she was a keen reader.

Mary: oh, still is

CP: Still is a keen reader?

Mary: mmm

CP: Did your mum's reading influence you?

Mary: not to probably

CP: Sorry?

Mary: not to

CP: Not to

Mary: not to read, yeah she used to do it . . . she used to read all the time. She just love it.

CP: her reading you felt put you off reading?

Mary: cause she was fanatical about it, where I didn't- where I wasn't am . . . confident in reading myself, it sort of hindered me. I said ooh, no, I don't-she's constantly read-my granddad used to say to us . . . when we was naughty "go in the cupboard and get a book," you know, that sort of thing, you know.

CP: like punishment?

Mary: yeah. that's another thing, with Jamal, as well, I try not to do. Cause . . . I do remember things that happen, and am . . . so I didn't like it. And I used to think why does mum- everywhere she goes it was literally-mum would walk with a book on the bus, to someone's house, mum would go round someone's house for dinner and as she gets a spare hour, she'd read . . . it's too much man. I don't want to do that. I want to have fun. You're just boring to me and books were boring. That's probably what it was. Books are boring. And you can have more fun with people and talk and have a laugh.

CP: where did that come from, the idea that books are boring? surely I mean . . . because obviously your mum is doing it, she must be having fun doing it.

Mary: I didn't see that at the time. I didn't think . . . she was just herself so I didn't see the fun in that. I know what you're saying, but I didn't see the fun in that as a child. I mean If she would have am, sat down and even told me about some of the books she was reading sometimes. But I never knew and I never wanted to know.

CP: She never said, Mary, this is what I'm reading come and read with me?

Mary: no, not like that. She probably did with us when we was younger. But no, not like . . . no. It was her book she was reading.

CP: and did she ever read to you?

Mary: she must have done. Can't remember. But my mum- ah . . . she must have done. I would have thought so, yeah. I can't remember it now, as such.

Mary's aversion to reading is made even more explicit in her comments below.

CP: Do you read Mary yourself?

Mary: Not as much as I should. No

CP: ok, why is that?

Mary: Cause I don't like books myself.

CP: really? Not reading? Then why?

Mary: I don't know, but my mum loves books. She reads and reads and reads and reads and me and my two- me and my second sister we can't stand reading. But my last sister adores books.

CP: But you're doing a degree.

Mary: I know.

CP: Don't you find that a contradiction? You must like reading.

Mary: No. What happened was from my school I didn't like it. I didn't like books, didn't find that there was anything- I don't think I really learnt as well as I could have done. As I've got older and I've gradually done different courses and seeing different things, am, it's slowly encouraged me, but then also, to do with like, doing the courses, it's help me with my English, with my grammar, so that that's the reason why the degree . . . I progressed onto the degree cause I can do it, it's just that I don't like to do it

BECOMING SUCCESSFUL: OVERCOMING LIMITATIONS

Given the fact that these parents received little or no support from home and school, what then can be attributed as the cause of their success, whatever success they may have achieved? One significant factor in the parents' quest for success was the role of siblings. In their initial educational development siblings, brothers in these instances, played a central role in the parents' effort to move from "zero to hero." Later on becoming successful for the parents involved the parents themselves taking control of their educational development by overcoming the limitations imposed on them by white and black mythologies and applying themselves to the task of learning. The parents were driven to overcome the limitations imposed on them not simply for their own purposes, but by their desire to better the learning opportunities for their children. This is more forcefully expressed by Mary.

SIBLINGS AND SUCCESS

Siblings did not play a central role in Mary's quest for success. But they played a fundamental role in Leona's reading development, a role repeated by Beres with his own younger sibling before his departure to a private school in Jamaica. Siblings were not the only agents in providing support in Leona's home. Other family members were recruited for this purpose. For example, Beres's cousin played a central role in his skills development, and the very same job that he performed for his brother, Leona's siblings played in hers. Leona's brother's and sisters were older than her and acted as models for her, both in relation to her skills development and in the decisions that she made in relation to her exams. The lack of success of Leona's Siblings in school motivated Leona to stay on in school and try harder.

CP: Ok, Leona, who taught you to read, would you say?

Leona: well am, I'll say, I got the same way my niece was with Rees, that's how my brother and sisters were with me. Cause I could count and I knew my ABC before I started school.

CP: ok, so they, your brothers and sisters played a central role in your education?

Leona: yeah, as well, yeah. That's why I think, I mean, and the way we was brought up, it sorta like rubs off on our kids. Cause even when I had my other one, with my-my other child he's four years younger than Rees, I'd say that time Alesha used to read with you, you know, go and do the ABC like Alesha used to do it with you, and like I bought them, like educational toys as well, them Btech stuff. Yeah, I bought them every Christmas. I used to buy them one of those each.

CP: And how many brothers did you have?

Leona: I've got three brothers and two sisters.

CP: And they are older?

Leona: they were all older

CP: So they were a sort of role model for you?

Leona: yeah.

Leona: I think what it was is that my brothers and my sister, they never did-they never-one brother, one sister never stayed on at school to do the exam, and then they had to turn round and go to college to do it, and I thought, I aint gonna do that. I said, you know what, I ain't gonna do that. I'm gonna stay on. I'm gonna stay in school and I'm gonna take my exams in school. I'm not gonna have to go to college and redo it again.

Siblings also played a central role in Clara's educational development, which was identified above, and a primary role in Esther's reading success. Esther's brothers taught Esther to read. They lit the spark. But Esther developed the process, took it further. Esther's success was due to her own internal motivation and her need to overcome the limitations and oppressive nature of her environment. She had to overcome her psychological turmoil caused by her home environment to achieve what success she achieved.

CP: so . . . ah . . . who would you say taught you to read?

Esther: am, must have been my brothers. My brothers must have taught me to read.

CP: But you would say that the process . . . ?

Esther: by my passion for reading. Came from my loneliness.

CP: And who was the central figure in your education?

Esther: in my education? Ah, it'd be me again. Determination to learn the things that I liked.

CP: But where did that determination come from do you think? Where did it come from?

Esther: I suppose am . . . I never had a lot of things that the kids have now. So I had to find avenues for my energies, and I suppose that's where it come from. I couldn't define it in any other way, because . . . my brothers . . . hardly went to school when I was going to school. My older brother had already left school am . . . and my middle brothers, one was on the verge of leaving and the other one hardly went to school.

OVERCOMING LIMITATIONS, APPLICATION AND MOTIVATION

Mary's quest to become successful was accomplished through her own efforts. Mary is not quite sure where the seeds were sown. The seeds may have been planted by school or her mother, she's not certain. What she is sure of is that her quest to master the art of reading and become successful was accomplished through her own internal desires, by overcoming the limitations and barriers imposed on her and applying herself to the task of learning.

Mary: I've trained myself to am . . . read, to be able to spell, cause I couldn't really spell very well and I have done that myself, since adulthood, not teenagehood. And I know that I have done that and wherever there is something that's going, to do with any courses, if I can get any extra English or any extra coaching in that area, I will take it up. I do do that now, just for the sake of going to help me achieve what I need to do in my course. So I need to . . . so I have done that. That's the main reason why I've got better, and I can read to Jamal, cause when I first started I couldn't really read very well to him anyway. He was a baby, but still to me, I could stumble, stumble. But now I'm much more confident at picking up a book. I could actually read a story to him and come . . . I felt like him, what he feels now . . . whereas he can't read a story like it flows. But I can do that now, but I couldn't before.

CP: Mary who taught you to read then?

Mary: No, knew how to read through school and through my home, but what I mean is am . . . basically I didn't . . . a lot of words I might not have been able to tackle. My phonics, I wasn't very good on, so I couldn't am . . . even now I'm not brilliant. But I'm a lot . . . you know, I'm quite confident that I can, you know, get through quite a lot of words and spell quite a lot of things pretty much. But I couldn't do that even when I left school. Am, there would be a lot of mistakes in my work. Not just a little bit, a lot, and well, like I said, a lot of times, you're in a big classroom and you're not really going to get the attention that you need are you, as such.? They didn't do Saturday school, or things like that, so instead I talked and got myself into trouble a lot.

CP: Mary who would you say is the most significant person in your reading development, for example ability to read, your development as a reader?

Mary: me

CP: you are

Mary: I was yeah. I can't think of anybody that I felt... well it was me because I couldn't still do it, and if I never pushed myself, very hard and believed that I could do it, like I say... I would about... up to four years, five years ago, I really did push myself to the limit. I started to try and do English again and things like that, take up that extra adult learning thing, it wouldn't have happened. I wouldn't... I still wouldn't be able to do what I can... still wouldn't be able to read very well. I wouldn't be able to do the spelling, the phonics...

A DIALOGUE WITH THE PAST, PRESENT AND FUTURE

Mary was motivated in her quest for success by her desire to help Jamal and herself. But in the need to uplift herself and her son, Mary was engaged in an interior dialogue with time and with society. Mary examined her position and status in the past, her situation in the present and recognised the need for change. What she did next was to place her gaze on a future goal and pursue it as unflinchingly as she could.

CP: But why? What made you push yourself? What is it? I mean what is it? Cause some people don't do that. what is it about you that made you want to push yourself? Cause some people would say, well... I'll just trod along, but you don't... you didn't

Mary: Partly because obviously, like I said, when I was reading with him as a little one, it was very hard for me, but also because am... I wanted to achieve and I felt like I had nothing and there were a lot of people who could do things that I couldn't do and I wanted to do it. And I knew that if I wanted to do it, I had to do certain things to get there. I knew that there's things... sometimes I don't like to do things, but I will do it, just because I know that at the end, I need to achieve something. I need to, you know. So I don't know.

THE PARENT, THE CHILD, SPATIAL RELATIONS, EDUCATION AND IDENTITY

Parents, on the whole, overcame the limitations imposed on them to better the educational opportunities for their children. In overcoming these psychological, educational, and social impediments, and in their efforts to improve the educational chances of their children, parents attempted to nurture positive and constructive interpersonal relations with their children, beyond what they themselves were used to, and applied themselves to their educational development. The parents purchased books for their children, spent time reading with them, and allocated time for helping them with their schoolwork. In some instances parents joined the library with their children. In their drive to develop their children's learning and nurture more positive relations, parents were acting in a way that was contrary to their own parents' behaviour. In their conduct these parents were ensuring that they did not repeat the failings of their own parents. This motivation to develop the children's educational chances and to nurture constructive interpersonal relations to ensure that the desired outcomes were achieved, were the sole preoccupation of the mothers. The fathers were on the periphery, never mentioned as being a significant figure in the children's educational development. But in some respects the parents were repeating the lessons of their own parents. They felt they had insufficient self-knowledge to transmit to their children. This inability to pass on purposeful cultural knowledge filled the parents with despair. The main concern of these parents was the fear that their children would have no self-identity, as they themselves were deprived of a self-image, in a society in which their colour and their race were the most dominant factor by which they were judged and which determined the degree of their success. It is the absence of this self-knowledge about their Caribbean culture, as Worrall (1981) suggests, that led African Caribbean youths to affiliate with, and appropriate the values of Rastafarianism. This self same lack results in their association with, and consumption of the negative aspects of rap cultures to form an identity, and to the pattern of behaviour identified by Sewell and Gilroy.

THE CHILDREN'S STORY

With the exception of Jamal, the children were all doing very well. They were performing as well as the top children in their class. They had positive attitudes to school, teachers and study. They were motivated and applied themselves to learning. In this they were actively encouraged by their parents and significant others. The children enjoyed good relations with their teachers. Where there was a breakdown in positive interpersonal relations between children and their teacher, the children often blamed teachers for igniting the flames of dissension. The children were influenced by popular culture, Tyrese and Jamal more acutely than Beres and Gabriel. The children's success was attributed to their parents, teachers, themselves and significant others, particularly siblings in the case of Gabriel and a cousin in the case of Beres. Jamal's underachievement was, amongst other things, due partly to the discrepancy between his requirements as a learner and his mother's approach to teaching, and absence of the one-to-one support within school that would improve his educational opportunities.

The children were motivated and engaged in seeking out reading at home and at school. They were supported in this within the home by their parents, their mothers by all accounts, and in the case of Beres and Gabriel by a cousin and sister respectively. Even though Jamal was not achieving as well as his peers, parent support and encouragement was a significant part of his educational development. However, the nature of the interpersonal relations between himself and his mother, Mary, was sometimes problematic. This was partly due to the method employed by Mary to teach Jamal. As it was with Mary and her mother, so it was with Mary and Jamal. Jamal's method of learning conflicted with Mary's approach to teaching. The incongruity between Mary's method of teaching and what she believed Jamal needed and Jamal's own requirements and approach culminated in the problematization of interpersonal relations between mother and child. Jamal's response was to rebel and refuse to work any longer. Mary in turn walked away leaving him to his own devices. This and other factors at home and school limited Jamal's opportunities for success. For example, Mary withdrew support from Jamal in order to concentrate on her newborn child, and did not know when she would be able to resume her efforts in supporting his educational development. Whilst Mary was in sympathy with the pressures on the school to cater to the needs of all children, and has only praise for the teachers in their past efforts to help Jamal, she was conscious of the fact that at school Jamal was not receiving the 1:1 support that would enable him to succeed. All these factors were identified by Mary as being of central importance in Jamal's underachievement.

The nature of the interpersonal relationship between the children and their teacher was overall positive. This was particularly the case with Beres and Gabriel, who enjoyed a better relationship with their teacher than Jamal and Tyrese. Jamal's and Tyrese's relationship with their teacher was more problematic. They were often drawn to peers who were engaged in poor behaviour. This often brought them in conflict with their teacher. Where the children had negative perceptions of school and teachers it was influenced by the teachers themselves. When the children believed the teacher had dealt with them fairly they were willing to accept punishment for their behaviour. However, when they believed that the teacher had treated them unfairly this led to resentment and conflict. Tyrese's response below demonstrates the extent to which his own response was influenced by the teacher's attitude to him. His language also highlight his awareness of the way events in his primary school may spill over into his secondary school and lead to his stigmatisation and mythologisation by teachers and the conflict this may cause, thus impacting negatively on his secondary school career. Gabriel's rather succinct response underlines this process further. In order for pupils to respect teachers, it is important that teachers respect children. Miss Winters in the excerpt below was a floating teacher, who taught the children in the absence of Emily who sometimes had other duties. I had the distinct impression that miss Winters resented my presence in the classroom and so I stayed out when she was teaching.

Excerpt 1

Tyrese: well miss Winters tells me to try and bite my tongue but sometimes I just can't do it, especially for teachers that I always just try to please and try to be nice to, and like five minutes later they just like abuse. It's like unfair. Just because you get- you might get told off from different teachers, teachers don't-it doesn't mean that you have to take it out off somebody else. That's my opinion.

Excerpt 2

Tyrese: if I get told off, if I think that it's fair I probably won't say something, I'll just moan it to myself.

Excerpt 3

CP: Do you get carried away?
Tyrese: Well firstly, sometimes I might just do it to get on the teacher's nerves because the teacher's already got on my nerves . . .

Excerpt 4

Tyrese: The thing is, what I don't want to happen in secondary school is, I don't want people to judge me from what's happened in school first and then just think that I'm going to be bad.
CP: Do you think they (teachers) have to listen to children?
Gabriel: if they want children to listen to them, then I think they should listen to children.

The conflict between Tyrese and his teacher did not have any significant impact on his school performance. He achieved very good grades in his SATS tests. This was perhaps due to the positive relationship fostered by Tyrese's mum and his permanent teacher, who together planned for Tyrese's transfer to a different class, away from the peers who were distracting him. It was also due to Tyrese himself who was acutely conscious of what he must do in order to succeed. He was aware that in order to succeed he needed to modify his behaviour and to concentrate on the task of learning. Media images dominated the children's consciousness, and influenced some children's career aspirations. In a minor projectionist experiment I found that the children were more adept at identifying pop and sport stars than black role models not involved in these areas. Jamal was actively encouraged by his father to affiliate, and identify with the designer label culture. He wore a Nike earring purchased by his father, who according to Mary believed that Jamal will get by without an education. He also bought Jamal other expensive designer objects. For Jamal's father therefore school and education were meaningless past times, mythologised and downgraded in relation to non-school activities as a path to success. Tyrese wore one of the symbols of this popular culture, a bandana, not in school but when he was out with his friends. Mills and Huff (1999) argue that it is not until their early adolescence when they are beginning the process of fashioning their identity, that the young are more susceptible to the influence of popular culture and form strong association with the counter-culture. It is at this critical phase that they affiliate with the counterproductive aspects of rap, and display more powerfully the negative patterns of behaviour identified by Gilroy and Sewell. This analysis of the formation of the counter youth culture and its attending negative forms of behaviour is reflected in Mac an Ghaill's (1988) study of black youths in an inner city comprehensive. In Mac an Ghaill's study the "Rasta Heads" began to develop a counter-culture and oppositional behaviour to those demanded by the school in their third year of secondary school. This was due to their growing awareness of the racism they perceived in their teachers and the wider White community. As one student said:

> At junior school, teachers pretend they like black kids, as soon as you leave junior school and you get into secondary school, and you reach third, fourth and fifth that's when you learn, you realize how you are being treated and the problems in the past. As you get older you understand what you are.
>
> (Mac an Ghaill, 1988, p. 94)

It is clear from this statement that the children's knowledge of the mythologies held about them by teachers and the wider White community is one of the key factors fuelling their desire to associate with the counter-culture and its oppositional philosophy. As Mac an Ghaill's study clearly demonstrate, the children's resistance, underpinned and given credence by the oppositional beliefs of the counter-culture, was a need to combat these White myhthologies. If the children in this study, particularly Tyrese, with his awareness of the potential of his mythologisation by teachers, continued to develop strong associations with the counter-culture as they journeyed through school as a means to form an identity, without the mechanism to critically evaluate the culture and mediate their teachers' negative perceptions of them, then this is likely to have a detrimental impact on their identity-formation and quite possibly their academic success.

THE TEACHERS' STORY

The teachers on the whole nurtured positive and constructive relations with the children. Where conflict arose, such as with Jamal and Tyrese, it was often quickly resolved, where necessary with the involvement and support of parents. The benevolent use of power and the development of a positive attitude to the children and the culture they represented, necessitated the overcoming, transgressing, (or even containment) of mythologies, which not only allowed teachers to nurture positive interpersonal relations, but to focus on the task of teaching based on equality and justice, irrespective of race or culture.

Tim, the head teacher, and Emily the deputy head, and the teacher of Tyrese and Beres, demonstrates this process of overcoming (or containment). Tim grew up in an enclosed Irish community where other cultures were outside his experiences and from a background where his mind was susceptible to prejudicial views about other cultures and other peoples. On going to university Tim experienced other cultures for the first time and new experiences opened up to him. This enabled Tim to overcome the limitations of his own environment and to develop a more open mind, allowing him to nurture ideas of equality and social justice.

Tim: ... until that point I'd only ever-this is astonishing-up to the age of 17, 18, I'd only ever mixed in White Irish communities, in the whole of my Leeds socialization. Once I was at home that was the community that we mixed in. So all my mother and father's friends for example, the same immigrant community in the UK, we all lived within a few streets of each other, in an area of Chapel Town, which was very Irish in those days. And am, so it was almost like a, a ghetto community that we lived in and am ... when I moved on to university and suddenly met people from different backgrounds, cultures, religion, it was just invigorating, cause I wasn't used to that.

CP: you were not mixing.

Tim: Not at all
CP: And then you went out and you began to mix. You begin to meet different people
Tim: Yes. Yeah.
CP: Did you have any kind of prejudice towards–?
Tim: Always a fear of the unknown. Cause it was alien to what I was used to. But there was also a very strong connection with what I'd experienced to what a lot of other people experienced, that I met in my first year in university. And am, it was actually something that brought us together as opposed to kind of am- because in the same social constructs in different cultural terms, children had experienced exactly the same thing as I had. And am, we soon discovered that we were actually survivors of the system, because we were the tip of the iceberg that made a move out of that social construct. The rest of our peers are still there. And am, therefore had you asked me that question, if I had stayed within that social construct of living in that same community I would probably know no difference. So am, my experience would have been much more limited, and therefore, my overview on how I think society operates would have been much more limited. And am it's through having that wealth of experience of mixing with different socio-economic cultural groups that really excited me, I think really homed in that passion that I had about opportunity and equality of opportunity. And it really taught me early on about what like, what equal opportunities mean.

Emily came from a middle class background and from an all white society in a rural setting. It was a totally different background from the multicultural environment in which she has chosen to conduct her career. Emily now keenly subscribes to multiculturalism. In Emily's discourse there is a shift in perspective and a shift in consciousness, which I believe is similar to the journey that Tim had to undertake in order to arrive at his present position. Emily has had to contain or overcome what was an essentialist and mono-cultural background and reinscribe herself in a multicultural setting.

CP: . . . Do you feel that am-what is your social and political background?
Emily: social?
CP: Yeah
Emily: Am . . .
CP: Would you say you're middle class, working class?
Emily: I guess middle class
CP: ok
Emily: Yeah

CP: And am . . . how does your background influence your teaching?

Emily: I think politically it affects it.

CP: In what way?

Emily: Well I've made a conscious decision now that I could never work in like an all White middle class school, because I know I wouldn't enjoy that as much as I enjoy working in a multicultural school, for example. And that, you know, when I have children, then I would always want those children to be taught in a multicultural school, because I think people, hopefully develop much better attitudes of living in a multicultural society. And I mean that's completely different than how I was brought up. I went to an all White, middle class primary school, you know, in a sort of deep in the countryside. That's completely different to what I would have thought that I would be doing, certainly when I grew up. Now having done it since I qualified, then I don't think I could do anything else.

I mean you've got to retain your own cultural identity. I mean cause I think a lot of people are very frightened that theirs is going to be completely lost, or sucked up in everybody else's, and that's not the case. Ideally you want everybody living together, but- and you've still got all that am, you know, certain aspects of your culture to share, and I think you can only do that when you live in-live somewhere like this.

CLASSROOM INTERACTIONS, OVERCOMING AND POWER RELATIONS

Classroom observations using proxemic analysis showed that teachers and pupils were engaged overall in cooperative patterns of behaviour and power relations. Teachers nurtured positive interpersonal relations within the classroom, and in the process created a positive environment for learning. Apart from their instructional role, the teachers' language and gaze were tools for control. But the language of control was used in a non-threatening way when speaking to the children. The teachers' voice was never raised to a point that was likely to intimidate the children and induce fear and apprehension in them. The teachers did not ignore the children. Their gaze was frequently turned to them at question time as they sought to involve them in the lesson. During these periods the teachers' gaze was focused and attentive rather than peripheral. The teachers did not restrict the children's movements unduly.

In the creation of this constructive environment, teachers were supported by the children, who overall were engaged in positive and co-operative patterns of behaviour amongst themselves and the teacher. On the occasions that I visited the school and entered the classroom a co-operative and harmonious atmosphere permeated the room. Children were busy at work, talking and enjoying the classroom and each other's company. Sometimes the serenity in the classroom was quite ominous. The children knew instinctively what was required. Children were applying themselves to the task of learning without fear of disturbance from their peers or the teacher. The language and behaviour of the children in the study were not different from those of their peers. This was true for Beres and Gabriel who were extremely reserved, to Tyrese and Jamal who were inclined to imitate their peers in unhelpful behaviour, which was never extreme. When the children went beyond the accepted norm of behaviour and were reprimanded they readily accepted their punishment, as Tyrese has already remarked on. This was true for him as it was for Jamal and the other children who had cause to be reprimanded. A lowered gaze was often a sign of contrition. The children challenged the teacher only when they felt they had been wrongly censured. Again this was as true for Jamal and Tyrese as it was for the other children who were castigated. At such times the children's gaze was fixed on the teacher. Sometimes the admonished child gazed away or peripherally at the teacher. Where the child's gazed fell depended on the nature of the reprimand and the feelings it induced in the child. But the matter was often quickly resolved and normal classroom activities were resumed. Boys were frequently out of their seats more than girls, were engaged in negative behaviour more than the girls, and had cause to be reprimanded more than the girls. In conclusion, it is clear from these observation that the nurturing and development of positive interpersonal relationships and the right environment for learning would not be possible without overcoming or containment of mythologies or cultural practices and beliefs that led to confrontation and conflict. As suggested above, it is this containment or overcoming of mythologies that ensured the actors involved subscribed to constructive and co-operative rules of social behaviour, that the nature of power relations was overall non-combative, that there was equality and respect, and finally that the right environment was created where learning could take place in a non-combative space.

POLICY AND RESEARCH IMPLICATIONS

What is clear from the research is that the causes of underachievement amongst Black children are complex, as are the factors that contribute to success. Reductive theories will not explain why Black children underachieve and succeed. In order to explain the complex process of failure and success a multidimensional approach, which embraces historical discourses, and examines the role of knowledge and power in shaping identity and defining interpersonal relations, is necessary. It is equally important that researchers do not focus simply on failure, but recognize that Black children do succeed. In fact it is high time that researchers focus on success, otherwise the fact of Black underachievement, which is so deeply embedded in people's consciousness whenever they think about Black children, will never be undermined. Programmes designed to curtail Black underachievement must place the Black community at its centre. The solution to Black underachievement does not rest solely with the White community. The Black community, the Black family and child, must play a central role. An important aspect of policy must be a commitment to changing the practices of institutions of power that preach equality and diversity, yet normalizes myth and inequality.

CONCLUSION

The paper presented here is an examination of the factors that contribute to success and failure among children of Caribbean heritage. I argue that research into Black underachievement is limited and neither explains why children of Caribbean heritage underachieve or why they succeed, because the research used is reductive in approach, and that the policies developed to tackle the issue relating to Black performance have been likewise inadequate, lacking in commitment. I further argue that children of Caribbean heritage underachieve because of historical and contemporary social and cultural forces associated with the nature of knowledge and power in the public and private sphere that determines the nature of interpersonal relationships, identity formation and educational performance. Success involves overcoming experiences that may lead to conflict, accommodation, and application in the teaching and acquisition of knowledge and skills. It also depends on the ability of Black children to evaluate Black and White mythologies without assimilating those mythologies into the internal structures of the mind, and the examination and overhaul of institutions of power and structures of knowledge that mythologise and exclude Black children.

REFERENCES

Argyle, M. (1994). *The psychology of interpersonal behaviour*. Harmondswrth: Penguin.
Barthes, R. (1973). *Mythologies*. London: Paladin Books.
Bruner, J. (1996). *The culture of education*. London: Harvard University Press.
Coard, B. (1971). *How the West Indian child is made educationally subnormal in the British school system*. London: New Beacon Books.

Department of Education and Science (1981). *West Indian Children in our schools: Interim report of the committee of enquiry into the education of children from ethnic minority groups.* (Rampton Report) London: HMSO.

Department of Education and Science (1985). *Education for all: Final report of the committee of inquiry into the education of children from ethnic minority groups.* (Swann Report) London: HMSO.

Driver, J. (1981). Classroom stress and school achievement: West Indian adolescents and their teachers. In: A. James & R. Jeffcoate (Eds), *The School in the Multicultural Society* (pp. 288–297). London: Harper & row.

Edwards, V. (1979). *The West Indian language issue in British schools.* London: Routledge & Kegan Paul.

Edwards, V. (1983). *Language in multicultural classrooms.* London: Batsford.

Fitzgerald, R. et al. (2000). *Black Caribbean young men's experiences of education and employment.* London: DfEE.

Foucault, M. (1991). *Discipline and punish.* Harmondsworth: Penguin Books.

Fuller, M. (1981). Black girls in a London comprehensive. In: A. James & R. Jeffcoate (Eds), *The School in the Multicultural Society* (pp. 270–287). London: Harper & Row.

Gilborn, D. (1990). *Race, ethnicity and education: Teaching and learning in multi-ethnic schools.* London: Unwin Hyman.

Gilborn, D., & Mirza, H. S. (2000). *Mapping, race, class and gender: A synthesis of research evidence.* London: Ofsted.

Gilroy, P. (1992). *There ain't no black in the Union Jack: The cultural politics of race and nation.* London: Routledge.

Gilroy, P. (2000). *Between camps: Nations, cultures and the allure of race.* Harmondsworth: Penguin.

Hall, E. (1963). *A system for notation of poxemics.* New York: Arno Press.

Hicks, D. (1981). Bias in school books: Messages from the ethnocentric curriculum. In: A. James & R. Jeffcoate (Eds), *The School in the Multicultural Society* (pp. 159–177). London: Harper & Row.

Hooks, B. (1992). *Black looks: Race and representation.* Boston, MA: South End Press.

Kincheoloe, J. L., & Steinberg, S. (1997). *Changing multiculturalism.* Buckingham: Open University Press.

Kirk, G. (1988). *Myth: It's meaning and functions in ancient and other cultures.* Cambridge: Cambridge University Press.

Labov, W. (1977). *Language in the inner city: Studies in the black English vernacular.* Oxford: Blackwell.

Levi-Strauss, C. (1993). *Structural anthropology.* Harmondsworth: Penguin.

Little, A. N. (1978). *Policies for multi-racial areas.* London: Inaugural Lecture.

Mac an Ghaill, M. (1988). *Young gifted and black.* Milton Keynes: Open University Press.

McCarthy, C. (1990). *Race and curriculum: Social inequality and the theories and politics of difference in contemporary research on schooling.* London: Falmer.

Mills, H., & Huff, A. (1999). *Style over substance: A critical analysis of African American teenage subculture.* Chicago, IL: African American Images.

Nehaul, K. (1996). *The schooling of children of Caribbean heritage.* Stoke-on-Trent: Trentham Books.

Ogbu, J. (1978). *Minority education and caste: The American system in cross-cultural perspective.* London: Academic Press.

Ogbu, J. (1998). Introduction. *British Journal of Sociology of Education, 3*(10).

Parekh, B. (1988). The Swann report and ethnic minority attainment. In: G. Verma & P. Pumfrey (Eds), *Educational Attainment: Issues and Outcomes in Multicultural Education*. London: Falmer.

Pearse, A. (1986). A case for black literature in the mainstream syllabus. In: A. Saba & A. Pearse (Eds), *Towards the Decolonization of the British Educational System*. London: Frontline Journal/Karnak House.

Phoenix, A. (2000). Research briefing paper number 17: Emergent identities: Masculinities and 11–14 year old boys . . .

Pieterse, J. N. (1992). *White on black: Images of Africa and blacks in western popular culture*. London: Yale University Press.

Sewell, T. (2000). Identifying the pastoral needs of African Caribbean students: A case of critical anti-racism. *Education and Social Justice*, *3*(1).

Stone, M. (1981). The education of the black child. In: A. James & R. Jeffcoate (Eds), *The School in the Multicultural Society* (pp. 45–57). London: Harper & row.

Taylor, M. (1981). *Caught between: A review of research into the education of pupils of West Indian origin*. Slough: NFER-Nelson.

Tomlinson, S. (1981). The educational performance of ethnic minority children. In: A. James & R. Jeffcoate (Eds), *The School in the Multicultural Society* (pp. 119–146). London: Harper & Row.

Watson, O. (1970). *Proxemic behaviour: A cross-cultural study*. The Hague: Mouton.

Willey, R. (1984). Policy responses in education. In: M. Craft (Ed.), *Education and Cultural Pluralism* (pp. 27–40). London: Falmer Press.

Worrall, M. (1981). Multiracial Britain and the third world: Tensions and approaches in the classroom. In: A. James & R. Jeffcoate (Eds), *The School in the Multicultural Society*. London: Harper & Row.

NAMING AND DEALING WITH INEQUALITY: IMMIGRANT STUDENTS' PERSPECTIVE OF UNEQUAL SPACES IN THE CLASSROOM

Ruth Silva

It is a necessary feature of action that, at any point in time, the agent 'could have acted otherwise' (Giddens, 1994, p. 56).

[the need] . . . to 'get behind the backs' of the social actors whose conduct they seek to understand . . . (Giddens, 1994, p. 2).

. . . theorize a 'subject' whose 'agency' – as constituted by discourse – requires no 'human' foundations (Zipin, 1998, p. 318).

INTRODUCTION

The current literature on the educational progress of immigrant students within the host system is encapsulated in the thesis that these students will face difficulties, and that these difficulties will more often than not lead to a failure to meet the demands of the system for the majority of the immigrant students. An apposite comment by Portes (1996), queried whether the children of immigrants would be able to work their way upwards into ". . . the middle-class mainstream" or whether they would be blocked in this ascent based on their migrant status, and become part of an "multiethnic underclass or join an expanded multiethnic underclass."

Ethnographies of Educational and Cultural Conflicts: Strategies and Resolutions
Studies in Educational Ethnography, Volume 9, 171–201

ISSN: 1529-210X/doi:10.1016/S1529-210X(04)09009-6

Súarez-Orozco and Súarez-Orozco (1995, 2000) completed this perception by uncovering the implicit viewpoint within which this query was nested. He foregrounded the domination of sensationalism and myth in discussions of the "natural process" of assimilation of minorities. Finally, current discussion on the issue of these so-called *at-risk* students centres on how they can be made successful at school.

Attempting to separate the myth from fact Trueba (1999), along with a growing number of educational anthropologists, pointed out that although predicting and explaining failure of some immigrant youth was by and large, a favoured topic in educational research dealing with minority youth, "explaining success where failure is expected is a bit more intriguing" (p. 3). This statement echoed Foley's (1997) observation that "school studies of minority youth tended to focus on why these youth failed in mainstream schools." Thereby tending to underemphasize the factors leading to success and empowerment (Valencia, p. 124).

This critical movement of the discourse term from failure to success led to a small but growing body of anthropologists studying minority education from a sociolinguistic perspective, and educational researchers doing so within a pedagogical setting, to refocus their studies. The locus now shifted to an emphasis on the "underemphasized factors leading to success and empowerment" (Foley, 1997, p. 124). Foley was referring to the role students can and do play in this process of "success and empowerment."

In the current discussions of these issues the success or failure of these students is explained by the presence or absence of "resilience" respectively. Resilience is further defined in therapeutic terminology, despite its origins in insurance industry parlance! Further, the development of resilience is attributed to existence of a set of what are known as protective factors. These factors seem to represent some sort of bubble or shield, which when once put into place, the *troubled* student's pathology will be, at best removed, or at worst held at bay.

It seemed to me, reading this research that the perspective was from the student as the one being "done to." The role of the student seemed to be relegated to merely responding to the circumstances. The Agentic role of the student was being either denied or ignored. In those circumstances where it was mentioned, it was a role that seemed to be created by the discursive situation (i.e. a situation which *allowed* the student to act), rather than any notion of foundational agency that the student is able to exercise in any and all circumstances, regardless of the discursive situation.

The nascent research study presented in this paper is grounded within this new/fledgling discourse of looking at how immigrant students view the labels attached to them, are they aware of these labels and if so how do they deal with these labels? The actions of these students will be examined against the background of a system that foregrounds the possibilities of their failure through the use of terms such as *risk*, *deficit* and *poverty*, rather than at the probabilities of their success. The student in this study will be placed at the center of the discussion – in other words the student's action/reactions are to be foregrounded and analysed.

The current study 2001–2002 is a follow-up of an earlier study conducted in 1997–1998. This first phase of the study investigated how first or second generation Latino immigrant students, in Grades 5 and 6 who were learning English as a second language organized their learning tasks and the nature of the support structures they had at school. These students were documented as low socio-economic status, were attending urban schools in low property tax areas, which in turn affected school funding, and identified as *at risk* students. Specifically the study focused on identifying students as educationally resilient or non-resilient based on their academic achievement.

The current phase of the study revisited these students now in middle and/or the first year of high school. The purpose was to explore their current educational achievements, as compared to their original identification as resilient or non-resilient. From the original 112 students we were able to locate 90 students, out which 68 agreed to be re-interviewed. One ethnographically-based interview was conducted with each of the students, lasting approximately one hour to one and half hours. The interviews were conducted in the subjects' school, but in a private room. The interviews were conducted during school hours.

As the pre-planning for analysis got underway a number of issues surfaced that seemed not to have been explored in the first phase. Unproblematised connections existed between being immigrants, low socio-economic and English language learners and being at risk. The preliminary questions that occurred to this researcher were:

> Why were they [students] at risk?
> What was the risk?
> Who was responsible for the existence of the risk?

The difference between being at risk and putting at risk seemed to require analysis.

> Why and how was resilience tied to success as defined by high grades?

This study examined these issues primarily from the students' perspectives, and descriptions of whether they are aware of these labels and if so how they deal with the labels applied to them.

Using the models of deficit thinking and cultural poverty I examine and critique, first the conceptualization of risk, resilience in educational research, and, the nature and implementation of the interventions by educational authorities under the umbrella term of support structures based on protective factors. Finally, perhaps there is a need to question the relationship that is posited between resilience and success. Resilient students are those who are [academically] successful in the conventionally accepted notions of success, and those who are not [academically successful] are labeled non-resilient.

This critique explores the notion that the use of the labels *at risk*, *resilient*, and/or *non-resilient* (used within deficit thinking models) as adjectival referents attached to the student allows for the blaming and victimizing of the student. It makes the students passive recipients of the largesse of the system, thereby although explicitly removing the risk, nonetheless implicitly maintaining an unequal status by keeping the students' progress dependent on the presence of the support structures. The support structures do not make explicit provisions for the student to develop an agentic role in the process. The student is *done to* rather than the *doer*.

As commented earlier there also seems, sometimes, to be a tacit acceptance by the school authorities that by some sort of osmosis the student will absorb and develop qualities of resiliency and maintain these when the intervention is removed. For example, the following comment by a teacher explaining what she expects:

> I give them the time [to do the work], I have already explained it to them – I have told them the results of not doing the work – not just in this grade, or school but also later in their lives.

And

> I pick him up and bring him to school everyday from his home.
>
> Q: Why?
> A: Because if I did not he would never get here in time – his mother is there sometimes at other times not.
> Q: What will happen next year when he moves [to middle school]?
> A: (shrugs her shoulders) I don't know – and that is the big problem you know – there is all this gang stuff – and looking cool – and coming to school on time is not cool.

The data from the present study seems to indicate otherwise. For example, for some students who had been identified as resilient in Phase I of the study, it seemed as if the removal of the caring support structures present in the elementary school had left the student adrift in middle and high school and they were now labeled as non-resilient, as in unsuccessful (low grades, unacceptable behavior, etc.).

This led me to another, what I begin to think, is a critical issue – the relationship between resiliency and school success – as indicated by high grades. In effect, the system seemed to be saying that if you work hard and you achieve high grades, you are resilient. If on the other hand you work hard but you do not achieve high grades, then you are non-resilient. A teacher in the study highlighted this issue when asked to identify four resilient and four non-resilient students in her class (in the criteria given for identification purposes resiliency was tied to factors like high grades, good attendance, etc.):

Q: You have put all your students in the resilient group, why?
A: Because they all work hard, and if they do not get good grades it is not for the want of trying.

The study is also in the exploratory stages of questioning the current system of dealing with at-riskness through the use of support structures based on protective mechanisms, but often not providing structures and scaffolds to enable a student-based decision-making process. As a counterpoint, I am in the process of exploring and developing an Agentic Model for developing resiliency based on both the notion of a foundational agency (Giddens, 1994).

Consequently, one has to deconstruct not merely the conventionally – accepted notions of success and failure and relationship to resiliency, but also concurrently examine the motivations of the students to either succeed or fail conventionally. The emphasis being on the students decision to do so – that is either fail or succeed. This does not ignore that there are school policies that may lead to this state of events – it merely intends to highlight how the situation looks from the student's point of view, rather than the school's.

In the discussion/interviews with the students, I had brief glimpses into their exercise of the agentic role. Not necessarily always in ways that the administration might approve of!, but perhaps vital to the survival of the student in the circumstances. The emerging and I think highly researchable theme is this agentic role of the student in using the so-called protective/unprotective factors in her/his environment as and when necessary. The student makes the call, and is therefore in a doing position, rather than a done by position.

To begin with I explore and examine the origin, scope, and practical influence of centralizing explanations of failure. Embedded within this exploration will be the concept of agency and its expression by the students in their daily dealings with their cultural peers, anglo peers, and system authorities – i.e. their actions as a result of the exercise of their agentic role. This discussion is centered in the students own descriptions of how they act, react and/or proact within the prevailing school culture. The analysis will include a problematisation of the definitions of the traditionally used term to describe these students as at risk per se, and application of the adjective resilient to describe them *only* if they are successful. To explain and analyse the agentic role of the students I utilise a conceptual model based on Giddens' (1994) notion of foundational agency. The agentic role of the individual student will be juxtaposed with the role and primacy of protective factors as explanations of resiliency-based success.

HISTORICAL CONTEXTS OF STUDYING "SCHOOL FAILURE"

Deficit Thinking

Tracing the history of the notion of deficit thinking Valencia (1993, p. 1) began with an explanation of the poor performance on grade level and standardized tests of low socioeconomic (SES) minority students. He attributed it [poor performances] to attendance at schools that are segregated, hence inequitably financed, and leading to "vapid" curricula delivery, and creating hostile learning environments. He also emphasised the fact that this was a situation that was pervasive, persistent and affected a disproportionately high number of minority students. In response, the explanation of the systemic authorities to this research had been based on "communication process" models, which emphasized the differences between teacher and taught. Since the students could not understand the teacher's verbal and sometimes non-verbal communication, they could not act appropriately. However, instead of focusing on improving or changing the language of communication the students were labeled as unmotivated to learn. This lack of motivation on their part led to their failure. The deficit was therefore attributed to the students.

Valencia's explanation on "deficit thinking" goes back to the 1600–1800 pseudoscientific racist discourses (Menchaca, 1997). Briefly, this model posits that the failing student does so because of internal deficits (ability, motivation) linguistic shortcomings, etc. The causes of this depend on the period in question and range from genetics to culture to class to micro family system. In effect the student and his/her immediate surroundings are responsible for the failure. For Valencia deficit thinking blames the victim, results in oppression, is based on pseudo-science, and influenced by the ideological and political climate of the time, and finally leads to solutions that begin in describing the pathological behavior and naturally following the medical model to predict the behavior and prescribe an intervention. However, once the intervention is removed the pathology may return. When it does not return, the cause is attributed purely to the success of the intervention in removing the "deseased element."

Strangely however, in this theory deficit thinking is a "person-centered explanation of school failure, [the student is responsible for his/her failure, but not necessarily for any success – that is attributed to the systemic intervention] with no reference to system within which the student is required to learn. Neither the student nor the system are problematised."

Cultural Ecology Theory

Ogbu (1978, 1987) based his explanation of why minority youth fail within the operation of a cultural ecology model. He, [Ogbu] "reintroduced the race factor" (Foley et al., 1999, p. 46) to explain their [students] failure. Briefly, Ogbu postulated that caste-like ethnic minority students living in a racist society perceive their life chances as limited and develop coping mechanisms that are dysfunctional and oppositional based on the belief that they cannot be ethnically different and academically successful. In developing his theory Ogbu differentiated between voluntary and involuntary minorities depending on the method of their entry into the host country, classifying involuntary minorities under the term caste. He argued that unlike the voluntary minorites who tended to meet the demands of the school system positively, the involuntary minorities dealt with their deficit labeling by developing oppositional identities to those valued by the system (see also Willis' lads). The system thus saw them as lacking in resilience and therefore unable to achieve system-defined success.

STRUCTURAL INEQUALITY MODEL

Pearl (1991) and Bowles and Gintis (1976) discussion of minority student failure based their explanation of minority student failure on the structural inequalities inherent in the macro and micro spheres of learning and living. Pearl brought into his discussion of failure not only the nature of educational system, but also encompassing politico-economic structures that dictated the functioning of the educational system. Thus for those who espoused this particular theory, minority student failure was posited under the system failure.

Culture of Poverty Explanation of School Failure of Minority Students

Foley (1997) ascribes the origin of cultural explanations for failure in school and ultimately life to the anthropologist Oscar Lewis' (1965). Lewis conducted a series of studies on the urban poor in Mexico, New York, Puerto Rico and Cuba from 1959 to 1966. He [Lewis] maintained that people living in poverty created and maintained over generations a life style characterized by negative values, norms and social habits. Designating such a lifestyle a culture of poverty, he identified list of 70 traits within 4 clusters that lead to it. The traits evoked a picture of dysfunctional, lazy fatalistic, violent and distrustful group of people. Ultimately, he concluded, because of the self-sustaining nature of this way of life they remain poor and therefore inferior to the mainstream.

Foley's (1997) critique is however more powerful than the original work. Nowhere in the original text, cautions Foley, is there any moralizing about the poor, and in the original Lewis' description of the culture is more nuanced than secondary accounts. The point however, is that it allowed a surface impression of the poor, which could be used as well as abused. Paradoxically, it was the very lack of moralising in the original [Lewis'] and its presentation in an objective manner that conferred on it the status of an absolute truth claim and allowed subsequent moralising based on a variety of subjective and gradually narrowing viewpoints. Further, since the original claim [Lewis'] was accepted as the truth, what was inferred from the original was also the truth. Finally, it paved the way for a resurrection of the Victorian notions of poverty and the poor – as in "the poor are always with us." Thus, since it is a fact, that their [the poor and/or minorities and/or immigrants] poverty is the result of their own actions, it absolves the powers that be from of any blame for the existence of poverty and its continued impact on their lives. Just as surely as it absolved them of responsibility, it also provided the basis for connecting deficit thinking with cultural poverty. Study after study (Bernstein, 1975; Hess & Shipman, 1965, 1967), expanded on the causes of school failure based on the notion of a culturally deficient poor (Foley, 1997, p. 116).

Katz (1989) brought these and other such studies together to demonstrate what he termed a "poverty discourse" that was used by policy makers across the political spectrum – conservative and paternalistic liberals for political purposes. This one-dimensional discourse of deficiency did nothing to enhance the status of the poor by blaming them for their own misfortunes, thereby keeping government expenditure low and at the same keeping their own middle-class constituencies happy on the conservative side.

DEFICIT THINKING AND CULTURE OF POVERTY AS SEEDBEDS FOR THE USE AND DEVELOPMENT OF TERMS "AT-RISK" AND "RESILIENCE" IN EDUCATIONAL RESEARCH

Recent and current writings in the field of school success amongst specifically defined populations, whether delineated by English acquisition issues (second language or bilingual learners), immigrant-student status, low parental socio-economic status-related issues, and the presence of social and emotional problems, have tended to emphasize the role of resilience in achieving and maintaining academic success. These students have generally and broadly been categorized as being at risk. When some, but not all, of these *at risk* students have succeeded in school, their success has been attributed to their ability to be resilient, and succeed despite the odds being against them. The development of resilience is further attributed to the presence of support systems in their environment termed protective factors. The presence or absence of these protective factors thus determines whether or not the student will succeed or not do so.

Furthermore, most of this body of literature spends a considerable amount of time on defining and discussing the concept of resilience, the concept of risk however seems to be either subsumed or accepted as synonymous with the notion of "risk factors" and/or "risk indicators." What it [risk] means is explained through how it [risk] occurs or is evidenced. The implicit assumption undergirding such a subsumption seems to be that if risk exists, than risk will occur, thereby either ignoring or negating the futuristic concept of risk – risk probability.

Explaining its subsumption within the concept of deficit thinking Valencia (1997), along with other writers on the topic (Fine, Weiss, Sleeter & Grant, Foley*) made the case that the use of at risk is also a form of deficit thinking. It is an adjectival term with the student as its noun referent. Thus being at risk is a personal quality of the student. Viewed thus it has no reference to the macro spheres of school and system within which the student has to operate to be either at risk or excellent. Failure is the result of "presumed personal shortcomings of the student" (p. 196). It is a discourse of personal deficiencies and personal failure resultant from these deficiencies. It is interesting to note that in dealing with achievement or the lack of it, the school and system are either left out of the equation or attributed a minor role, in dealing with at risk qualities attributed to the student, at riskness is more often than not extended to the family and physical environment of the student in question. For example, the following explanation by a teacher:

> You know there is not a lot we can do – it is the parents – they are the ones that can make or break [the student??]. You know I had this parent – the kid needs to be tested and put into special ed. I think – but she won't have it – You know what – I think kid knows this too – that he would do far better in the other class.
>
> Q: Did he say this?
> A: Not exactly, but when I talk to him about what is done in the other class [special ed.] he goes like – yeah that would be good – I could do that. – it is easier.

A separation of these concepts will also serve to highlight the additional and pertinent distinction that needs to be made between *being at risk* and *putting at risk.*

CONCEPT OF RISK AND THE STATE OF BEING "AT-RISK"

Education got the term at-risk from the field of medical epidemiology, which in turn adopted the term from the insurance industry. In both these fields "risk is identified by defining and measuring probabilistic outcomes" (SEDL, 2001). In the chemical industry the concept of risk is closely tied to the concept of hazard. While hazard is the intrinsic ability of a chemical to cause adverse effects, risk is the probability that such effects will occur in the various applications in which the chemical will be used and/or discharged; and risk assessment takes into account both the hazards of the chemical and exposure to it. Two things become apparent in the above definitions and descriptions of risk – first, that risk has a futuristic component to its occurrence, i.e. of something that has not happened, but may happen, but then again may not happen either; and second, it is possible to view risk as a subjective concept. For example deconstructing the following conversation with a student highlights these issues:

Q: Why were you in the bilingual class?
A: Because I had just come from . . . I had only been here [U.S] for 3 months
Q: So you were having trouble with English?
A: No, I learnt to speak it at home in . . . My mother speaks a little, but my father is good – so am I.
Q: So why do you think you were in the bilingual class?
A: Because of my name [Hispanic] and they put everyone who has just come in there.

Howard and Dryden (1999) traced the medical origins of the concept of risk and its subsequent adaptation and use by educational researchers to describe students who entered school with "serious needs that schools frequently have difficulty accommodating" (p. 1). Werner and Smith (1982) defined "risk factors" as "biological or psychosocial hazards that increase the likelihood of a negative developmental outcome in a group of people" (p. 3). Howard and Dryden however, specifically exclude biological factors from their definition of risk factors. Risk in their study refers mainly to environmental factors "that singly or in combination have been shown to render children's failure to thrive more likely" (p. 2). Sleeter and Grant (1999) trace the use of the term at risk to the Soviet Union's launch of the Sputnik in 1963 and the subsequent publication in the U.S. of the document "A Nation at Risk" in 1983. The nation [U.S.], this document argued, was in danger of losing the competitive edge internationally, which in turn would adversely affect its economic capacity unless it improved the quality of its human capital. Subsuming it within the broader concept of deficit thinking, Valencia (1997) associates [being] "at-risk" as a key contruct in the predictive scheme used for the identification "of characteristics of students who are predisposed to dropping out . . . " (p. 195). Whilst not tracing its etymological history, he traces its popularity in educational research, to its use in "educational policy circles as a reaction to the notion of excellence in the early 1980s" (p. 195). Margonis (1992) first used the term to critique the "excellence" movement in American educational system. This movement tied success and/or failure in school solely to individual effort. These critiques of the excellence movement were intended to highlight and foreground the role of the system and further contended that school failure was largely systemically based. Within this critique some students were thus put at risk. Perhaps the most compelling point made by Margonis was the coopting of the term [at risk] by the excellence movement proponents "that it was first used to challenge" (p. 196). A use that was further strengthened by the fact that the excellence proponents were able make the "goals embodied in the ideas of excellence become the standard, and students who could not reach these goals came to be at risk" (p. 196). Valencia in fact further identified the use of the term "at risk" as a major "strategy" used by system authorities to "understand and solve the secondary school dropout problem – particularly among low-income and racial/ethnic minority students . . ." (p. 195). Thus, in practical terms, the achievement of immigrant minorities was benchmarked against those standards set out by the host [excellence] community. And an integral part of this standard was the element of individual effort as related to success or failure, with little or no reference to the system and its actions and responsibilities in the educational endeavor.

In summary, returning to issues risk – that may or may not happen – the futuristic nature of risk – and fact that in current literature the underlying assumption seems to be that it will happen simply because the student belongs to a low SES group and is an immigrant – being an immigrant student is a hazard. What therefore are the applications under which risk will occur? Or in the case of the immigrant student in the current paradigm – risk will occur under any application. A few like Swadener and Lubeck (1995) conducted a sustained and detailed critique of the use of the term and its personal and ultimate societal impact.

RESILIENCE: INDIVIDUAL EFFORT OR SYSTEM INTERVENTION OR BOTH?

The field of research into the concept of resiliency is a growing and robust field. The pioneering work of Rutter (1985, 1987, 1995), Garmezy (1991, 1993), and Werner (1993), heralded the growth of the study of resiliency as a construct in explaining success where success was not predicted but achieved despite adverse circumstances. Garmezy's findings particularly are interesting. He concluded that some disadvantaged children turned out competent and did not display any behavioral problems, thus leading to the question about why is it that they were able to beat the odds. This is the key issue in resiliency research – what are the factors that enable some to cope and become successful [that is successful in the manner of dominant paradigm – succeed at school and then at an occupation] and that similar others [disadvantaged] are not able to do so. What does success mean to the system and more to the point, to the student? The following is an excerpt from an interview is both highlights and problematises the notion of success:

Q: Do you think you will stick it out to the end of high school?
A: (shrugs – as if it does not matter) Yeaaah – maybe, I'm thinking why should I? – They –
Q: Who?
A: They, the teachers – think that I should finish school – and that that is good.
Q: And you don't think so?
A: No, my brothers are mechanics – they work on indy-type cars – they are doing good.
Q: Is that what you want?
A: Yeah – but why should she [teacher] tell me?

(NOTE: And, in another school, a mainly middle class anglo school – the success of the reform effort in school was being gauged by how many of its students got into "good" colleges. The records in this school indicated that only about 40% of their students even applied. Most of them applied to Junior Community Colleges. The generally held view was that something was wrong in this school!)

Continuing from this introductory work, resiliency research then focussed on how young people acquired resiliency traits that had been identified in the first wave of resiliency research. Richardson (1995) described this as a process and experience of adapting to disruptive, challenging, and stressful situations and discovering ways to adapt that provide the individual with skills and knowledge they did not have before. He quotes a student comment "*. . . is about choosing to bounce back from problems and stuff with more power and smarts*."

Current research in the field of resiliency has continued with the notions presented in the previous wave, with the addition of focusing on the critical disruptions that occur in the process of achieving resiliency traits (Richardson & Nixon, 1997). It is within this general field of resiliency research that studies of resiliency amongst specified population groups are based. Research studies in the adapting mechanisms of Latino students in particular are beginning to grow in number. Alva (1991), Gordon, Padilla, Ford and Thomson (1994), Gonzalez and Padilla (1997), Súarez-Orozco and Súarez-Orozco (1995, 2000), and Trueba and Bartolome (2000) are amongst the many studies that have specifically explored Latino adaptive issues. Whilst some of these studies specifically use the term resilience to explain positive and successful behaviors, the descriptions and analyses are mostly from the point of the systemic view of success – achieving high grades and going to "good" colleges seems to be the pay-off from these Olympian heights view. Thus for this study the "frog's eye perspective" *a la* Nietzsche begins perhaps by asking what these students see as success? How did they achieve it? Or, intend to achieve it? How do they see themselves in relation to the system? One student comment on homework seemed to be full of subtexts:

> We have homework, I finish it at school most times. Then when I go home I don't have to do it. And besides it is easy. But they [not clear who] say I have to do homework – that it is good for me – that it will help me do classwork better. So I must sit for two hours at home, after school – even if I don't want to.
>
> Maybe because I have been here only a year?

Whatever action they [students] take, what spurs them on to this action? AND How do they use the environment? Do we know how they use the environment? Does thc bubble manage to hide and/or neutralize what they think and/or want to do? Does the system see only what it wants to see because it has a master narrative to define success? Where in all the research and literature on the resilient student, does the student herself explain the not only the how, but also the why of their actions? And if they do explain this, does it get incorporated as part of the so-called protective factor scheme?

Thus Sagor's (1996), straightforward question "Why do some youths overcome insurmountable odds during childhood to become productive happy adults? . . . how do they manage not only to survive but to thrive?" (p. 38), encapsulates the problematics undergirding resiliency research. Rephrased it should perhaps read "Why do minority students in classrooms when faced with sometimes insurmountable odds within the school system act in a certain way and others in a different way?" The conventional answer is that the successful ones are the ones who had supportive protective umbrellas and therefore were successful. My question is: there are students given similar protective umbrellas, some use them others do not – why not? In fact should one be querying the nature of the protective umbrella, rather than user of the umbrella? Phrased this way it allows for the contextualization that critical social theorists deem necessary to understanding epistemological and sociological issues in the acquisition of knowledge Students who question single sources of knowledge assumptions and the certainty of others' knowledge assumptions show a sophisticated level of epistemological development (Kuhn, 1994). These minority youth can and do use contexts beyond the dominant discourse to question source and certainty of knowledge beliefs. Sagor continued his discussion by deciding that increasingly the "term used to describe the critical factor that some youths possess is resilience" (p. 38). Once again one returns to this concept of resilience with positive connotations.

CURRENT DEFINITIONS OF RESILIENCY

Definitions of resilience vary slightly across the spectrum of its use. Grotberg (1995) however, pointed out that "Recognizing features of resilience did not mean there was agreement on what resilience is; how to define it. Defining resilience is a continuing problem" (p. 2). Masten (1994) defined resilience "in an individual" as referring "to successful adaptation despite risk and adversity." Garmezy, Masten and Tellegen (1984) operationalized resilience as "manisfestations of competence in children despite exposure to stressful events." Rutter (1985) defined resilience as facing "... stress at a time in a way that allows self-confidence and social competence to increase through mastery and appropriate responsibility." Gordon (1995) defined it as "the ability to thrive, mature, and increase competence in the face of adverse circumstances." Sagor (1996) defined it "as a set of attributes that provides people with the strength and fortitude to confront the overwhelming obstacles they are bound to face in life." Winfield (1991) narrowed the question for educational purposes (getting even closer to the frog's perspective) by posing the question as to how specifically is the term [resilience] defined to make it meaningful and useful for educators and policymakers. In doing so she tied the definition of resilience to the doing or fostering of resilience by educational authorities.

As I pondered on these issues centered on the notion of the critical role of resilience in achieving success, the issue that arose was the effect of some of the definitions based therapeutic origins of the term as used by developmental psychologists in the field of psychiatric risk research. Whether the failure of immigrant/minority students was predicated simply by virtue of the fact that they were a subject culture within the dominant host culture? Accordingly bringing into the picture the "deficit thinking" construct – that a minority group was by definition lacking or deficient in the ways of the dominant host and therefore required restitution into operating normative structures (p. 181). Hazard and risk relationships. Was immigrantness the disease, protective factors the medical intervention, and achieving resilience/success the cure?

Foley, Levinson and Hurtig (2001) believe that the answer may lie in "student agency." These researchers believe that this agency can be found by "studying the small everyday cultural practices of ethnic students" (p. 59). They (Foley et al., 2001) suggest ethnographers study the way students of color use their communities, families, and peers as cultural resources. They also suggest a study of the way these students deploy expressive identity practices to negotiate school. And further, what practices do these students with agency create on their journey of negotiation?

It seemed therefore that explaining the educational journeys of immigrant students by analyzing the effects of the so-called protective factors were at best simplistic and at worst crass. The assumption that these students were tabula rasas to be written on by the system through the implementing of an intervention seemed to ignore and negate completely any agentic role in deciding their actions. When a student explains that:

> They think I can't do it [get good grades] as the anglos can. But I am going to show them. I am going to be better – yes better. I work hard and I play hard.
>
> Q: What kind of play.
> A: Oh I part on weekends.
> Q: With whom?
> A: With my Latino friends.
> Q: Why not with your white friends?
> A: laughs – Oh because – you know – **white girls can't salsa**.

– this requires an examination of the complex subtext present here. And therefore a new discourse to explain the student's action. Giddens' notion of the acting subject provided a basis for this new discourse.

CONCEPTUAL BASIS OF THE AGENTIC MODEL

The concept of agency as advocated by Giddens (1979) involves "intervention [by subject] in a potentially malleable object world . . ." (p. 56). Agency refers to more than just discrete actions, or even a series of discrete actions "but to a continuous flow of conduct" (p. 55). In more specific terms Giddens delineated the role of what he termed the acting subject involved in action or agency. "An adequate account of human agency," he stated, "must, first be connected to a theory of acting subject; and second, must situate action in time and space as a continuous flow of conduct . . ." (p. 2). He elaborated on the concept of acting subject by explaining the choice of the agent at any point in time to decide between available courses of action. This is Giddens' notion of *could have acted otherwise*. Allied with this emphasis on the acting subject Giddens presented in his theory the *intentionality* feature of human conduct. He explained intentionality not as meaning that the acting subject consciously has definite goals in mind during the course of action, but rather that purposeful monitoring of action follows the action and motivation to act rather than preceding it. He termed this the reflexive monitoring of action. The ability to reflexively monitor action, he further explained, is possible because of the "capabilities of human agents to explain why they act as they do by giving reasons for their conduct" (p. 57). Giddens argued that this reflexive monitoring of action was the distinguishing feature of human action as compared to the behaviour of animals.

Bruner (1996, pp. 35–36) tied his definition of agency to the notion of self. The formation of selfhood he attributed to the culture within which it developed. In addition he also argued that agency was delineated and constrained by the culture within which it operated. "A solo agentive view" he believed was "wildly off the mark" (p. 93). The agentive mind, Bruner stated, sought out dialogue and discourse with other agentive minds and through this shared discourse with other points of view a living dynamic culture was sustained.

Like Giddens, Bruner explained choice by juxtaposing it with strict causal explanations for events in human existence. Stimulus-response situations he argued did not require moral reasons to explain them; intentional actions, on the other hand implied responsibility for the actions, and responsibility implied choice.

In summary, one always has agency, and this means one always has the ability to act one way as opposed to another way. Both Bruner and Giddens see agency as taking place within conditions that more or less constrain it or more or less resource it.

Butler and Popkewitz (1998), however argue that the degree of ability one has varies and the degree of voice one has also varies in relation to agentic ability. This variation is the result of the discursive situation the acting subject is operating within. The theoretical concepts of agency in both Bruner's and Giddens' theses support the notion of an active agentic role in human action; the presence of choice to act otherwise at any point in time in the process of events taking place. Thus, the picture of an intentionally acting subject achieving intended results is given textured levels of dimension.

ORIGINS OF THE MODEL

An Agentic Model of Resiliency Development

The Agentic Model proposed in this discussion is based Giddens' notion of the "acting subject" possessing foundational agency as described above. However, it also takes into account the agency conferred on students within a discursive situation (Butler & Popkewitz, 1998), created by the school. The discursive situation is presented to the student in the form of the support structures based on protective factors. It is the situation where the student is taught how best to act in any given instance. All of the above provided the conceptual basis for the construction of a model based on the Agentic Role of subject within which one explains the success of the students in a school situation in this study. The model is an adaptation of Giddens basic 3-stage model. Moving from a "primitive process" to a fully agentic process where their success is the result of them taking steps in a time-space interaction.

Briefly, to reiterate the concept of Agency as Giddens explains – it refers to the intervention in a potentially malleable object world by an acting subject (the agent), who at any point in time *could have acted otherwise*. At the same time the prevailing discursive situation has the possibility of influence action or inaction.

THE STEPS TO BUILDING THE MODEL

The Model in Theory: Three Dimensions

Dimension # 1 – Homoestatic Causal Loop
Action taken by the student within the Homeostatic Causal Loop operates at the most primitive level. It is a functionalist explanation of action based on the interdependence of system parts usually interpreted as Homeostasis and involve the operation of Causal Loops – i.e. circular causal relations, when a change in one item leads to a sequence of change which ultimately returns to affect the original item and bring it back to the original state. It resembles a physiological or mechanical model incorporating the deterministic or mechanical notion of events, where the forces operate almost "blindly" (Giddens, p. 78).

Illustrating it with issues faced by students in the study: The Homeostatic Risk Cycle would operate as below:

- At-risk student faced with a situation with hazard.
- Leads to engaging in risky behavior.
- Leads to trouble in school – low grades, lack of motivation, poor attendance, etc. (Non-resilient behavior?)
- Reverts to or continues to be an at-risk student.

In the process above there is no controlling filter that acts a crucial filter in the other elements in the cycle to affect the actions of the student. Although the student acts, the action is almost a mechanical reaction (not fully agentic) to the operation of the system – nothing is being considered outside the causal loop. The at-risk label is not questioned either, the system assumes that immigrantness is a hazard which will inevitably lead to risk behavior. There is no suggestion of certain combinations leading to risk (*extend discussion – subjective notion of risk*).

Dimension # 2
Self-regulation through feedback – An institutional analysis of action. In this model an intervention is put in place, which acts as the controlling/crucial filter on the other elements in the cycle. In examples in the study an intervention is activated by the teacher, administrator, and/or the school district at the system level to deal with the "at-risk" labeled students.

- At risk student faced with a hazardous situation.
- Engages in risky behavior (does not do homework, etc.).
- Intervention by the system (controlling/crucial filter).
- Remediation, retention, counseling, in traditional models of protective factors.
- Leads to the student improving grades, attendance, punctuality, etc. In other words develops acceptable behavior – Resilient [i.e. successful] Behavior.
- Becomes a "not at-risk" student.

In the model above the student has changed during this process. The critical questions however are/should be: Why did the student change? Only because of the intervention? What else motivated the student? Is there any attempt made to find this out? And secondly, will this change last? Change has been brought about by feedback from the system to the student through the intervention. The message is that the risky behavior will not be accepted, the message may be punitive or it may be sympathetic. Is the student acted upon or acting voluntarily? The question remains however whether removal of the intervention will lead to return to the original behavior and put the Homeostatic causal loop into play once more. As long as the agentic role of the student is ignored the explanation and its effects should be viewed as problematics.

Dimension # 3

Agentic model of resiliency development – Analysis of strategic conduct. Reflexive Self Regulation is based on a strategic analysis of conduct by the subject (Agent – student), not only on an institutional analysis of conduct. Here the system in operation is examined not from the vantage of the system in action, but rather through an analysis of the strategic conduct of the agent – through an analysis of the mode in which the actors (in this case the students) draw upon structural elements (*Explain Giddens' Rules and Resources used*) in the progress of their social relations. This model examines the students' use of the structural elements of school and schooling to achieve and maintain success, within the normative definition of school success OR not to do so.

- At-risk student faces situational hazard – in this case environmental? Circumstance, immigrantness which has the intrinsic ability to cause adverse effects.
- Student as agent (acting subject) has to make a choice of whether to allow the environment to dominate or dominate the environment – either/or
- Choice is made based on their knowledge of the social situation – monitoring of the setting and of the interaction.

• **As competent social agents**	**As incompetent social agents**
make positive choices	make negative choices

What is examined in this model along with how the Agentic choice is made is the ecology of action situations. In the resilience literature these tend to focus on the support systems or the protective factors in school system that enable the student to develop resiliency. The Agentic model posits that the critical factor in developing resiliency is not only the existence of the support systems, but also that part of the student's ecology that lies outside the parameters and influence of the school. How the student either reacts to or uses all these environments is interconnected and intertwined.

It is critical to note that the working of the model at this third stage, involves an analysis of the choice-making process within the ecology of the action situation. In other words not merely the event, but a sequence of events needs to be analysed. Finally, at this stage the homeostatic loop as well as the institutional intervention (simple feedback loop) is broken. A fully functional Agentic model does not promote stasis nor merely institutionally-controlled directed change, but rather a self-regulated, directional change that is made by the student-agent with knowledge of the situation and process of interaction. The data provides examples of such student-directed agentic action in dealing with the school and the system. An important point to be made at this point, is that both resilient and non-resilient behavior must be analysed within the social interaction in which it is meshed – as reflexively monitored conduct – i.e. reflexive self-regulation by an acting subject. Resilient or non-resilient behavior is the result of the student making a definite choice at stage 3 through the manner in which the risk situation is negotiated within the context of the protective mechanisms.

THE MODEL IN PRACTICE

At the outset it became evident that the model as outlined above to explain the comments of the students in this study would not allow for a consistent classification of the students into neat categories. What it allowed however, more importantly, for this particular study, was the opportunity to view the students' behaviour outside the usual binary explanations of successful/unsuccessful, resilient/non-resilient, or the more overarching and oftentimes vague, but popular classification of good/bad students. Furthermore, these binaries usually tended to be classifications that were made from a system-initiated, and evaluated perspective. It [the agentic model] allowed the focus of the explanation of student behaviour to be placed on the *acting agent – the student*, based on the belief that

> Students are capable of reflecting upon their learning in meaningful ways... and that to include the voices of our students not only adds another perspective, but also ensures that the conversation remains relevant (Innes, Moss & Smigiel, 2001).

Owning Success

Annalisha is a ninth grade student. She does not fit the operational definition/s of "immigrant" that was employed in the first phase of this study. Immigrant was used to refer to students who were either in bilingual or ESL (English as Second Language) classes. These students were usually referred to as ELLs (English Language Learners). Annalisha has an Anglo mother and a Mexican father. She was classified as *at risk* because of her Mexican father. She has Mexican step-siblings with whom she has very little regular contact. She speaks fluent English, additionally she manipulates the language idiom with complete ease.

Analytic Comment: The *at risk* label here is an significant issue to note. Annalisha was not and had never been in either a bilingual or ESL class. The immigrant label seemed to be attached to her by reason of her Spanish surname. And this name it would seem labeled her as an at risk student. However the concept of at risk is defined and used, at the particular stage Annalisha did not seem to be suffering from any significant adversity.

In the first phase of this study she was classified as resilient. According to her current school-based (in all subjects) and standardised test grades (in English, Writing, and Mathematics) she consistently makes *A*s. She informed me that that she intended to maintain this straight *A* record in Junior High and High School. When asked why she worked so hard to achieve these grades, she stated unequivocally

> Good grades are very important to me because I want to go to a good college. I do not want to get bad grades. Bad grades would reflect on the fact that I do not have backbone. I also know my parents would expect me to get good grades.

The decision that these ends [good grades] are beneficial to her are based on a variety of influences, primarily her parents – more specifically her mother

> My mom – oh she'd be – the first she'd tell me by you know – you need to work harder – she wants me to go through high school and then get into college and then graduate. She doesn't want me to be like her – uh because she my mom is going to college now – and so she kinda pushes me too

and the conclusions she herself has reached from observing some of her less successful friends

> I have friends who don't care. Actually I have a friend and he gets many Fs. And he doesn't care. Maybe because his parents don't say anything to him. I tell him –'why don't you do it?' and he is like I don't care – I don't wanna do it – first he says I don't understand it and then I don't wanna do it.I really don't understand . . . ummm.

Analytic Comment: In discussing her friends who did not get high grades her speculations as to why this was so were done in a thoughtful and sympathetic manner, taking into account the consequences that follow not doing well at school, not going to college and effect of this on one's future. It also seemed implicit that she accepted their right to do so, and that they remained her friends nonetheless.

Enlightening too was her reply to the question as to what she did when she first arrived at school in the morning. Most of the other students had either sought out their friends for some socializing before classes began, or those on free lunches went to the cafeteria for breakfast. Annalisha

> When I come to school in the morning I don't go to the cafeteria or anything – I go to the first class teacher, then when the bell rings I go to my locker for my books.

The system existed to be used by her, and in a sense to be "manipulated" to achieve the ends that she has decided are beneficial to her ultimate needs. When asked how she would handle an extremely difficult homework problem, and whether she would ever consider giving up, she replied

> First of course I would try every possible method to solve it myself. If I could not do it I would then go and find the teacher for help you know – if I don't get some of the questions – and I would probably ask him to stay for tutoring – that's what I usually do – if I don't get something I ask for tutoring.... Sometimes my mom can help me – if I give her enough time to read the chapter. And you know I have some smart friends too whom I can ask for help.
>
> (softly but firmly) I would never give up – never – because you know that's kinda weak – I would just try to find somebody who understands it. Giving up – is kinda like shows you have no perseverance you – ahh it's hard for me to put this into words – it just means you know that you let everything go – that you don't care about anything.

Analytic Comment: Annalisha is very clear here as to the choices *she* makes. The at-risk situation she faced was the difficult homework. She chooses to seek help, and furthermore she ensures that she gets the help she needs, thereby putting Dimension # 3 into play. Within the conventional definition of a competent social agent, she makes the socially-accepted positive choices to ensure that she achieves academic success. She is able to choose those elements of her environment that she recognizes as able to help her achieve these ends.

In summary Annalisha was one of the few examples of students who used her agentic ability (foundational agency), the available resources around her (the discursive situation, i.e. the existing situation), both in school and outside school and adjusted the interaction to ensure that the desired goals are achieve it. Annalisha's success cannot be explained simply, for example, by examining the activities of the school's curricular and pedagogical practices, or the supportive atmosphere in the home. Annalisha herself clearly explains the choices she makes, this is particularly evident when she muses on the reasons her friend will not change his habits to get rid of the Fs he gets.

Viewed therefore from the perspective of the student, success can be explained as the result of an *ecology in sync*, where the student is an equal and active contributor in the teaching/learning process.

Owning Failure and Explaining Success

Q: Lauro what grades are you getting in Math
A: I am barely passing Math, get about 60%. I find Math a little bit difficult now – You know I think I was good at Math in elementary school.
Q: Why was it good then?
A: Ahh – umm – I think the teacher made me do it – Also I liked doing it so I did.
Q: Do you think you can improve?
A: Yes ma'am, like pay attention to work – and not talk to my friends. The teacher sometimes moves us – than I pay attention but sometimes I don't understand – but I don't say nothin'.
Q: Why?
A: I don't know – maybe because sometimes I tell him – he helps me – then sometimes I understand. Sometimes I feel embarrassed.

Lauro is a ninth grade student. His father is Honduran and mother Mexican. He was born in the U.S. Parents came to U.S. just before he was born. He has two sisters and a brother. The brother is older and lives in Honduras. One sister lives in Honduras too, and the other sister is in high school in the U.S. His English whilst good, is strongly Spanish-accented and not completely fluent. He speaks Spanish at home, and told me he learnt English "*from my friends*."

Analytic Comment: Even though he was born in the U.S. and went to elementary school here, he does not attribute his knowledge of English to the school. Interesting is the fact that he articulates this fact clearly, despite accepting at other times that school is a place to learn. He seems to be aware at an implicit level that he does have some say in what he does and does not do, and in what he chooses to do.

In the exchange cited above Lauro is aware that "talking to his friends" is his problem. That is the *risky* behaviour. His behaviour can be explained within Dimension # 2, in so much as when the system intervenes in the form of the teacher moving him away from his friends, or as in elementary school when "she made him do it," he achieves required results. However, Lauro makes a conscious choice not to say anything when he does not understand the problem, knowing the consequences will be failure. He goes further in explaining his behaviour when he explains that "embarrassment" is the reason. In doing so he moves his behaviour into Dimension # 3. He very definitely owns both his successes and failures.

The above however is only one aspect of explaining Lauro's behaviour, that is within the context of the school. There is a whole other influential area of home and friends which together form an interlocking and interacting system that affect his actions.

Lauro's behaviour seesaws between doing as the system deems acceptable, i.e. when an intervention is in place, and reverting to unacceptable behaviour when it is not. However, in explaining his behaviour, when for example he says "*I don't say nothing*," he is taking responsibility for his actions. As Giddens (1994) pointed out he could have at any point acted otherwise. Hence, what at first superficial glance may seem to be simply reverting behaviour on Lauro's part, is actually for either tacit or implicit reasons a choice he makes. At another stage Lauro explained in detail what happens when truancy from school take place consistently. It ranged from D-Hall (detention), to Saturday all-day detention, to finally appearing before a magistrate in juvenile hall. When asked whether he had gone through these stages, he replied

> I know when to stop. My dad would not like it if I got to juvie

Analytic Comment: Note use of "I" – he makes the decision, and for a reason, it may not be the reason the school wants. Nonetheless he has one. "Acted otherwise" issue comes fully into play here. It has nothing to do with what the school wants or threatens.

OVERLAPPING DIMENSIONS

In looking at the operation of Dimensions # 2 and 3 in the portraits above Dimension # 1 is explained in the default. To explain a student's behaviour within the simple and rather deterministic homeostatic risk cycle is to ignore the inherent ability of all humans to make choices, to either explicitly own their choices or to imply them on a tacit level. If the tacit issues are not made explicit, they may superficially seem to be operating within Dimension # 1.

Perhaps the crucial issue separating action in Dimension # 2 from that in Dimension # 3 is the delineation between the type of agency being exercised in each case. Annalisha for example seemed to be exercising, as much as is possible in a situation which involves other acting subjects, a foundational agency as advocated by Giddens (1994) and Bruner (1996). Although the decisions Annalisha made were influenced by others around her, the final choices were her own. In explaining her choices, implicit is the notion that she could have acted otherwise. On the other hand, Lauro's efforts at exercising his choices seemed to be almost hampered, in some instances, by the situation he was in. When he [Lauro] stated that his teacher made him do it, he also added that he liked doing it. The overriding influence however seemed to be the teacher's influence. The teacher created the discursive (a practical) situation, which almost guided the choice-making process for Lauro. In the final instance therefore Lauro's agentic ability varied depending on the discursive situation.

This paper began by citing three quotes, two from Giddens (1994), supportive of the notion of a foundational human agency, and one by Zipin (1998), placing constraints on the functioning of a pure foundational agency. These quotes encapsulate the operational difference in the exercise of agentic ability between Dimensions # 2 and 3 of the proposed model.

IMPLICATIONS FOR POLICYMAKING AND PRACTICE

The model originally adapted and designed from Giddens' (1994), discussion of the operation of foundational agency, was intended to provide a template to theoretically interpret the data collected in this research study, and to develop conceptual abstractions. It is however, ultimately based on a basic educational premise that what we do in schools is not teaching and learning as two separate binary-based activities, as it sometimes seems to be, rather that teaching and learning are a community of activities within a community of learning. In this community both the teacher and the learner should be able to contribute to the conversation that leads to education. We are not short on rhetoric around the concept of inclusion of students in the learning community. Unfortunately, as Lensmire (1998), pointed out, student voices have not fared very well in American schools

> Whether spoken or written, they [students' voices] have too often been reduced to lifeless, guarded responses to the questions and assignments of powerful others (p. 261).

The model therefore has other uses besides as a research tool. If one accepts the validity of the rhetoric on the integral role of student voice in the teaching/learning process, as opposed to a top-down, transmission model of education, then the creation of opportunities for student voice to be heard and integrated within the learning community is not a matter of choice, but rather and indispensable element in the process.

Its [student voice] use in research is a metaphor for its use in the classroom, and in administrative offices of education. It is a metaphor for the conceptualising and implementing of teaching/learning relationships at all levels of the educational enterprise. The notion of agency is at the heart of model. If agency is denied explicitly to any member of the teaching/learning community, it will make itself felt tacitly in a number of ways. In classrooms, for example it will be through resistance. As early as 1985 Apple discussed the importance of understanding how students made sense of their everyday life in classrooms. The phrase *everyday life in classrooms* may of course be interpreted in a number of ways. In its narrowest form it refers in an immediate sense to what happens in the classroom during the teaching/learning event, and in its broadest sense to all the other events in the life of the teacher and the learner that have an impact on how they handle the teaching/learning event in process. Specifically in the case of the learner, if the narrow perspective dominates, then it is possible that the behavior of the student will tend to be explained by powerful others, and lead ultimately to the marginalisation of the student in a process which in the rhetoric, is intended to keep him/her at the centre. For the teacher in the classroom therefore finding ways and means of not only collecting information of their [students] whole lived experience in and out of the classroom, but also ways of using this information to benefit the learning process is essential. This is particularly crucial for those students who start out being marginalized by the labels attached to them by the system, *immigrant*, *language deficient*, *at risk*, *language learners*, etc. These are the students are assigned *unequal places on the educational* playing field, often not only academically, but also physically, these are the students who either sit in the back, or are so regularly withdrawn from classes, that they begin to see themselves as visitors. And different often gets translated to inferior. These are the students whose lack of fluency in the medium of instruction is interpreted to mean lack of academic ability.

Another perspective on the value of actively and consistently attending to the ways in which students view their learning processes is perhaps to invert the conventional manner in which the work of schools is linguistically described – *teaching and learning*, to *learning and teaching*. While it may seem semantically superficial, an examination of most curricular documents, and/or implementation programs, reveals the majority of space is given to preparing what and how to teach. Comparatively, a minimal amount of space is devoted to how learning takes place, and to matters of practical pedagogy. Much of what we know of how learning takes place often remains in the domain of theoretical foundation courses in teacher education programs. In the everyday life of the classroom, teachers spend most of their time perfecting how to teach. Conversations with students is most times limited to telling them what did they did not learn, and the consequences of not learning. Very little time is spent in sincerely trying to uncover the *why*, and more importantly the *why as enunciated and explained by the students themselves*. Neither is this conversation taken further to find out how they [the students] think they would learn, to ask them to reflect

> On the experiences they have undertaken . . . to generate an awareness and responsibility for learning on the part of . . . students. To ensure education remains relevant and meaningful, surely we need learners who are able to identify what and how they are learning – to understand as well as to describe (Innes et al., 2001, p. 220).

In the midst of this paucity of what Shor (1987), alluded to as "a culture of silence in mainstream first world classrooms," there are, gradually, studies being done researching the importance of student voice, and how it can be used to improve the learning process. A majority of the studies however, at this stage are of course being done with the general student population. Studies with minority students, so-called at risk students, and other marginalised student populations are still much fewer and far between. So, amongst the unequal hearing of student voices, voices of minority students are even fewer. Nonetheless, a start is being made in a positive direction in the publication of theoretical discussions on the value of including student voices in framing and implementing curriculum, and in the conduct and evaluation of empirical studies. Garcia, Kilgore, Rodriguez and Thomas (1995), is one of the more interesting studies as the first three of the aforementioned authors are students, and Thomas is an university professor of education. The study is in the form of conversations, comments and particularly some very perspicacious reflections by the student authors. Innes, Moss and Smigiel (2001), report on two studies "which addressed this issue [student voice] by listening to the opinions of students in regard to their own learning." Amongst the authors conclusions was one that the study provided an unique insight into the learning dynamic by presenting the students' point of view. Brooker and Macdonald (1999), provocatively titled study "Did *we* hear *you*?: issues of student voices in a curriculum innovation," used constructivist perspectives on teaching/learning strategies to examine amongst other issues the role of power and nature of power relations in curriculum making as it exists, and what it could be if student voice was taken into account.

From Policy Text to Classroom Practice

"Education policy," Spillane, Reiser and Reimer (2002), acknowledged, "faces a familiar public policy challenge. Local implementation is difficult." The process of translating abstract policy ideas into concrete classroom practice requires a host of skills at a number of different levels. For example, in the research studies cited above all of the researchers went into schools in what one could characterise as ideal conditions. They went in for short period of time, they were visitors to the schools and hence enjoyed a "novelty value" with the students, they had a specific research agenda, which they were testing and they did not have to concern themselves with the everyday stresses of school life faced by the regular teachers. What these researchers had done was created the policy text, a text which had to be translated into a policy agenda, and which in turn required translation into an implementation agenda. The implementation agenda in turn had to be translated into action on two levels at the administration level and at the classroom level. There therefore is a vast chasm that requires bridging at a number of points between the creation of policy text and an implementation policy.

Furthermore, oftentimes in education it is outside researchers such as those based at universities and/or central education offices who create the policy texts and it is either the administrators at school district and individual school level who interpret these texts and hand them down for implementation. As Scott (2000) pointed out, as a result

> An educational policy text is always underpinned by an ideological framework: that is the text itself, explicitly or implicitly, offers a viewpoint about the nature of knowledge, forms of child development, teaching and learning, and organizational issues which relate to these (p. 19).

Thus it is possible that the ideological framework that guided the formation may differ at best either in degree or at worst in kind from the educational ideology guiding the implementation site. Hence, between the policy text creation site and the implementation site Fairclough (1989; Scott, 2000, p. 25), suggests there maybe constraints relating to

- Content – claims made in the text
- Relations – the way social relations are inscribed in the text
- Subjects – the positions that various players are assigned in the text

In other words the nature of the discourse as created by the policy text may differ markedly from the discourse existing in the implementation site. Each of these sites have their own set of rules about how truth is constructed, interpreted and implemented.

In sum the implications for makers of policy texts, agendas, and implementers is first, to be aware of the gaps that needs to be carefully bridged between each site. The concept of contextualization of discourse is crucial particularly at the agenda creation and implementation stage.

CLASSROOM TEACHERS GIVING STUDENTS VOICE

In this particular case of dealing with the concept of student agency and its role in creating effective learning/teaching contexts, creators of policy texts need to be aware that agents at all the other sites will need to *make sense* of the policy before it can be effectively implemented. Further, creating policy, and communicating policy does not ensure effective implementation (Spillane, 2002). Sense-making will remain a cerebral exercise until and unless suitable opportunities are created to provide for learning, critiquing, and contextualizing a policy.

This need to make sense operates in all directions. Sometimes, unfortunately rarely, a policy text is created at the implementation stage. In the case for example of sites where the concept of teachers-as-researchers of their own classrooms operates, teachers in these sites often seeking out stories about their students is an essential activity (Kincheloe, 1991). However, the method that these teachers follow will not necessarily conform to the notions of what is termed scientific inquiry. Within the conventional hierarchies of educational administration, the alternative methods used by these teacher researchers to incorporate student voice into their curricular and pedagogical decision-making processes may be in conflict. It is then incumbent on the teacher researchers, who may not be used to do so, to be aware of creating a "text." They [teachers] should accept the responsibility of communicating and structuring appropriate opportunities for all stakeholders.

Unfortunately of course, given the hierarchical, top-down, nature of most education bureaucracies, a Catch-22 situation may come into play when policy texts originate at the classroom level. Unless the creator of the text has sufficient "bureaucratic" stature within the school, and with district authorities, the opportunities to communicate may be few and far between. On the other hand, this lack may be turned into a positive by creating professional learning communities within and between schools, if both the central office administrator and the school-based personnel policy evolves as it is implemented (Spillane et al., 2002), and "Implementation is evolution" (Majone & Wildavsky, 1978; Spillane et al., 2002, p. 419).

CONCLUSION

As one interprets the words and actions of students within the lens of their [students'] ability as acting agents capable of reflexively monitoring their own actions and contextualising them, one needs to move away from essentializing theories that omit the complexities of students' everyday interactions and negotiations within and without the school. The minority and/or immigrant student, is no longer inherently *at-risk* but is equally *at-promise* and capable of "acting otherwise," and should occupy an "equal" place in the classroom. I am suggesting that the current interventionist discourse of resiliency with its protective factor solution, based deficit notions, leading to unequal status of the immigrant student, be replaced with a new discourse of resiliency based on the concept of student agency.

AFTERWORD

The title of this study has its origin in a vignette (from interview notes) about a young boy who was put into ESL simply because he had a "Hispanic-sounding name" and because he had only been in the U.S. for five months. His comments led me to wondering how many others were handicapped similarly? Or were being talked to loudly in the hope that they would be understood? Secondly, as commented earlier, there seemed to be some implicit injustice to merely explore the actions of the students interviewed from the system's point of view – when they [the students] were taking the time and trouble to explain their actions and feelings!

REFERENCES

Alva, S. A. (1991). Academic invulnerability among Mexican-American students: The importance of protective resources and appraisals. *Hispanic Journal of Behavioral Sciences*, *13*, 18–34.

Apple, M. W. (1985). *Education and power*. New York: A. R. K. Paperbacks.

Bernstein, B. (1975). *Class, codes, and control*. Berkeley, CA: University of California Press.

Bowles, S., & Gintis, H. (1976). *Schooling in capitalist America: Educational reform and the contradictions of economic life*. New York: Basic Books.

Brooker, R., & Macdonald, D. (1999). Did we hear you?: Issues of student voice in a curriculum innovation. *Journal of Curriculum Studies*, *31*(1), 83–87.

Fairclough, N. (1989). *Language and power*. London and New York: Longman.

Foley, D. A., Levinson, B. A., & Hurtig, J. (1999). Anthropology goes inside: The new educational ethnography of ethnicity and gender. *Review of Research in Education*, *25*, 37–98.

Foley, D. E. (1997). Deficit thinking models based on culture: The anthropological protest. In: R. R. Valencia (Ed.), *The Evolution of Deficit Thinking: Educational Thought and Practice* (pp. 113–131). London: Falmer.

Garmezy, N. (1991). Resiliency and vulnerability to adverse developmental outcomes associated with poverty. *American Behavioral Scientist*, *34*, 416–430.

Garmezy, N. (1993). Children in poverty: Resiliency despite risk. *Psychiatry*, *56*, 127–136.

Garmezy, N., Masten, A. S., & Tellegen, A. (1984). The study of stress and competence in children: A building block for developmental psychopathology. *Child Development*, *55*, 97–111.

Gordon, K. A. (1995). The self-concept and motivational patterns of resilient African American high school students. *Journal of Black Psychology*, *21*, 239–255.

Gordon, K. A., Padilla, A. M., Ford, M., & Thoresen, C. (1994). Resilient students beliefs about their schooling environment: A possible role in developing goals and motivation. Paper presented at the 1994 Annual Conference of American Educational Research Association. New Orleans: LA.

Grotberg, E. H. (1995). The international resilience project: Research, application, and policy. Paper presented at the Symposio Internacional Stress e Violencia, Lisbon, Portugal.

Hess, R. D., & Shipman, V. (1965). Early experience and the socialization of cognitive modes in children. *Child Development*, *36*, 869–886.

Howard, B., & Dryden, J. (1999). Resiliency: A comparison of construct definitions arising from conversations with 9–12 year-old children and their teachers. Paper presented at the Annual Meeting of American Educational Research Association. San Diego, CA.

Innes, M., Moss, T., & Smigiel (2001). What do children say? The importance of student voice. *Research in Drama Education*, *6*(2), 207–213.

Katz, M. B. (1989). *The undeserving poor: From the war on poverty to the war on welfare*. New York: Panteon.

Kincheloe, J. L. (1991). *Teachers as researchers: Qualitative inquiry as a path to empowerment*. Philadelphia: Longman.

Lensmire, T. J. (1998). Rewriting student voice. *Journal of Curriculum Studies*, *30*(3), 261–291.

Lewis, O. (1965). The culture of poverty. *Scientific American*, *215*, 19–25.

Majone, G., & Wildavsky, A. (1978). Implementation as evolution. In: H. Freeman (Ed.), *Policy Studies Annual Review* (Vol. 2). Beverly Hills, CA: Sage.

Margonis, F. (1992). The cooptation of 'at-risk': Paradoxes of policy criticism. *Teachers College Record*, *94*, 343–364.

Masten, A. (1994). Resilience in individual development: Successful adaptation despite risk and adversity. In: M. Wang & E. Gordon (Eds), *Educational Resilience in Inner-City America*. Hillsdale, NJ: Lawrence Erlbaum.

Menchaca, M. (1997). Early racist discourse: Roots of deficit thinking. In: R. Valencia (Ed.), *The Evolution of Deficit Thinking: Educational Thought and Practice*. London: Falmer.

Ogbu, J. V. (1978). *Minority education and caste: The American system in cross-cultural perspective*. New York: Academic Press.

Ogbu, J. V. (1987). Variability in minority school performance: A problem in search of an explanation. *Anthroplogy & Education Quarterly*, *18*, 312–334.

Pearl, A. (1991). Systemic and institutional factors in Chicano school failure. In: R. Valencia (Ed.), *Chicano School Failure and Success: Research and Policy Agendas for the 1990s* (pp. 272–330). London: Falmer.

Rutter, M. (1985). Resilience in the face of adversity: Protective factors and resistance to psychiatric disorder. *British Journal of Psychiatry*, *147*, 589–611.

Rutter, M. (1987). Psychological resilience and protective mechanisms. *American Journal of Orthopsychiatry*, *57*, 316–331.

Rutter, M. (1995). Psychosocial adversity: Risk resilience and recovery. *Southern African Journal of Child and Adolescent Psychiatry*, *7*, 75–88.

Sagor, R. (1996). Building resiliency in students. *Educational Leadership*, *541*, 38–43.

Scott, D. (2000). *Reading educational research and policy*. New York: Routledge & Falmer.

Spillane, J. P., Reiser, B. J., & Reimer, T. (2002). Policy implementation and cognition: Reframing and refocusing implementation research. *Review of Educational Research*, *72*(3), 387–432.

Suárez-Orozco, C., & Suárez-Orozco, M. M. (1995). *Transformations: Family life and achievement motivation among Latino youth*. Palo Alto, CA: Stanford University Press.

Suárez-Orozco, C., & Suárez-Orozco, M. M. (2000). Some conceptual considerations in the interdisciplinary study of immigrant children. In: E. T. Trueba & L. I. Bartolome (Eds), *Immigrant Voices: In Search of Educational Equity* (pp. 17–36). Lanham, MD: Rowman & Littlefield.

Trueba, E. T., & Bartolome, L. I. (Eds) (2000). *Immigrant voices: In search of educational equity*. Lanham, MD: Rowman & Littlefield.

Valencia, R. R. (Ed.) (1997). *The evolution of deficit thinking: Educational thought and practice*. London: Flamer Press.

Werner, E. (1993). Risk, resilience, and recovery: Perspectives from the Kauai longitudinal study. *Development and Psychopathology*, *5*, 505–515.

Werner, E. E., & Smith, R. S. (1982). *Vulnerable but invincible: A longitudinal study of resilient children and youth*. New York: McGraw-Hill.

Winfield, L. F. (1991). Resilience, schooling and development in African-American youth: A conceptual framework. *Education and Urban Society*, *25*.

Zipin, L. (1998). Looking for sentient life in discursive practices: The question of human agency in critical theories and school research. In: T. S. Popkewitz & M. Brennan (Eds), *Foucault's Challenge: Discourse, Knowledge and Power in Education* (pp. 316–347). New York: Teachers College Press.

IDENTITY FORMATION OF FEMALE STUDENTS IN A PREDOMINANTLY FEMALE, MULTIETHNIC HIGH SCHOOL

Kathleen Gewinner

RATIONALE

Researchers have demonstrated that the individual and social identities of adolescents are constructed through interaction with other people as they move through various social sites: home, school, the community, and within the virtual social site created by media (Raissiquier, 1994; Weir, 1996; Willis, 2000).

Wexler (1992) explored the importance of school culture in this process. He wrote that:

> The main thing about schools is that they are one of the very few remaining public interaction spaces in which people are still engaged with each other in the reciprocal, though organizationally patterned, labor of producing meaning . . . indeed, the core meaning of self-identity (p. 10).

As part of the public educational system, schools are subject to the organizational structure and policies determined by administrative bodies. However, schools are also part of the private sphere in that they are the sites of socialization, cultural reproduction, and individual meaning construction. A school is, therefore, a public/private context and resource for student identity formation. This dual character, encompassing both private and public lifeworld perspectives (Habermas,

Ethnographies of Educational and Cultural Conflicts: Strategies and Resolutions
Studies in Educational Ethnography, Volume 9, 203–224

ISSN: 1529-210X/doi:10.1016/S1529-210X(04)09010-2

1981, 1987) makes schools significant research sites for studying both the symbolic reproduction process by which youth negotiate identity meanings concerning class, ethnicity, and gender, and the penetration of this process by systems imperatives.

However, both quantitative and qualitative studies have indicated that identity formation is not a gender-neutral process (McGinty, 1999; McRobbie, 1978; Orenstein, 1994; Raissiquier, 1994; Weis, 1988). Recent qualitative research suggests that female students construct identity within a "matrix of domination" (Collins, 1990) consisting of class, gender, and ethnicity. These socially constructed conditions intertwine to form meaning about identity that young women must negotiate.

"Shortchanging Girls, Shortchanging America" was a 1991 study updated in 1999 (AAUW, 1991, 1992, 1999). Conducted by the American Association of University Women, it identified disparities between the self-esteem and identity formation of female and male adolescents, suggesting the need for continued research into the individual and social identity formation of female students in the context of public schools. The study indicated that the educational system often failed to support the success of female students. It reported that female high school students had more problems building and maintaining positive identity than their male counterparts and often experienced a drop in achievement in mathematics and science courses as a result. The survey indicated that the self-esteem of girls never caught up to the level of boys and that they were more vulnerable to feelings of depression and were four times as likely to attempt suicide. The researchers found a variation among ethnic groups; more African-American girls retained their overall self-esteem than did White or Hispanic girls, who had the greatest self-esteem problems. In light of this research, there is a need for further exploration of identity formation of female students.

The following study was designed to investigate the process by which high achieving female students make meanings about class, ethnicity, and gender, and develop self and social identities. Therefore, the study had two main goals. The first goal was to explore how students make meaning about their own identity. The second goal was to examine the school as a social site significant to the identity formation of female students.

It was shown that students negotiated the expectations and limitations from both family and school and worked to integrate conflicting identities into a coherent sense of self. It was also shown that the school, as a public/private social site, was significant to the identity formation of female students in that it provided the context for the challenges to and the renegotiations of meanings by students. Achievement ideology, which permeated school culture and influenced policy, was shown to serve as a link between economic and bureaucratic systems and identity formation. The high level of rationalization of the lifeworld at the school which served as the research site made it more vulnerable to the overinfluence of systems which were allowed to penetrate and distort the individual and social identities of students.

THE RESEARCH SITE

The four young women who participated in this study were drawn from the population of female students at a small, specialized high school within a large urban school district in the USA. The Medical High School was located in Houston's medical center, the second largest in the United States. Houston, a large, ethnically diverse city on the Texas Gulf Coast had a large immigrant population reflected in both the medical center and the public schools. Founded through a partnership of the metropolitan school district and a college of medicine in 1972, the Medical High School offered a vocational health professions program embedded in a traditional college preparatory curriculum. Students began the program in the 9th grade and by the 11th grade they spent part of the day in the medical center participating in internships.

Drawn from the entire metropolitan area, the 2000 student population of 715 was predominately female and multiethnic. The ethnic breakdown was as follows: African American, 269; Hispanic, 187; Asian, 177; and White, 82. Eighty different flags hanging in the school halls represented the ethnic origins of students and staff. Extremely diverse in ethnicity, race, and religion, students were, however, nonchalant about differences. Tolerance was a characteristic of the school culture and was part of the mission statement. Thirty percent of the student population benefited from a national free lunch program for economically disadvantaged families. Many were from families that had recently immigrated to the United States, although all were proficient in English, reflecting some degree of assimilation.

Unifying factors in the student body were the general conformity to the value ascribed to academic achievement, middle class behavioral values, professionalism, competition, social mobility, economic success and access to consumerism. Therefore, although students were largely minority, immigrant, and from working or lower class families, they conformed to the middle class social norms of the school culture. Student behavior in the school halls and classrooms, on buses to the medical center, and at lunch was subdued; the behavioral norms carried over to the halls of the medical center where the students interned. Their decorum, attitude, and appearance met standards set by medical professionals.

As a vocational school, the Medical High School was valued by the community, not only as a public college preparatory school, but as a source of trained medical volunteers, labor for low and medium skilled positions in health care, and students for pre-med programs in local universities. With these priorities in mind, a curriculum heavily weighted in science and math was developed.

RESEARCH DESIGN

Carspecken's (1996) critical ethnographic research design was employed in the two-year study in order to facilitate the uncovering of the underlying assumptions that structure meaning making by female students, and the process by which they negotiate expectations and limitations from both family and school. Carspecken (1996; Carspecken & Walford, 2001) recommends five stages for critical research design: (1) compiling the primary record through the collection of monological data; (2) preliminary reconstructive analysis of data; (3) dialogical data generation; (4) description of systems relations; (5) implementation of systems relations in data analysis. In order to achieve the goals of this study, the researcher gathered data on the following: social routines across related social sites, setting constraints affecting social routines, cultural forms associated with social routines, partial life history narratives, and subjective experiences of participants in social routines. The following data was collected: field notes, audio-tapes of observations, and audio-tapes of interviews.

Field notes were made concerning social action in various social sites on campus, such as the classroom, cafeteria, main office, school halls and social gathering areas. Notes on informal conversations with faculty members, administrators, counselors, and students were recorded. Since the researcher was a teacher at the research site for six years, observations of students in various areas of the school and in many different types of social interaction took place over an extended period of time. School routines and the patterns of behavior of students and staff were experienced from participant-observer perspective. The four young women who were the participants in the study were often observed in classrooms and other locations on campus.

Participant selection began with observations of a 10th grade Honors World History class. Audio-tapes of classroom observations of student discussion groups in the class were recorded simultaneously with field notes. Participants in the study were part of a pool of twenty students – male and female-who were observed and audio taped as they engaged in discussions about school life. Of the twenty, the twelve female students were interviewed. Of the twelve, four girls expressed interest in the goals and the process of the research study and were then interviewed extensively. Their "stories are presented in the research report. As one of the girls commented, "You found us and wanted to hear our stories." A flexible observation schedule was employed. Audio-tapes were supplemented with notes on body language, voice intonation and social setting, which were inserted into the transcripts of the audio tapes before analysis of data. Topic domains for interview questions were generated from this data.

Audio-tapes of individual two hour interviews with four female students who participated in classroom observations were recorded. Each participant was interviewed privately in the researcher's classroom, a minimum of two times, so, that follow-up questions could be asked after the initial interview. Protocol questions for interviews focused on participant perceptions of home life, school norms and culture, individual and social identity formation, and achievement ideology. Before the interviews, covert categories that related to the research questions were created in order to guide the researcher's inquiry. Covert categories are defined as items from each of the topic domains that the researcher wants to address in the interview without leading the participant's responses.

Paraphrasing and summarizing during the interview helped the researcher validate her understanding of participant speech acts. As with the observation audiotapes, transcripts were produced and shared with participants who were asked to verify their accuracy and offer comments. Then transcripts were supplemented with observer comments, notations by the researcher, which included her impressions and reactions to the social interaction observed, and the body language, voice intonation, and facial expressions of the participants. Data was analyzed using the reconstructive data analysis methodology developed by Carspecken for critical ethnography and began after the audio taped observations of classroom activities and group discussions on school life were transcribed and supplemented by observer comments.

Low level coding then began. Several segments of each interview transcript were selected for in-depth analysis using meaning fields. Meaning fields fall under Habermas's (1987) three ontological categories: objective, subjective, normative-evaluative. Every social act is constitutive of validity claims in each category. In the reconstructive analysis employed in this study, the researcher interpreted the range of possible meanings for each category in speech acts from the transcripts. Meaning fields were interpreted, as were identity claims, binary oppositions, homologous strings, metaphors, roles, semantic categories, and interactive power relations. These elements suggested coding categories. Coded transcripts were then analyzed for central cultural themes and implicit cultural assumptions that were used by the participants in constructing and maintaining individual and social identity. Through the use of this methodology, the intersubjective process by which the female participants negotiated expectations from both family and school was revealed as well as the tension between emancipatory and distorting effects on identity generated by the school culture.

RENEGOTIATED MEANINGS AND SCHOOL CULTURE

The four young women profiled in the research study were very different in personality, ethnic background, position in the family, class, experience, and life narrative. However, they shared in the work of identity construction and the negotiation of meanings about class, gender, and ethnicity described by Weir's (1996) identity formation model. Each girl had to comply with one set of meaning codes at home and adjust as those codes were challenged and renegotiated at school. They were engaged in the difficult task of sustaining and integrating multiple identities into coherent individual and social identities. These young women were developing "a capacity to reflexively and practically accept, live with and make sense of difference and complexity" (Weir, 1996, p. 185).

The girls were able to employ intersubjectivity in the process of constructing identity. They took the position of the other in social interaction, established mutual recognition, engaged in critical self-reflection, and critically examined the social norms of both home and school. When they were confronted with complex, conflicting meanings about gender or ethnicity, they examined their internalized norms, the general social norms of the Medical High School, and those of their peers. This process led to a redefinition of meanings and a shift in identity claims. Social identity and individual identity were interactive.

The participants – Carol, Tam, Anna, and Jane -were subject to traditional, intertwined gender/class/ethnicity codes in their homes. Carol was frustrated in her efforts to challenge the traditional gender codes established by her Hispanic mother. Although she asked her two daughters to clean the house on weekends and based their allowance on the chores that they completed, she exempted her son from this practice.

> Carol: I would ask my Mom, "Why doesn't he do anything? He's lazy. He doesn't know how to do anything." And she was, like, "Well, this is the way I've been brought up. You're girls. You should have to do the chores and take care of the housework and everything like that."

The gender different practices also extended to privileges and expectations, and indicated that Carol's mother had an entirely different manner of regarding male and female children.

> Carol: My Mom puts more pressure on me than she did on my brother, because that was her only son. He's all it is.

> *I: It sounds like you feel like gender is rewarded with privileges, but not responsibility. So that behavior doesn't really have a connection with privileges that follow. Is that correct?*

Carol: Uh-uh. Yeah. It's exactly like that. My brother, he was a guy. He got to do what he wanted. I'm a girl. I should be all proper and I can't socialize past certain times. I have to be in bed, because that's the right thing for girls to do. Girls shouldn't be staying up at all hours of the night doing homework and stuff like that. And on top of that, I have to do the chores. I have to do the housework.

"You're a girl" was a phrase that Carol repeated throughout our interviews in reference to the restrictions concerning curfew, social activities, driving, phone and computer access, and bedtime, that were placed on the sisters, but not the brother in the family. She expressed her distress and frustration in attempting to negotiate equal privileges with her mother. She referred to her mother having a "mentality that she recognizes, but can't fight."

I: Well, how has this situation affected your self-image, the fact that you feel responsibilities don't reap rewards but that gender does?

Carol: It just makes me feel like everything that I do is, like, useless, like I can't . . . there's nothing I can do to change her mind . . . to improve my standing or whatever . . .. I have given up. I hate to beg. It's too much effort. I think that I should be allowed to do it without . . .. I shouldn't have to fight for it. It should be understood that I should be able to do this.

Tam was raised with an integrated set of Vietnamese cultural values that severely restricted women. Although her mother broke with Vietnamese tradition in regard to women's education, she was very traditional in her views of proper behavior and roles for girls and restrictions on female children. In this regard, Tam was raised as a traditional Vietnamese girl. The gender meanings she constructed at home were in sharp contrast to those she experienced at the Medical High School.

I: Could you tell me how your parents have, uh, instructed you on being a young woman?

Tam: My Mom used to say, "Girls have to watch what they say, what they do, and where they stay." . . . It's like this Vietnamese proverb . . .

I: Could you explain that for me?

Tam: For them, they say that girls are like these ticking time bombs. [Chuckles] That having a girl in your house is like a ticking time bomb. She's going to go off and get married one day. (And her in-laws will blame deficiencies on the girl's family.) They're going to say, "Your Mom didn't teach you right."

"Your father didn't instruct you right." So my Mom says, "Girls have to watch what they do and what they say."

I: Do your parents have different rules or attitudes toward your brother than they do towards you?

Tam: Yes. They do.

I: Could you explain that to me?

Tam: When I was a kid, or now, I could never go to like a sleep-over. Never.

I: What was the reason for that?

Tam: They just feel that girls shouldn't stay overnight at anyone's house . . .. My brother, it's like, "Okay, go." . . . I told Mom, "What if I go to college in a far away place? And she's like, "I'm going to go with you." [Chuckles]

Tam: I asked my Mom, "What if my brother goes to college?" It's like, "He's a boy. He can take care of himself."

I: So do you bring up the differences that you see to your parents and ask them to clarify

Tam: Yes. I'm like, "That's not fair," because my brother gets all these things, you know. He gets to do all these things, and I don't. And she's like, "But, you're a girl." I'm, like, "So?"

Tam: I'm older than him and I don't get to do all the stuff he gets to do.

Tam: Because of my culture, my family, I don't express myself as much at home. I'm younger, so I don't say as much. And I'm female. Boys speak up more.

I: Does that bother you?

Tam: No, never. I just think it, but I don't say it. My parents criticize other girls who act modern. They say, "Don't ever act like that." They also point out good role models.

In the interview data, Tam referred to speech as an exercise of freedom for males and restriction on females. In speaking, a girl represented her family; her views were not only her own, but reflected on her parents. Tam was taught to be aware of the age and gender of the person/persons she addressed and modulated the expression, tone, and forcefulness of her discourse accordingly.

Tam was raised to believe that girls were "ticking time bombs" that would explode (become sexually active, embarrass their families) if not strictly controlled. The restrictive gendered social norms of her traditional family were internalized by Tam; she conformed and complied. Her individual desire for independence was subordinated to family stability and happiness. However, she expressed a wish to raise her own children differently.

Tam: My children are going to be, like, you know, I'll be there for my children. They're going to be free. They can do whatever they want, you know, and I wouldn't be so strict on them.

Tam: I will raise my kids like Mom, but less judgmental and not say things she says to me. Like, "You're a disgrace." "I'm disappointed in you." She always lectures me about the sacrifices she's made for us. It's just to manipulate me with guilt.

Anna's father was Lebanese and her mother was El Salvadoran. In her home, male family members dominated space and discourse, restricting her attempt to build a positive self-identity as a young woman. Her father's actions toward her were characterized by a need for absolute control and the fear that she would escape his domination, become pregnant, and therefore, cause him embarrassment and shame.

Anna: Because I'm a girl, he thinks that once I lose my virginity, that's it. That's the biggest mistake a girl can make in their lives, and that's the only chance they have . . .. Just the

> other day, I asked him if I could go to a birthday party . . . and he yelled at me. He threw the invitation at me and yelled at me. "Well, you know, I'm going to shoot you if you end up pregnant." He didn't even say if I could go or not. And he just said that, and I'm like, "Okay." And then he told me really sarcastically, "Yeah, you can go. Just go." And I told my friend I couldn't go.

The lack of privacy for all family members was a source of tension and revealed power relationships within the family. Anna's bedroom, which contained the computer, was also the family room, so Anna attempted to do homework and sleep while her brothers played computer games until early hours of the morning. Family life was strictly regulated by gender.

> I: *Since you have brothers and sisters both, do your parents make a difference with gender according to chores or expectations or restrictions? Could you tell me a little about that?*
>
> Anna: Um, they make a difference with gender with everything. There isn't an exception on anything. Um, the girls wash the dishes. The girls do the clothes. The girls cook. The guys don't go into the kitchen. The guys are, "I'm not gonna wash that 'cause I'm not a girl." And the guys don't even fix their beds. And so the girls pretty much do all the housework. And then the girls, they're not allowed to do certain things that the guys are allowed to do, even at the age the guys were. For instance, (the boys went) to camp in fifth grade. Both of my brothers got to go and I had to stay at school. And I was one of two or three children who didn't go. And then, my sister, the same thing happened to her.
>
> I: *Why do you think they didn't want you girls to go to camp?*
>
> Anna: They said it's because we were girls, and that was their reason.

> I: *Well, how do you feel about these gender differences?*
>
> Anna: They're unfair. Because the guys, it seems like they'll always have more than us.

> Anna: Everything in my house is pretty much gender-based. It's either females or the males and everything. They separate everything. We have different duties and things to do. And basically it's like the women do one thing and the men can never do what the women do. They, even though they know how to wash dishes, they won't do it. It's the girl's job, you know.

During the summers Anna worked in the family auto-parts store and found it to be an extension of her male-dominated home.

> Anna: I don't even like going and working in the auto parts store because it's a male dominated environment. It's just men. They hit on you and they don't think you can do things and there are a lot of issues there.
>
> I: *Have you talked to your mom about your need to, um, get away from the male-dominated environment of both the store and home?*
>
> Anna: Yeah. I've asked her if I can work somewhere else. I've been offered a job . . . but my parents were like, "No. Because you don't, you aren't in need of the money." And things like that. But, I do need that independence, and they, they don't allow it.

I: They haven't recognized that need that you have?

Anna: They feel that it's all money, and I don't know. They don't see it as me just wanting to interact with other people and things like that.

Gender meanings were also central to Jane's identity construction and were still being negotiated during the period that we conducted our interviews. Issues of gender and sexuality had affected her family life, her choice of schools, and her own gender identity. Jane's parents divorced over her father's bisexuality. Her adored older sister was a lesbian and was estranged from their mother. Jane wanted to attend a prestigious Catholic school, however, her mother insisted that she find program in a public school, away from the rumors about her father and sister. Jane made several observations about homosexuality, which she identified with her closest family members, her father and sister.

Jane: Question posed to everybody, "And when did you choose to be straight?" They're normal people with a different preference that's about as close as "I like the color red. You like the color blue."

Jane: It's just a preference, and maybe if you send somebody through countless therapy sessions, you might... They'll see being gay as being something bad or something. I'm not saying that they'll change their preference, because they won't. But they'll see it from the point of view of somebody else instead of as, "It's an acceptable thing because it's me." Because, like, with my sister, they sent her in a whole bunch of different therapy classes to try to convince her that she wasn't bisexual and that she didn't like girls.

Jane: All that does is say, "Well, this person over here thinks that I'm doing something wrong."

I: Can you tell me a little bit about what you have in common with the other kids here?

Jane: Well, okay. When I was at the other school, the whole gay issue was, "You're way over there. You're way different, and that's bad." And then so I, I was still in the whole mentality that, "What's wrong with these people? Am I so messed up? Or do these people have a very limited perspective?" kind of thing. So I kept my sister's bi, my dad's gay thing underground. I didn't talk about it. I just didn't deal with it. And when I got here I became friends with Nan and her aunt, and both of her uncles are gay. She's grown up in the same situation.

Anna, Carol, Jane, and Tam believed that their brothers had undeserved status in the family based on their gender alone. The girls reacted to their families' restrictions and anxieties with a mixture of negotiation and compliance. Each girl complied with family gender and ethnic codes while trying to various degrees, to renegotiate them. And, for each, achievement ideology with college and career was viewed as a way to escape traditional family social codes. Each girl assumed that she would have a career, a component of the Good Life; each wanted to rise in class and escape stereotypes by engaging in an important medical career. Praxis, the connection between work and self-actualization was a value for each.

Tam: I want to join Doctors Without Borders. When I grew up in Vietnam, it was a Third World country and people still suffer from easily curable diseases. I want to do something that will make a difference.

I: How do you think a job could become part of your self- image?

Tam: For awhile I worked at Texas Children's, and I worked in the playrooms, and I played with the kids. And they're so sick, you know, but they're so happy. And the people, they treat you so nice, you know. Certain jobs, it's like your identity. If you work at Kroger, you know how to cashier, you know how to deal with people. If you work at certain jobs, it's like your identity. If you're a doctor, they just assume that you're intelligent. And they assume that you're honorable and you're prestigious, but you might not be. [chuckles] Certain identities, they just form these, like, you know, judgments before they see you on your job.

I: So, you're saying that maybe jobs can define a person to the outside world?

Tam: What people choose to work kind of represents them. If you like what you're doing, then that kind of represents you. If I want to become a doctor, and I want to help people, then that kind of represents me, you know. If I want to become an accountant or an architect, and I want to build things, that represents what I would like to do, but certain people don't get to do what they want to do. They have to do whatever to make money. That kind of shows what kind of personality. They have to withstand all this stuff to do what's best for their families, to do what's best for their children.

Anna: I feel that girls should have a profession, girls should have everything. And if it's up to me, I want both things, and I don't think anything would really keep me from having both.

Carol: Because if you don't like what you're doing, you're, you're just going to be sad. You are not going to be happy with the way your life is. Even if you're making all this money, and you don't like what you're doing, you're still going to feel some emptiness.

I: What other things are components of the Good Life?

Carol: Good relationships with whoever you're with. Good family ties. Time to spend with your family. Being able to talk to your kids. Being able to be there.

Data from interviews showed that the participants valued the equalized power relations between students, which were maintained by school social norms having to do with tolerance and equality. While individual students and teachers may have privately held intolerant beliefs, the campus norms supported equalized power in gender, ethnicity, and class. In the lives of the four girls studied, campus social norms offered freedom from the gender codes of their homes. The student body, administration, and staff were predominately female and so offered positive, alternative role models of high achieving, multiethnic, academic women, including many who excelled in science and math. As Anna explained,

Anna: I feel that it's better at school than at home, because at home, it's like you're being pressured by your parents, and everything . . . and at school you can just be yourself, and . . . because everyone else is so different, you don't need to really think about that. It's like here you can put that aside.

Much like defense mechanisms, isomorphisms were invoked by each girl at school in order to protect her individual identity. These isomorphisms were cultural themes constructed at home and transferred to other social sites. For instance, each of the four girls had thought of herself as an intelligent, high achiever from an early age; her role and status in the family were tied to academic achievement and approval from parents in elementary and middle school. Carol, Jane, and Tam felt pressure from their families to be academically successful. Anna's achievement was not supported as it led her away from the traditional female roles of wife and mother, to independence. Achievement ideology led to renegotiated identity for all four girls.

Each struggled to separate her sense of self from the opinions and judgements of others or from cultural stereotypes. As Carol said, "Know who you are and don't let anybody get you down." Anna, Tam, and Jane made similar statements about their rejection of others' judgements about their ethnicity, achievement, sexuality, gender, and class. They were engaged in the identity work described by Benhabib (1992).

> The identity of the self is constituted by a narrative unity, which integrates what 'I' can do, have done, and will accomplish with what you expect of 'me', interpret my acts and intentions to mean, wish for me in the future, and so on (p. 5).

All four participants experienced Honor Roll Syndrome, a mentality imposed by schools in which students come to believe that they must receive A's in all classes. Students caught up in this mindset confuse ability with effort and often suffer a rude awakening when they reach a level of education in which their peers have similar ability, and effort alone separates student achievement (Reis, 1998). Anna, Carol, Tam, and Jane spoke of high grades that came easily until they entered the Medical High School, where everyone had the ability to achieve.

The Impostor Syndrome was another pattern of thinking that affected two of the girls. Tam and Carol attributed their slipping grades to internal faults or lack of ability while successes were explained, in part, as luck, parental support, or as undeserved (Clance & Imes, 1978). By not completing homework assignments, Jane manufactured a reason for her own slipping grades, which were, more often, due to mediocre test scores. Only Anna seemed to have a balanced view of internal and external factors in her own achievement.

> Anna: Grades are important in the sense that I have to do good, and I want to do good. I'm not going to put myself down about it... I'm not gonna whine about it, or complain about it. I mean, maybe I'll be upset about it for a little while, about the grade, or maybe I'll think I deserve better or I worked hard enough to get better. But, if I didn't I don't feel like it's my fault. I really don't. I think that however I do is okay with me. Pretty much. I'll work hard to get good grades and I'll do my best, but, um, if I'm too tired, if I've only gotten a few hours of sleep, but I've tried my best, maybe I didn't finish reading

> the whole chapter or something, but I read as much as I could, well, I think that's me trying my best, even if I could give more.

Internalization or naturalization of achievement ideology was the basis of the semantic category, "good kids," used by all four young women in the study to describe themselves. The full sense of good kids depended on its contrast to students who willingly attended zoned, comprehensive high schools and who did not connect work ethic, sacrifice, and academic achievement with future success and the Good Life.

> Tam: We're a good school. We're good kids.
> *I: What do you mean by "we're good kids"?*
> Tam: We're good kids. I mean, we don't, we're not like the other kids in the other schools that have problems with guns and fights and stuff.
> *I: So, you're not violent?*
> Tam: We're not very violent... We're academic people. We know what's right and what's wrong. We know what to do and what not to do. But, we're still kids.
> Jane: Here you're not trapped in your zoned school. You, also, seen to get this status in your family. That you're, like, special or something because you're going to a hard school.

Although the category, good kids, may imply elitism, at the Medical High School it crossed gender, class, and ethnic lines, and constructed a diverse group. Good kids also included internalization of middle class social norms such as decorum, respect, and compliance. Each of the girls mentioned that the administration expected them to act like adults, even though the girls, themselves, were aware that they were "still kids."

All desired positive regard and approval from their teachers and made efforts to establish the model student role in their various classes. They appreciated being respected and treated like adults by their teachers and recognized that their opinions, intelligence, and high achievement on standardized tests and course work were the basis for teacher approval. Often there was a great contrast in the adult relationships they established with teachers and their relationships with their parents in which they were still regarded as children.

Ironically, the model student role was sometimes in opposition to the policies of the school administration. The perceived injustices in the dress code, book bag policy, sanctions against cheating, and the punitive attitude of the administrators challenged this social identity claim. The girls employed emotional, logical, and common sense arguments in their opposition to school policies. They believed that as good kids, in the role of model student they should be respected and privileged for their sacrifice and compliance instead of suffering increased restrictions. Students made a distinction between administration and teachers according to how their identity claims were recognized. Therefore, they were much more critical of the impersonal administration than the teachers with whom they had personal relationships. Surprisingly, none of the girls regarded cheating as incongruous with the model student role; all had a relativistic view of whether cheating was right or wrong. Factors such as work load, quality of the assignment, competency of the teacher, and grade weight of the task figured into whether or not cheating in a particular instance was justified. However, all four girls admitted that they felt better about themselves and their academic performance when they did not cheat.

Interview data revealed that each of the girls gradually withdrew from whole school activities during their 11th grade year and focused instead on individual volunteer work and academics. The Advanced Placement (AP) program in which they participated left little time for anything but studying for the continual round of tests, reading, and doing homework. The girls also had less time for family activities. Both Jane and Anna spoke of missing everyday experiences in order to study. Carol found that trips to visit her great-grandmother took up time that could be used to study. Tam talked about growing apart from her younger brother as they each became involved in school.

None of the girls had lasting intimate relationships with peers. Their friendships tended to be emotionally distant. Although Carol, Anna, and Jane had boyfriends during part of the study period, the relationships were casual. The lack of emotionally involving relationships enabled the girls to focus on schoolwork. Each of them ended friendships that they felt were not supportive of their achievement or took up too much time. Friendship groups established in 9th grade also fell apart during the 11th grade year. Cheating, which had served as a bond in many 9th and 10th grade friendship groups, declined in AP courses. Carol, Jane, and Anna each experienced a falling out with close friends during junior year. Only Tam maintained close friendships with her two Vietnamese friends, both of whom were in her AP classes and were well-liked by her parents. Classmates in AP classes were mutually supportive and often called each other for information about missed classes; all four girls expressed the need to maintain friendly relationships with fellow AP students.

Despite problematic personal experiences, all four girls studied placed their energies and focus on education and their hopes for the future. Although they had little control over their home lives, they believed that school was one area of their lives wherein they could take control. School provided a setting in which they could construct narrative unity, and so individual and social identities. Their emotional, indignant responses to perceived injustices by the school administration underlined the importance they placed in the school as a context and resource for identity construction. However, the school also provided a site for distortions in individual identity formation through naturalization of achievement ideology.

ACHIEVEMENT IDEOLOGY AND SCHOOL CULTURE

Students at the Medical High School surprised campus visitors with their ability to reflexively articulate their lives; they were aware of the education grid formed by SATs, class ranking, and AP programs. They also employed strategies to traverse the grid in order to present the image expected by selective college and scholarship committees. Time management, achievement ideology, and competition dominated their lives, however, they had to deal with the fear of failure to measure up to self-expectations and the expectations of their families. Since the research participants in this study were largely from minority and immigrant populations, their achievement ideology included the social mobility of their families, putting intense pressure to succeed on very young teenagers.

With the introduction in 2000 of a full AP program, the achievement ideology that was already present in the school culture was ratcheted up. Course work in AP classes focused on the high stakes exams that offered the opportunity for college credit, to the exclusion of other curriculum designs or teaching methodology. As course work became more focused on exam performance, on action consequences, so did the students' action orientation toward learning. Although the value of knowledge for its own sake was recognized, it was overshadowed by the value put on grades. Teachers were respected for their expertise and effectiveness in preparing students for exams, but also resented as potential obstacles to getting a high grade; a demanding teacher could be a "bump in the road" to high class ranking.

The Medical High School curriculum left little time for elective courses and not many were offered. However, students chose electives, clubs and organizations, and even their required volunteer work with consideration of how these activities would enhance their "paper" identity and impress admissions or scholarship committees. Activities having to do with the arts and humanities were not valued as highly as those connected to science, math, or medicine. The school culture did not encourage students to think of self-development or exploration of personal interests when choosing their courses or activities. Within the context of the school culture, instrumental goals superceded purely educational interests.

As Anna explained,

> I think that education, for me . . . I don't think that I do it so much for intrinsic values, but more for extrinsic values because I have to. But, I like learning the things I wanna learn. I'm not in the classes I want to be in, or doing what I want. But, later on, I'm guessing I will go to college . . . and take courses that I really want to take.

An unintended consequence of the achievement culture of the school was the widespread practice of cheating, an adaptive strategy used by students to cope with the difficulty of the academic workload, the shortage of time to complete the work for four to six AP courses, the intense competition among students for class ranking, and the high levels of stress experienced by students. Maintaining high grades, even through cheating, helped students protect the identity claim of high achiever, important both at school and at home. Students were aware of the contradiction between the identity claim of good kids and the practice of cheating; however, its widespread use made cheating a school social norm.

Students entered the Advanced Placement program in the 11th grade. Extra weight was assigned to grades in AP courses, and so their value increased. Not only were AP courses impressive credit for college applications, but each AP course potentially increased a student's grade point average and, therefore, class ranking. Students wanted to take as many AP courses as their classmates so as not to fall behind in the race for the top ten. Individual choice was curtailed; competition drove enrollment in AP courses to high class numbers. Over two-thirds of 11th graders enrolled in the United States History AP course in 2000.

Anna: And now all the AP classes are filling up. And it's people who never really cared before, but now everyone's really trying because they think, "Okay, I have one more year to go."

Carol: The only reason I took AP classes is because I needed to maintain my rank. And I knew everyone else that was at my level was taking these certain classes. And I have to maintain my rank.

AP exam scores from 11th grade classes were received the summer before senior year and were reported to prospective colleges. Course choices and AP scores from the 11th grade were therefore more relevant to college admission than were those of the 12th grade. However, the importance of AP classes to the achievement system continued into the 12th grade year, and all seniors were required to pass the AP calculus course in order to graduate from the Medical High School, a requirement insisted on by the sponsoring College of Medicine.

Ninety-five percent of graduates from the Medical High School entered college. Students applied to colleges all over the United States and competed for scholarship money from a wide variety of sources. The class of 2002, which consisted of approximately 150 students, was awarded $10.6 million in scholarship offers. Students from minority ethnic groups who ranked in the top ten of their class earned entrance into prestigious universities and were offered multiple scholarships. In accordance with tradition, ten seniors were awarded full scholarships to both the local public university and the private College of Medicine that helped to found the high school.

HABERMAS'S INTERNAL COLONIZATION THEORY

Achievement ideology was generated by the imperatives of the economic and bureaucratic subsystems. Students at the Medical High School were subjected to conditions determined by educational policy on national, state, and district levels. The interlocked achievement system that connected AP courses, standardized exams, and class ranking with college admissions and scholarship money was beyond the control of the local school community. There was no discussion of whether or not students' interests were served by the achievement ideology that permeated the school culture; it was accepted as a natural state of affairs, beyond question. Even the wisdom of requiring each student to pass AP calculus in order to graduate from the Medical High School was not available for discussion by students or teachers; the decision was made by the anonymous educational committee of the College of Medicine. Because a menu of AP exams created by the College Board was available, the state recommended that those courses be offered in high schools as early as 9th grade. This policy was rationalized as a democratization of education. Teachers, students, and campus administrators struggled to adjust to changes in the high school curriculum, which were imposed as imperatives from the educational system. There was no opportunity for the population of the Medical High School to discuss what curriculum design would best serve students or to challenge the homogeneous notion of success that underlay the policies. These decisions were removed from the realm of what Habermas (1981, 1987) termed communicatively structured consensus, decisions made by social actors after argumentation. Instead, policy was split off from individuals and determined by the bureaucratic sub-system (the state educational system, the College Board, the University system) whose mechanisms limited the voluntary decisions of social actors and whose integrated, strategic action had unintended consequences. Aggregate action consequences functionally interconnected to produce a system with self-maintaining tendencies. From 2000, when it was introduced, to 2002, the AP program at the Medical High School took on a life of its own, greatly affecting class ranking, college admissions, and scholarships and directly affecting the identity formation of the four girls profiled in this study. Habermas raised concerns about the colonization of the lifeworld, or the over-influence of economic and bureaucratic systems on areas of life, like schools, in which culture was reproduced. He warned of the replacement of the desires and intentions of social actors with the means-end rationality of coordinated systems. Habermas theorized that schools, the sites of cultural reproduction, could become satellites of systems.

He identified two problems that occurred when expectations of social reproduction contradicted imperatives from systems. The first was the splitting off of expert cultures (such as the College Board) from the realities of contexts of communicative action in daily life (such as a particular high school campus and its student population). He also identified the problem of the penetration of forms of economic and administrative rationality into areas of action, like schools, that specialize in cultural transmission and social integration. The homogeneous notion of success at the heart of the achievement culture at the Medical High School was interlocked with the employment system of the medical center, a penetration in the form of which Habermas warned.

Habermas (1987) expressed his concern about the unintended consequences of the over-influence of systems on schools, including distorted identity formation. "Identity problems are inevitable in conditions of over expanding bureaucratization . . . socially integrated . . . relations are separated off from the identities of the actors involved" (p. 372).

Students, stripped of personalities, values, and social norms, or neutralized by subsystem imperatives, are, instead, regarded as bearers of certain performances: grades, standardized test scores, class ranking. In the process, they may lose the meaning or implicit value of learning and may internalize values, roles, and social norms shaped by system imperatives. Carspecken and Cordeiro (1995) also raised concerns about the loss of praxis that students may experience as personal identities become disjointed from student activities.

THE EFFECT OF SYSTEMS ON IDENTITY

Wexler (1992) investigated the relationship between the systems of larger society and individual and social identity formation in high school students. One of his research sites, which he called Pembrook, was characterized by the same achievement ideology that permeated the Medical High School. He described the school culture and its effect on the construction of social identity, which he believed to be the primary project of high school life.

> Achievement goals are what most immediately represent the larger society to the students . . . What are learned are strategies for managing infinite expectations and as a by-product, the formation of self as a process of environmental calibration control . . . Achievement, society's product, stands between self and society, blocking direct attachment to something larger than its own sign of individual achievement (p. 122). Socially created performance pressures carry along with them built-in defenses against limitlessness itself. Society, both the progenitor and antithesis of individual achievement performance, is really united with that performance. Both are means of self -affirmation, but also threats to the self . . . The success ethic requires ability to engage limitlessness, but in a controlled way (p. 131).

Jane commented on the limitlessness of the achievement system:

Jane: I don't see it stopping because, like, it continues when you go to undergraduate school. So then you're, like, you have to keep your grades up to get in whatever grad school you wanta go to. And then you have to do well to go on, like, to grad school if you wanta have a decent-looking application for, you know, whatever job you wanta go into. And then maybe the pressure lets off some, but then you probably have, like, a family. And you have, like, your job to worry about. There isn't any let-up, lessening of the pressure until, like, maybe you retire or something. So . . .

Students at the Medical High School, faced with the limitless character of performance on the achievement track to college, medical school, and careers, and focused on time management and workload, tended to pull away from whole school activities that would take an indefinite time commitment. Volunteer hours, required for graduation from the Medical High School, were recorded, hour-by-hour, in the counselor's office. If volunteer credit, like the hours awarded for tutoring other students, was not offered for a whole school activity, attendance was poor. School dances were so sparsely attended that, eventually, only one per year was scheduled. Students were, however, enthusiastic about whole school events scheduled during the school day; these activities precluded regularly scheduled classes and did not require extra time. Wexler (1992) commented on the apathetic attitude toward whole school activities that he observed in his high achieving student participants and linked it to the over-influence of achievement ideology. "Apathy is the student's way of describing compensatory defense against the limitless demand which is represented by both performance and society" (p. 131).

Wexler also argued that the school culture could limit or shape student identity to the purposes of impersonal systems imperatives. He saw identity formation as a combination of two processes that interact; as the school culture selected cultural resources of students to reward, students acted with agency to construct an image of self on campus.

At the Medical High School only cultural resources that were consistent with features of achievement ideology were recognized. Talents and interests in music, art, sports, technology, or drama were not acknowledged, and students had few opportunities to showcase them. The names of students who placed in any academic competition were recognized during the daily school announcements. This was a frequent occurrence as students participated in UIL and Health Science competitions and entered numerous essay contests. As Wexler (1992) wrote, "Identity was the pay-off for deposit of organizationally usable interactional resources" (p. 7).

The curriculum of the Medical High School favored students with a particular learning style that enabled them to work with texts, to memorize, and to analyze, and to be successful in advanced science and math courses. Students with the ability to focus on academics for extended periods of time were successful. However, they were sometimes compelled to drop outside interests, such as music lessons or sports, due to the time needed to complete homework or to study.

Students also internalized the dominant middle class social norms that were found both at the Medical Center and the Medical High School. Norms such as decorum, talking in low conversational tones, punctuality, restrained gestures, correct grammar and pronunciation, walking purposefully, and meeting another's eyes when speaking, all were components of a professional persona that students were encouraged to adapt. They became socialized to a professional culture that would enable them to fit into various health professions. Middle class norms formed an isomorphism between social sites, including the Medical Center, penetrated by systems. However, these social norms may or may not have been compatible with the student's home culture.

Academic achievement became an over-determined part of individual identity of the students at the Medical High School. The paper identity they constructed for the purpose of college admission and scholarships became internalized. Students saw themselves in relation to others, in part through their class rank or SAT score. If they were not in the top ten, they were somehow lacking. They were aware of the variables on campus that affected the paper identity and even manipulated them, but sometimes lost sight of the reified character of achievement identity. Students switched from playing the game to forgetting it was a game.

> Tam: I don't feel like I did my best. I always feel like what if that 89 could have been a 90. To me, if I try, I have to be the best. Either I should go all the way or don't try. I want to achieve. I want to be significant in my field.

> Carol: If I can't get an A, then I shouldn't do it at all, like, I've given up . . . I'm just going to try and keep my rank. It's like impossible to move up. You can only move down. And I know when I get the rank this year, it's going to be lower than the other year. And they're going to tell me, "Oh, it's okay." But I know they're going to be disappointed . . . because it's like now you have a reputation . . .. People expect more of you . . . I'm disappointed in myself. Now I'm like, in everybody else's shoes . . . A 10 or 20 rank would make me feel average.

However, the participants in this study did express implicit insights into the achievement system in which they were enmeshed. Under the pressures of the school culture, each girl described her attempts to separate her sense of self from the codes of achievement ideology and put rank, grades, and test scores in perspective. A bad grade did not make a student a bad person; neither did cheating. Both Anna and Jane realized that the concentration on achievement robbed them of everyday experiences that could not be recaptured, a condition Wexler (1992) identified as "an emptiness of everyday life" (p. 61).

Anna: If you're always trying to be a high achiever, you miss out on a lot. And there's lots of little things. Like on Halloween I didn't go trick or treating with my sisters. Instead, I stayed home studying. And little things – you end up missing them and you're all grown up and you're missing all these things and then you wonder what happened and where your experiences are.

Jane: I think life moves too fast as it is. And, basically, if we don't slow down, we're going to miss it.

Although achievement ideology encouraged all students to "live in the future and rationalize the present" (Wexler, 1992, p. 132), Wexler argued that minority students demonstrated a more complex challenge in identity formation. He argued that because minority students were the subjects of oppression in society and in the schools, for them, the drive to achieve rests with a more evident and pressing need for self affirmation – in the present, at school, in the future, in the attainment of "safe" occupational positions and the indisputable power and certainty guarantee of money (p. 76).

Collins (1990, p. 19) used the phrase "matrix of domination" to express the intertwining of gender and class with ethnicity meanings. Tam, Carol, and Anna expressed their self-doubt and the burden of low expectations from peers, or family, or society that they experienced as women from ethnic minorities.

Anna: I know they don't care about seeing my report card or anything. They never see it . . . I still feel like I have to tell myself, "Well, my parents, you know, they want me to do good and everything."

Tam: When I do the best that I can, and it's not enough, I just feel so depressed. I feel like I'm not, you know, up to standard.

Carol: When I got my rank, I was like, "Wow!" I was really impressed with myself and I felt kind of proud . . . and everybody thought that I was just someone stupid, that I didn't deserve it. But I knew I did, and I wanted to prove them wrong.

Achievement was empowerment; it was a way to connect with the larger world. Each of the four participants expressed the desire to become a doctor, a profession connected in popular culture with status, respect, and affluence. As Carol explained, "We like to show off that we're future doctors and look how professional we can be."

Achievement ideology, a penetration of the economic and bureaucratic systems, permeated the school culture of the Medical High School. Students constructed identity within this culture and used elements of it as material for meaning-making. The school served an emancipatory function in expanding and rationalizing the lifeworlds of students and providing a space in which they could renegotiate meanings about class, gender, and ethnicity, and construct identities. However, it also functioned as a space for systems to penetrate and remove central normative themes from discussion and negotiation, creating distortion in student identity construction.

The tension between the emancipatory and distorting effects of school culture on student identity formation is related to the tension between the public sphere and private sphere perspectives that schools occupy. Critical ethnography may be our best tool for exploring the contradictions inherent in school culture since it reveals the effects of the contradictions as well as their causes.

REFERENCES

American Association of University Women (1991). *Shortchanging girls, shortchanging America: Executive summary*. Washington, DC: American Association of University Women.

American Association of University Women (1992). *How schools shortchange girls*. A joint publication of the AAUW Educational Foundation and National Education Association.

American Association of University Women (1999). *Gender gaps: Where schools still fail our children*. New York: Marlowe.

Benhabib, S. (1992). *Situating the self: Gender, community and postmodernism in contemporary ethics*. New York: Routledge.

Carspecken, P. F. (1996). *Critical ethnography in educational research*. New York: Routledge.

Carspecken, P., & Cordeiro, P. (1995). Being, doing, and becoming: Textual models of social identity and a case study. *Qualitative Inquiry*, *1*(1), 87–109.

Carspecken, P., & Walford, G. (Eds) (2001). *Critical ethnography and education*. London, Amsterdam and New York: Elsevier.

Clance, P. R., & Imes, S. A. (1978). The impostor phenomenon in high achieving women: Dynamics and therapeutic intervention. *Psychotherapy: Theory, Research and Practice*, *15*, 241–245.

Collins, P. (1990). *Black feminist thought*. London: Unwin Hyman.

Habermas, J. (1981). *The theory of communicative action* (Vol. I). Boston: Beacon Press.

Habermas, J. (1987). *The theory of communicative action* (Vol. II). Boston: Beacon Press.

McGinty, S. (1999). *Resilience, gender, and success at school*. New York: Columbia University Press.

McRobbie, A. (1978). Working class girls and the culture of femininity. In: Center for Contemporary Cultural Studies (Ed.), *Women Take Issue*. London: Hutchinson.

Orenstein, P. (and the American Association of University Women) (1994). *School girls: Young women, self-esteem, and the confidence gap*. New York: Doubleday.

Raissiquier, C. (1994). *Becoming women, becoming workers: Identity formation in a French vocational school*. Albany, NY: State University of New York Press.

Reis, S. M. (1998). *Work left undone: Choices and compromises of talented females*. Mansfield Center, CT: Creative Learning Press.

Weir, A. (1996). *Sacrificial logics: Feminist theory and the critique of identity*. New York: Routledge.

Weis, L. (1988). High school girls in a de-industrializing economy. In: L. Weis (Ed.), *Race and Gender in American Education*. Albany, NY: State University of New York Press.

Wexler, P. (1992). *Becoming somebody: Toward a social psychology of school*. London: Falmer Press.

Willis, P. (2000). *The ethnographic imagination*. Cambridge: Polity Press.

THE RISK ZONE: INTERSECTIONS OF IDENTITY AND LITERACY IN A MULTIAGE, MULTILINGUAL CLASSROOM

Katie Van Sluys

INTRODUCTION

It was a typical Wednesday in Room 4. Wednesday mornings meant time for Invitations. A time cherished and enjoyed by the intermediate students in Ruth's elementary classroom. Invitations were a time for small groups of students to work together across disciplines on self-selected topics offered by the teacher but grown from student interests. On a weekly basis students signed up for Invitations – sometimes sticking with a topic for several weeks and sometimes attending to a new topic each week. Topics ranged anywhere from using technology, taking apart CD players to discover how they work, exploring media coverage of current events, debating social issues, dissecting plants, to making maps. Students then worked cooperatively in student-facilitated groups to use multiple ways of knowing, and available resources and materials to ask important questions, to investigate issues of significance, to pursue possibilities, and to inquire with others.

On this Wednesday Ana Cristina, in her fifth month of school in the United States as recent immigrant from Mexico and sixth grade student in this multiage intermediate classroom, opted to work with Adam, Brandon, and Jessica on an Invitation entitled My Maps. Being late March of the school year, Ana Cristina

Ethnographies of Educational and Cultural Conflicts: Strategies and Resolutions
Studies in Educational Ethnography, Volume 9, 225–253

ISSN: 1529-210X/doi:10.1016/S1529-210X(04)09011-4

seemed settled into the class routines. Her familiarity with life in this classroom was demonstrated though her adherence to classroom norms through her written entries about friends, recopied stories from her past schooling experiences, poems, and important artifacts such as Valentines, notes, and photos collected within the pages of her Writer's Notebook. In her day-to-day participation she used her knowledge of Spanish to write, talk with other Spanish-speaking peers, as well as explain her thinking to others in a slowed, more deliberate version of Spanish. Her role as a frequent translator and friend to a newly arrived student, provided evidence that Ana Cristina understood much of the English and classroom practices that surrounded her. Also, as time passed, one could hear Ana Cristina's voice more and more in small group settings. She would talk about her work, ask questions, and at times guide the group's interactions. And her actions on this particular day seemed to mirror her growing comfort and familiarity with life in her classroom. In the hour of work time, Ana Cristina had created a detailed map of her neighborhood in Mexico infusing a bit of fiction when she added Jessica's house to her Mexican neighborhood. As she worked she told stories to me, another teacher who had stepped in the room, and to her nearby peers about her school, the playground, playing basketball, and living with her extended family. However, when this week's Invitation Presentation time arrived she continued her pattern of shying away from sharing her learning publicly, but her teacher and classmates nudged her to make this the day where she would share.

> Standing shoulder-to-shoulder, but one step back, Ana Cristina stood between Jessica and Adam on the carpet in the center of the room. Ana Cristina silently faced the class all the while clinging to her map.
>
> Shelia (a younger classmate seated in the audience): Ana Cristina, Ana Cristina are you going to share yours?
>
> Ruth: Can you tell us about it? . . . Tell us four things that are on your map . . .
>
> Another student in the audience: School?
>
> Adam (a group member standing alongside Ana Cristina turns toward her, looks at the map where the map labels were visible): Grandma's house?
>
> Ruth: Ok . . .
>
> Sara: Grandma's house . . . everyone wants to know.

And everyone did want to know because in this classroom, articulating your process, what you learned from your experiences, and what it might lead to next were norms that permeated across the curriculum including Invitation Presentation time. So, on this particular day, Ruth and the students of this classroom allied together to help Ana Cristina see herself in a new way, as one who shares her work.

As readers will come to see in the continued story of Ana Crisitina's presentation experience narrated in the first portion of the findings section of this paper, Ruth and the students encouraged her to try-on a different "me," to step outside her normal comfort zone, and to experience what it might be like to participate in new ways. Ruth and the children in this class were initiating work in Ana Cristina's *risk zone* as they crafted their moves to nudge this child to new places in a way that continued to validate who she was and reflect their intimate understandings of each other.

The *risk zone* is the name I have given to a core feature of this constructivist classroom – a feature that I came to understand over the course of a yearlong ethnographic study of a multiage (4th, 5th, and 6th grade) classroom in a public school located in a midwestern university town in the United States. As a researcher, I entered this classroom at the beginning of an academic year interested in the literacy lives and practices of the children as they navigated the year together as a diverse multiage age, multilingual working class community. I was interested in the literacy practices available to students, what they took up, and who they became along the way. Data collected from this year long study offers insights into the use of cultural resources, critical pedagogy in action, as well as the interactions and discourses that shape this classroom as an open, critical, and constructivist learning culture.

A special analytic focus for this paper concerns the ways that learning situations for these children always involve issues of identity. Examining classroom practices, events, and discourses unveils the ways in which the students and teacher engage, affirm, resist, and construct the literacy culture of the classroom. The study of these interactions foregrounds features of the classroom community, curriculum, roles, and identity claims in the interest of understanding who students become as literate beings as well as the nuances of such work.

Teaching moves, by both the teacher and students alike, are shaped by their mutual understandings of each particular learner's sense of identity and security in their classroom community. Taking risks here was about the self. It was about positioning and the taking up or resisting possible identities. Because in this classroom culture taking a fluid, flexible stance toward becoming was valued over assuming a fixed identity. Therefore the notion of *risk zone*s describe the space surrounding students where others bringing together their understandings of classroom norms and discourses as well as understandings of each others to craft interactional moves to push others just beyond what is comfortable to experience what another identity might be like.

Episodes such as the one begun above with Ana Cristina are not unique, rather woven into the fabric of daily living and learning in Room 4. The children and teacher in this classroom live in a space characterized by a permeable curriculum (Dyson, 1993) where students' experiences, knowledges, resources, and identities are the threads that determine the patterns of interactions, the curricular decisions, and the practices enacted. Prior to returning to the data episode begun above as well as other classroom examples for further analysis, it is necessary to understand the theoretical foundations upon which this classroom culture and research analysis is constructed.

INFORMING THEORY

One size fits all notions of curriculum, the proliferation of prescriptive curriculums, and the testing culture of current political agendas positions teaching and learning as something that can be simplistically defined and uniformly mandated. As these sorts of efforts push achievement discourses to the forefront of what it means to be educated and literate, teachers and students alike are working to honor the complexities of learning creatively navigate these narrow visions of educational practice. Such work involves risk, a rethinking of what is meant by literacy, and the recognition of identity work and mediational moves alive with educational practices.

Negotiating Educational Climates: Taking Risks in Teaching and Learning

Risk taking is a fundamental to learning and an essential characteristic within practices aimed at reorienting the focus of discursive practices. Turning to professional literature, discussions surrounding risk are often associated with notions of risk reduction, the minimization of risk, the decreasing of risk factors, the probability of potential risks, and the state of being at-risk (Lawy, 2002; Levine, 2002; Robertson et al., 1998; Tulloch & Lupton, 2001). In such instances, risk is treated as an entity or fact rather that something associated with a sense of choice or agency. There are discussions about the institutional technologies that work to position workers in environments of "less risk" (Adkins, 2002), work to position students as successful or failing students (Davidson, 1996; Varenne & McDermott, 1998) and how social mechanisms such as the media work to narritivize risk – suggesting scripts for living that tell people to avoid or take risks while masking underlying issues. Within the aforementioned references, risk is often associated with "costs" and is conceived of as an undesirable condition.

Life in Room 4, will offer images of risk taking where risk is associated with delving into uncertainties of the self – where uncertainty is thought of as hope-filled opportunities to explore various ways of being. Student and teacher action contribute to sorts of interactions where the use of such technologies are absent and risk is brought to a more discursive level. Action in this classroom suggests that people are more than passive recipients. Rather, students here are given the agency to construct and revise temporal biographies of who they are.

Redefining Literacy: Literacies as Configurations of Social Practices

Broader notions of learning have shifted the focus from individuals obtaining knowledge to notions of knowledge construction occurring between individuals in activity with others. Wertsch (1991) uses activity theory to describe learning through the lenses of human action – actions that are goal oriented, occur within relationships, and are inseparable from the cultural, institutional, and historical milieu in which they are enacted. Vygotsky (1978) positions "mind in society" and writes about how participants draw from available tools and discourses to mediate their participation and to craft possible meanings. Vygotsky sees learning as occurring first on an interpersonal plane, meaning that thinking must first take place socially before it is internalized. From a Vygotskian perspective, there is a need within social learning interactions for more capable others to apprentice more novice participants into given activities through assisted performances. Bakhtin (1994) theorizes that we do not own words individually, rather we appropriate the words of others from previously configured texts that are saturated with meanings from larger social spheres. Thus, as one then works to manipulate language for their own intentions, they are constrained by the social ideologies and possible meanings wrapped up in the language that they select for use. Together these scholars, along with numerous others, contribute to the social turn or theoretical shift that aims to redefine a theory of literacy as a social theory where literacy is conceived of in the plural as sets of social practices.

Literacy, learning, is a social process of apprenticeship into the social practices of a culture. "Becoming literate," taking on the practices required for participation and manipulating cultural artifacts within the orchestration of one's participation, is a process of discovery of possibilities and actions as learners work through situated activity to become inside participants in practice. Literacy is not autonomous. It is not the end result of a process or the evidence of appropriation of a set of predetermined skills (Wells, 1999), nor a set of context-free, neutral skills to be learned, or a set of universals "out there" waiting to be acquired (Kucer, 2001; Street, 1995). Scripted literacy programs, such as those like Success for All (Slavin et al., 1996), instrumental approaches to instruction (Jeffrey, in press) are based on an autonomous visions of what it means to be literate work toward single, correct answers that negate the complex social variables that surround literacy. Moving toward understandings of literacy as sets of social practices, literacy itself is not "the problem to be solved" rather literacy is embedded within social issues and practices, systems of power, domination, and oppression, that often go unquestioned when the blame is turned to individuals and fabricated into a "literacy crisis," seeking a single solution or panacea that can fix and remediate deficiencies and offer false promises of changing an individual's position in the world.

Literacies are multiple, dynamic, malleable, and inextricably linked with particular histories, life possibilities, and social trajectories (Gee, 2000; New London Group, 2000; Street, 1995). Literacy practices, which always include issues of identity, are used as mediators in the world to produce, consume, maintain, and control knowledge (Kucer, 2001). Practices are wrapped up with cultural attitudes, values, norms, beliefs, and power (Gee, 1996) and are located in context – within social, economic, religious, political, educational, and historical spheres.

Participants in Room 4 are a community of learners constantly involved in the apprenticeship of others into their community. Practices are both local and global. Each situated practice is enmeshed in the collective understandings of community members. Practices include frequent interaction with others as they learn – talking, passing notes, commenting on each other's progress, recognizing classmates area(s) of expertise and learning from other classmates' experiences and/or knowledges. While social practices enacted in Room 4 embody aspects of social learning as theorized by the above mentioned scholars as they work in their classroom each day, activity in this classroom also suggests ways for continued rethinking of notions regarding learning in the company of others.

Studying Cultural Enactments of Literacy Practices: Moving Beyond What is Happening

When talking about Room 4's culture, it is not something we join, rather something we enact with each enactments being a product of social and cultural histories (Levinson, 2000; Peacock, 1986; Spradley, 1997; Wolcott, 1991). Literacy acts are cultural acts, constructed through the positioning work of one's own actions and their interactions with others (Bloome & Katz, 1997). Participants work to situate themselves within the discourses and come to know the world through the representations offered and constructed within such contexts. Because as Gee (1996) points out, literacy practices make claims to "what [participants] are doing" as well as "who [participants] are" (p. 68).

We know and take part in the world through the representations we make of it (Bakhtin, 1994). Our particular ways of representing events, through language, influence how we think about such events, the action we take, and who we are to both ourselves and others. Individuals negotiate a place for themselves as "stance-taking entit[ies], a[s entities] that take up a position somewhere between identification with an organization and opposition to it, and [as entities] ready at the slightest pressure to regain its balance by shifting . . . involvement in either direction . . .. Our sense of being a person can come from being drawn into a wider social unit; our sense of selfhood can arise through the little ways in which we resist the pull (Goffman, 196?, p. 319–320 as cited in Levinson, 2001, p. 342).

Who we are in the world, how we participate with others, and our decisions for actions are shaped by our understandings of who we are and who we can be in a given context. Our "[i]dentit[ies] exist in the remembered, the lived and the projected relations of our daily experience." (Sumara, 1998, p. 5). Approaching the study of literacy as sets of social practices calls for analysis that examines the texts, contexts, and actors within a scene that compose our remembered, lived, and future experiences. It calls for understandings of self drawn from studying human communicative action as people work through social understandings and issues of power in their desire to be recognized (Carspecken, 1999). When considering human actions and identity construction within cultural scenes, richer understandings of discourse become useful.

Gee (1996) uses the term discourse with a lower case "*d*" to refer to the "connected stretches of language that make sense, like conversations, stories, reports, arguments, essays, and so forth." (p. 127). When capitalizing the first letter, Gee (1996) then uses the term to move beyond language alone. Discourse then refers to "ways of being in the world," this use of the term brings together "acts, values, beliefs, attitudes, social identities, gestures, body position, clothes" (p. 127) as resources that inform and shape communicative acts. One's acts then define one's position in reference to a cultural group – they define one as an outsider or an inside member. Membership, which is marked by ones' use of the group's Discourse, is gained through apprenticeship within a social group. Becoming a member of various social groups calls for control and use of multiple secondary Discourses beyond the primary discourse into which one was socialized as a family/cultural member within a particular setting (Gee, 1996).

D/discourses that make up cultural contexts act as possible identity kits (Gee, 1996) for constructing possible selves. Learning in social contexts thus involves communicative action in anticipation of others (Bakhtin, 1994; Carspecken, 1999; Mead as cited in Aboulafia, 1991). Participants' actions reflect a generalized other and aim not only to accomplish literacy work but aim to shape and name who they are in that moment with present company. To become an inside member of a group, one must not only gain control of the secondary Discourse but be accepted by group members as an insider who "knows how to be in this group" (Shannon, 2002). Appropriation of a particular Discourse is not neat, clearly defined, or free. Boundaries between Discourses are often intersecting, overlapping, sites of tension. Taking on a secondary Discourse involves not only understanding the words to use, the moves to make, the ways to act and be recognized as a cultural insider but it also involves identity costs (Gee, 2001). In other words, looking at who one is or gets to be within a literate culture is not a matter of looking to the individual. It is a matter of studying interactions in light of entire cultural configurations. It is a matter of looking to human action and social practices. It is a matter of looking to the "processes of cultural production as the making of meanings by reflexive social actors in specific and diverse contexts of structured power" (Levinson, 2001, p. 326).

Educational ethnographies such as those by Davidson (1996), Willis (1977), Olsen (1997), and Valenzuela (1999) offer accounts of how social practices within schooling offer or deny access to opportunities, Discourses, and/or social positions. These ethnographies detail how students subsequently negotiate identities that, for the most part in these studies, resist the pull to affiliate with mainstream, middle-class notions of schooling. This work reminds us that it is not enough to label an identity or name a Discourse because neither are passive descriptions of the world rather we must look at the available Discourses and subsequent identities within the complex matrices of language and power as they are enacted and claimed by participants as they learn to be certain kinds of people or draw upon their own sense of agency and intention to negotiate positions as a different kind of person. These studies suggest that in schools, we need to look to positions, practices, Discourses, and identities available for student manipulation and meaning making in order to understand their actions as well as the subsequent meanings for their life trajectories.

Critical pedagogy calls us to interrogate what literacy is for, which practices are privileged in schools, and how widening the space for possible discourses and practices creates opportunities for participation where actors have a sense of agency to challenge and change the world (Comber, 2001a, b). Classrooms, like Ruth's, committed to critical pedagogy make curricular decisions that reflect their commitment to disrupt the commonplace, explore multiple perspectives, consider the sociopolitical influences to action, and take action in working toward a better world (Lewison et al., 2002). To accomplish this, participants need environments where they are safe to try on new identities without surrendering the security tied with their sense of self, environments where they can imagine new ways of being, and environments where they can develop a voice for change.

Current researchers in the field call us to explore accounts of critical language practices in classrooms (Janks, 2001; Luke, 2000; Luke et al., 2001; Nieto, 2002) and to investigate classroom practices that build from students' cultural and linguistic resources (Gutierrez et al., 2001; Moll, 1992; Orellana, 1994; Thompson, 2001). Concerns are focused on understanding literacy practices where becoming literate doesn't equate with jeopardizing or surrendering one's sense of self and/or where becoming literate means moving forward in ways that value a multiplicity of voices. Yet stories of actual practice where focus is turned toward becoming rather than curricular products and projects are scarce within the literature, especially within classrooms not deemed or supported as "bilingual" classrooms. So, it is toward that end that this slice of my research looks to nuance the nature of interactions in this classroom to offer classroom stories of literacy and critical literacy practices built upon student resources that are intimately concerned with who students become as literate beings.

Mediating Interactions: A Focus on Becoming

Vygotsky (1978) *Zone of Proximal Development* (ZPD) offers one way of thinking about the mediational work in social learning. Möller and Allen's (2000) *response development zone* offers another way of theorizing interactions between learners as students in literature discussions move through tensions in search of safer places as readers. Gutierrez's (Gutierrez et al., 1997) work with a *third space* offers a theoretical tool for considering spaces where students are not required to assume a singular identity.

Building on the work of Vygotsky, Möller and Allen, and Gutierrez in regard to the mediation of social learning, I aim to offer the *risk zone* as a conceptual tool for understanding how classroom work is very much about identity work. Also drawing from notions of literacy as sets of social practices and identity as being tied up in participation in situated practices, I would argue that deliberate interactions occur within particular student's risk zone – a zone defined by the intimate understandings of others, the appropriate risks for the particular student, the social forums of learning offered, the planful interactions among participants in this classroom culture, and the work toward creating different sorts of literate human beings.

Returning to Ana Cristina and the scenario at the opening of this paper, we see a young girl comfortable with an identity claim of one who is quiet, one who has accomplished important work during Invitations work time, and one who is reticent to articulate the work she has done with a public audience. Making a move to present her learning involves more than a mere articulation of words to others. It involves a risk, it involves motivation, and is contingent on the response of audience members. For Ana Cristina to claim an identity of one who articulates her learning publicly, she must be willing to take a position that involves a renegotiation of self within a particular moment in time. She must be able to imagine the responses of her audience and feel secure with their replies as well as possess a sense of agency toward being the sort of person who participates with confidence in the classroom community. Imagining an identity, making a claim to be a different sort of person, and reflecting on others' possible actions are all conditions that make it possible to try on new identities and move forward safely. Responses to Ana Cristina by her teacher and peers take place within her "risk zone," the theoretical tool that I suggest encompasses the understanding of the people and discourses that permeate this classroom. Interactions then become much more than merely words spoken but the conditions that create the culture which honor or deny options for new literate practices and new ways of being.

METHODOLOGY AND RESEARCH DESIGN

This research is concerned with literacy practices, human actions, and the social consequences of such actions. Pursuing this agenda calls for a dialogical understanding of human communicative action where action is studied in context and understood in terms of possible meaning horizons as actors act in ways that inevitably place their identity and need for recognition at stake (Carspecken, 1999). This requires methodological means that address the interconnectedness of identity and action, consider motivations for action (from the intentional and foregrounded to the backgrounded and barely noticed impetuses) as well as honor the complexity of human actions (Carspecken, 1996, 1999).

Narrative inquiry and critical ethnography are both dialogically structured means of inquiry involving dialogues between participants; between researchers and participants; between participants and local cultures; and between participants and social systems (Fariclough, 1995). Critical ethnography and narrative research traditions offer research options that invite multiple voices into the research process, call for prolonged engagement to gain intersubjective understandings of the participants studied, and work to understand participants' actions and meanings in light of their situated contexts. Critical ethnography approaches analysis in terms of understandings drawn from the reconstructive analysis of cultural scenes through position-taking and the articulation of validity horizons to deeply understand the options and actions of participants within the studied scene (Carspecken, 1996). Narrative inquiry also foregrounds understandings in light of human action in working to capture how human characters, acting in sequenced events, experience the world (Connelly & Clandinin, 1990; Riessman, 1993). Narratives constructed from or within research contexts also represent a means of constructing understandings of self and experiences. I found that blending these two methodologies offered means to honor participants' voices, examine the construction of cultures through discourse, and study human actions in light of both local and larger levels. For these reasons, the methodology was drawn from the wells of both critical ethnography and narrative research to study the discourses, actions, and texts produced and used in this literacy environment.

Research Site and Participants

The site of this research is a multiage classroom at public elementary school housing nearly 600 students during the 2001–2002 academic year. The voices heard in this space include the teacher; those of the 27–29 fourth, fifth, and sixth grade students; as well as my own voice. The students living and interacting in this place come from the homes of community professionals, university associated families, and working class homes where parents often hold multiple jobs to make ends meet. The student population is susceptible to frequent change, as students both joined and left this class throughout the academic year. Girls comprise roughly 60% of the class, boys the remaining 40%. An array of linguistic and cultural experiences are brought into this cultural scene – including experiences of recent immigration from Mexico, Israel, Korea, and Northern Africa; experiences that collectively reflect understandings and/or knowledge of 12 different languages; experiences of living in households with grandparents; as well as experiences of living lives in transition between various parents, step-parents, and/or adoptive parents. The teacher in this classroom is committed to holistic practices, involved in local and national professional communities, as well as dedicated to reflective study of her own practices. This year she expanded her multiage classroom setting by one year, adding fourth grade students to her previously 5/6 classroom. Also, when approached by the principal regarding the option to include students who were to be part of the ENL (English as a New Language) program, she accepted the offer with enthusiasm saying, "Count me in." As a teacher, her curricular decisions are theoretically grounded and informed by the notes that she is constantly taking as she interacts with students. When thinking about learning and working in her classroom she believes that being in school is about learning to,

> read and write and think and talk about everything that they need to do. And [to] live here . . . with all of the tools for solving problems, figuring out how to answer questions, and [how to] learn from each other. [And to do so], reflection is so important. [It is my job] to help them see the possibilities, to notice what they're doing and to help them see it too.

She also articulated her concerns for school practices that limited how students were supported in developing their sense of self-referencing specific instances where they were pushed toward a collective identity that excluded some members of the community (End of year interview). School for students in Ruth's classroom was about using what you know as a reader, writer, and speaker to question, reflect, and take action in the course of becoming critically literate. And this vision of critically literate students could be seen daily as students interacted with one another and engaged in inquiries that questioned policies and decisions connected to high-stakes testing, read newspapers bringing critical issues to classroom discussions, raised questions of gender equity, and used writing as a tool for social change.

The primary focus in this particular paper is on three focal children based on gender (two girls, one boy), primary languages (Spanish and English), years in this multiage classroom, their socioeconomic status, and the context of their interactions (whole class meetings with teacher interactions and a small peer group meeting). Analysis of three interactive sequences was conducted using Carspecken's (1996) research design. Throughout the gathering of the primary records, on going reconstructive analysis (including articulations of validity horizons, codings of discourse, roles and power, as well as reconstructive analysis in consultation with peer debriefers) as well as dialogue with participants regarding my understandings of their actions and their intentions.

FINDINGS

Examining transcripts and field notes from weekly classroom visits reveals cultural norms that are both directly and implicitly communicated through participants' actions and a range of social practices that are manipulated for classroom learning. By first understanding the typology of this classroom context (the nature of classroom norms and interactions) offers ways of considering the literacy practices offered in light of contextual use. Knowing the foundational norms that shape interactions in this classroom, it then seems possible to understand and articulate patterns of mediational moves between the students and the teacher and among students themselves as they work within risk zones to push each other to new places and new literate identities, in ways that preserve a secure sense of self and honor resources key to students' core sense of selfhood. This might mean drawing upon what they know about a particular student to safely support them in making new identity claims and/or it may mean work that challenges a student's secure sense of self when the sense of security seems to be impeding further movement as a learner.

Drawn from codings of classroom transcripts, fieldnotes, and artifacts such as written notes, charts, signs, and photos, current findings indicate classroom practices where participants are called to:

- Work from experiences, are oriented toward meaning making, and are valued for what they know.

- Take risk takers.
- Help others.
- Communicate across languages and semiotic systems.
- Do the best they can and accept approximations.
- Build on their history and reflect on their growth.
- Name and value the work (including processes) that happens here by crediting others when referring to their thinking.
- Listen to all voices.
- Articulate their learning processes and plans.
- Respect conversation participants and facilitators.
- Revoice what has been said to emphasize a point or to seek clarification.
- Pay attention to the words they use.
- Support others in their work.
- Value multiple perspectives.
- Communicate with your intended audience (do not speak for others, ask important questions/share substantive feedback).

Participants' implicit, and often explicit, understandings of classroom practices are evident through their orchestration and use of practices. For example when Sara, a native Berber speaker with beginning knowledge of French, uses a French book that she has brought with her from home as she writes in her notebook she understands that she can communicate her thinking across languages. Listening to Jessica play her grandfather's violin or watching Shelly paint in response to music illustrates that these girls know meaning can also be constructed via various semiotic systems. In another episode featuring Elisabeth, a student with Latina heritage that identified herself as an English speaking American born in this town, was called to reconsider what she "knows" about speaking Spanish when asked by other students to try her best with what she knew as her classmates attempted to construct a multilingual birthday calendar for the classroom because here in this classroom they help others, build on their histories, and accept approximations. Students support each others' efforts – as seen when Brandon clearly read his poetry into the microphone in front of a large audience and when Travis reconsidered his Vietnamese parents as potential resources to turn to when conducting a focus study on Vietnam. And Alissa's words, "So what you're saying is girls can't play?" reflects her efforts to continue an important conversation in a way that revoices what she's heard and pushes others to think about the issue at hand from other perspectives. As a final example of classroom practices in action, follow the interactions of a small group during an Invitation exploring *Images of Mexico*, when native English speakers seemed to take on other languages being spoken in their environment:

Four students are gathered around a table in the center of the room studying a large foldout photograph of Mexico City in a National Geographic magazine. Ana Cristina walks around and stands at Shelia's side.

Shelia: You lived here? A little bit? (pointing to the picture)
Ana Cristina: yeah.
K: Whose house?
Ana Cristina (facing Shelia when she is talking): *La casa de mi abuelita* [My grandmother's house] – *no de mi abuelo el vive mas por acá . . .* [Not my grandfather's he lives farther over here]
Shelia: grandma? grandpa? grandma/grandpa?
Ana Cristina: yeah
Shelia: Hey I know Spanish.
Ana Cristina: *No, solamente mi abuelita* – [No, just my grandmother] *nada mas que mi abuelita por que mi abuelito vive allá* [Only my grandmother, my grandfather lives over there]
K: *Un pocito mas despacio para ella* [A little slower for her]
Ana Cristina: *Abuelita sola* [Only my grandmother]
Shelia: Grandma? (looking to Ana Cristina for confirmation)
Ana Cristina nods affirmatively.

It is okay for students to be uncertain, have a go, and do the best they can. Their actions seem to reflect an understanding that their classroom honors multiple possibilities and questions rather than one set of correct responses. They seem to value each others' experiences, lend help when needed, take risks to attempt tasks, call upon others for their expertise, recognize particular student contributions, and interact in ways that reflect their classroom beliefs that literacy is about sets of social practices that weave together the experiences of participants to create their classroom culture.

While this list is far from comprehensive, these key norms inform classroom literacy interactions. The examples provided illustrate the range of implicit understandings of action that inform the students' and teacher's interactions with one another as they nudge each toward trying on new literate identities within each students risk zone.

To further demonstrate the intricacies of classroom practices in action, I will first narrate two episodes in whole class presentation-like settings and then use one episode where a group of girls are working on their own during Invitations time. Ana Cristina's story of learning to articulate her processes and work as a learner; Mitchell's story of struggling to be one who has learned something new; and Amber's story of working pursue questions with peers surrounding issues of language, identity, linguistics, and specifically within the highlighted sequence – Ebonics become powerful examples detailing how student and teacher interactions in Room 4 are connected to who the students are and who they are to become.

Ana Cristina, Coming to See Herself as "One Who Can be Articulate her Journey as a Learner"

Ana Cristina, whose story opened this paper, was a sixth grade student had come to this town with her mother, leaving behind two younger siblings in Mexico. Her cousin Maria also joined this class as a fifth grader and she often gravitated toward Maria. Early in the year, Ana Cristina seemed to prefer the peripheries and often seemed to busy herself with tasks that appeared unrelated to the work at hand. She often seemed to be "doing her own thing" as she rummaged through her pencil box at her table as the group gathered on the rug. However as noted earlier, as the year progressed she made shifts in her participation. As noted in the introduction, she was a confident writer in Spanish. Her foray into written English was noted as she first painted a picture about her memories of living with her family in Mexico and then wrote English text to preserve her story in print. Weeks later, in another Invitation about the challenges of learning English she seemed to speak more freely and be more interested in understanding her peers' thinking and work. And careful observations in early January suggested her deeper understandings of the happenings of this classroom as she sat beside a new Spanish speaking student, Fernanda, and softly translated what was happening around them and guiding Fernanda through classroom routines and structures detailing such things as students' responsibilities during Writing Workshop to the ways that students were to sign up for Invitations and conduct focus studies.

The snippet of data that opens this paper is drawn from an interactive sequence that is part of a stream of student presentations of their work during their Invitations. Ana Cristina and four of her classmates had spent the hour prior to their presentation investigating maps using *My Map Book* (Fanelli, 1995), atlases, and various other resources that suggested options for mapping. The group had decided to make their own maps (of their day, neighborhood, and homes). During their group presentation when Adam and Brandon had finished sharing their work, they turned to Ana Cristina suggesting that she begin explaining her portion of the group's work. To best understand how class members moved Ana Cristina toward the identity of one who verbally articulates her work publicly, I have elected to narrate this sequence from the actual transcript because turns and utterances made within the verbal exchanges tend to be short, choppy, and difficult to follow when only a portion of the transcript is examined.

Ana Cristina stood there, one step back from the group, in silence. Her classmates pleaded with her. She left the carpet and walked over to Ruth. Ruth offered her an option of passing the map around the room – another option that didn't seem appealing to Ana Cristina. From her observational work during the hour of Invitations work time; Ruth knew what Ana Cristina had accomplished. Ruth knew Ana Cristina had already talked through her work and the appearance of another teacher on the scene allowed for her to draw in his presence to further the sense of an audience eager to learn about her work. Ruth rephrased her request, not as a the usual range of choices, but as a statement requesting the listing of four things that appeared on Ana Cristina's map. Classmates offered assistance by guessing things that they imagined to be on her map and/or actual things they could see on her map and then posed them to her in a questioning manner. The other students seemed to understand Ruth's intentions as well as the workings of this classroom as they turned to help Ruth pursue her intentions to differently position Ana Cristina.

Initially Ana Cristina nodded as a means of acknowledging and responding to her peer's questions/suggestions. Ruth and others accepted her nods as meaningful contributions and approximations toward full participation. After affirming that "Grandma's house" was one item on her map, they moved on. Classmates encouraged her, Adam moved in closer and looked over her shoulder and told others what he could see on her map – a school. It seemed as if Adam felt like Ana Cristina had then reached a point of needing help. Again a nod serves as a meaningful gesture that moved Ruth on to finding out what a third item was on her map. Adam continued to be the talker, oscillating between interactions with Ana Cristina and the class revealing item number three as the library. Ruth moved forward requesting the fourth item to which Ana Cristina quietly whispered, "My house." Adam revoiced her response in a more audible volume. His move seemed to serve dual purposes, one of making her response more audible to her classmates and another of recognizing that she has done "the hard part." She'd used words to communicate her work publicly. Another classmate replied, "What?" which prompted a louder repetition from Ana Cristina.

Ruth began the work of pushing Ana Cristina to do something and be someone that she felt Ana Cristina could do, other students aligned themselves with the agenda and Ana Cristina's few quietly spoken words after a patient stream of non-verbal interactions on Ana Cristina's part led to a conversation that seemed to position Ana Cristina as someone who could verbally share her work, as well as someone who could use life resources to participate in school learning, and as someone whose work was of interest and importance to other class members. Both Ruth's and the students' decisions for action were informed by their understanding of the classroom norms and were aimed at nudging Ana Cristina to attempt to be one who contributes, to be one who is confident as a learner while knowing that they supported her in this risk toward change – change that need not become *the* way to conceive of who Ana Cristina *is* rather *another* was Ana Cristina might act. Their movements seemed careful and supportive. They seemed so show that they cared while expecting that she really make a move in her performance to situate herself differently within classroom discourses. Their patient persistence in this interaction seemed to take Ana Cristina to a new place as both a person and learner in this classroom community.

Verbalizing learning aloud in the presence of others was a risk not only Ana Cristina but also for her classmate Mitchell. However Mitchell's was considerably different and called for a different sort of risk zone work.

Mitchell, Moving Beyond the Safety of Being "One Who Always Knows"

Mitchell was a returnee to Room 4 and was experienced in the workings of this environment. When the class gathered for group meetings, Mitchell could always be found at the front of the group – sometimes sitting near the big green armchair where the teacher often sat and sometimes lying on his stomach along side the chair or tucked under a nearby table. His up-close physical position allowed him to add comments or experiences that related to the topic at hand. He saw himself as a capable reader, writer, and resource for others. He faithfully carried and kept his Writer's Notebook filled with pages of sports recaps, quotes from read-alouds, important family memories, games with friends, and reactions to classroom experiences captured mostly in written narrative with poems and pictures occasionally mixed in. His own words describe him best, "Me. I am a writer. I love to write. It takes me off to another place. When I'm writing, I don't feel like anything is around me. I just feel changed. It's hard to describe. It's me, the pencil, and the paper. Then there's the other extreme, when I'm kind of stuck . . . [Writing can be a way to] relax. [When I'm writing,] I'm not in that world [where] you're always moving. I'm not in the world where you change right away. One thing throws you. Writing is like my escape. It's a loophole way from 21st century like. It's really something that makes me me . . ." (fall Writer's Notebook entry). Mitchell's notebook entry continued drawing in the role of reading in his life noting that he loved them both. This and other reflective pieces mirrored his actions in the classroom as one who was confident, one who knew, and one who readily displayed what he could do with others.

However, studying a particular interactive sequence with Mitchell, his peers, and his teacher offers further understandings of the ways in which the students and teacher interact in Room 4 as they work toward pushing each learner to new places and possible identities throughout their learning lives.

On the day this sequence took place, the students had been engaged in DEAR (Drop Everything And Read) reading time. It was 2:00, the time that they usually transitioned into Writing Workshop. Mitchell had not been reading a book during this time rather he had been permitted to continue his work on his PowerPoint presentation. Ruth began the interaction by addressing the class in a way that referenced a prior conversation with Mitchell in which they had agreed to allocate some time prior to Writing Workshop to look at his progress with his PowerPoint work.

Students are returning from various locations around the room where they had been reading and are settling back into their home seats at their tables. They turn their chairs toward the center of the classroom where Mitchell is sitting in front of the computer by the meeting area rug.

[1] Ruth (teacher): Before we have our author's reading continued, I told Mitchell that we would all take a look at his PowerPoint. We're just all going to look at it from kind of far away right now and then there will be other opportunities to look closer and I think you (to Mitchell) are going to need to move away. (Mitchell is sitting directly in front of the computer.)

[2] Mitchell: Yeah, I am.

[3] Trevor: Does it go automatically? (to Mitchell)
(Mitchell begins to present his PowerPoint silently)

[4] Ruth: Do you want to read it to us?

[5] Mitchell: Yeah. Ok. (Zooming sound effect) GO Xxxxxxx! (team name) Got questions about X University, go no further your questions will be answered here. (He reads the entire presentation as he clicks through the slides – his voice inflection has changed into "announcer" mode; all students with the exception of Sara and Sandra are faced toward the computer for the entire presentation) . . . rely on sophomore sensation. . . . (During his reading there is quiet occasional laughter.)

[6] Ruth: Mitchell, are you available for questions or comments?

[7] Mitchell: Yeah, of course. Mary –

[8] Mary A: How long did it take you to do that?

[9] Mitchell: Probably about an hour.

Mitchell continued to take feedback from peers, Nikki commented on the quality of his work, Amber appreciated his layout decisions, and Amy noted how his use of sound effects enhanced his presentation. He then called on Ruth who had also raised her hand and awaited her turn to respond to Mitchell's work.

[17] Mitchell: Ms. Peterson

[18] Ruth: I'm kind of curious because I'm not sure about your history with PowerPoint. Could you tell us about that?

[19] Mitchell: Ummm . . . I'm still learning how to do it really um I like of course have heard of it and maybe seen a PowerPoint presentation but I mean I really don't –

[20] Ruth: So did your experience really start on Monday?
[21] Mitchell: Ummm . . . probably when we started these presentations. Mary
[22] Mary A: Um – Xx really made me go "ooooohhhh"
[23] Mitchell: Amy
[24] Amy: Like maybe you could put action buttons like Alissa's dad mentioned.
[25] Andre Yeah, do you know how to do that?
[26] Mitchell: I'm sure that I could learn.
[27] Ruth: I'm sure that, can we hang on one second, I think the people who know how to do it might like you to ask them.
[28] Mitchell: Ok.

Unlike Ana Cristina, Mitchell could stand in front of his peers and talk with ease but positioning himself as one who did not know something was not an identity that Mitchell readily identified with. This sequence seems to illustrate intricate moves by both Ruth and Mitchell in their attempts to move toward and away from taking on the identity of learner as one who doesn't know things and learner as one who may need others to learn.

Ruth had made time in the day for Mitchell to share this, not so much because it was a great presentation, but rather because it was an instance of Mitchell moving into something new. His comment in turn 7 seems to portray his confident stance toward participating in this classroom however his subsequent actions seem to communicate a different message. Mitchell took control of facilitating the questions and comments session following his presentation but used this role to steer away from the identity Ruth suggested he try out, an identity of one who doesn't know something and one who needs others to learn. There seems to be a sense of tension present as he responded to Ruth's query in line 19 and then moved on to Mary in possible hopes of abandoning that line of questioning. Accepting Ruth's bid for this new-to-Mitchell identity appeared to involve a cost of abandoning his one-who-knows-it-all stance. However these intentions were not lost as Andréa seemed to follow Ruth's initial agenda with her comment in line 25 when she asked if he knew how to use action buttons within a PowerPoint presentation. Mitchell's response that he was sure he could learn suggested that he was still a confident person. Ruth's final turn [27], seemed to allow Mitchell to safely adhere to his identity as a confident learner but pushed him to reach out to others and learn *from* them rather than always being the one who knows. The moves in this episode were echoed in future reflective conversations by the teacher, the intentions were inline with the agenda to move Mitchell toward being a learner who still had things to discover and one who saw others as valuable resources to draw upon in the course of learning.

Learning in this room was about taking on various identities, learning with and from others, developing and articulating positions, and being able to share how understanding occurred. Uncertainty was valued. Working out one's thinking through writing and talking were understood as acceptable practices, however using these tools as they were intended is not always easy. The topics the students explored and the questions they asked were difficult. They did not involve easy black and white answers and often called students to explore important social issues that required additional risks to the self as participants took stances and framed their positions, understandings, and identities.

Amber, Defining Where She Stands Discussing Issues of Language, Identity, and Self with Classmates as "One Who is Uncertain"

On a Wednesday morning later in the year, Amber and five other girls gathered for the third session of a continuing Invitation exploring issues of language, standards, dialects, and language policies. This diverse group of girls had self-titled their Invitation Linguistics based on some of their Internet research that provided them with resources from the Center for Applied Linguistics. Amber and her two classmates Jenna and Amy are African American, Missy identified herself as Persian American and the other two group members, Alissa and Mary, are Caucasian. Prior to beginning this day's conversation, Mary and Jenna briefed Missy and Alissa as to the history of their discussions because Missy and Alissa were new to this group's conversation. During the previous week's work, the girls' talk had led them to issues of Ebonics wondering exactly what it was and where they stood regarding issues surrounding Standard English. Jenna initiated the conversation by referring to the written questions that she had composed in her personal notebook. Early on in the day's talk, Jenna and Amber exchanged turns in the conversation focused on Amber's position regarding whether or not Ebonics should be considered "foul." Amber had commented that Ebonics was "foul language" and Jenna was working to push Amber to articulate her exact position by asking her to restate her position, offering opposing statements, and asking Amber to say more about her thinking.

[1] Jenna: I don't understand so tell me why.
[2] Mary: Well,I think that (drawn out) –
[3] Jenna: Let her talk.
[4] Mary: I'm not sure we're talking about Ebonics here at this table.
[5] Jenna: Amber, just tell us what you think you've learned and why
[6] Amber: I'll say why I think it is related to foul language because it is not really a standard English when you're runnin' around sayin' cus words all day long
[7] Mary: But Ebonics is not cus words are not
[8] Jenna: You're, so what you're saying is that the language is foul?
[9] Mary: But that doesn't define it right?
[10] Amber: (smiling without comment, nodding as if Jenna or Mary has hit her point)
[11] Jenna: But you speak Ebonics?

[12] Missy: There is foul language in any language. Nobody really knows what Ebonics are. It could maybe be in any language.
[13] Mary: Ebonics is a so-called black language and is spoken by African Americans, a lot of them (beginning to read from a printed article on the table)

Within the opening lines Jenna has positioned herself as an inside member of this classroom community echoing a very Ruth-like statement, "tell us what you think you've learned and why" in line 5. She continued to take this inquiring position as she pushed Amber further when she queried into Amber's position and her personal identity. Jenna shifted the issue into personal territory when she asked Amber if she was calling her own language foul. The conversation circled around the issue that Jenna seemed to be pursuing and the other group members' current understandings of Ebonics. When the conversation turned to attempts to speak in Ebonics rather that addressing the "foul language" and identity issues, Jenna continued in her 'persistent and focused role' and returned the conversation to this issue claiming that she did not understand Amber's positions and wants to hear what she is saying. With this attempt, Mary seemed to articulate Amber's position as one who was confused and Amy seemed to ally with Jenna's pursuit for an understanding of Amber's position by specifically asking, "Well, what do you mean Amber?" Jenna continued to respond to Amber's position from a place of confusion. She seemed to try multiple routes to understand Amber's thinking and eventually steered the girls to turn to a dictionary and their previous experiences with the social and historical nature of word meanings.

Mary shifted the conversation to a "right-wrong" debate where the girls then discussed language as a means to claim their heritage; maintain connections to their roots, family and histories; and shape/define social conceptions of "proper language" use. Within this new line of conversation, Jenna continued to push Amber to take a clear stand with regard to her thinking and her identity as an intelligent African American girl and one who was taking a position in opposition to her own language practices. They discussed language in terms of the need to understand others and stay connected with family; the difficulties of following societies notions of proper; and the messages sent to people about who they are if only one way of speaking is acceptable. Eventually, Amber seemed to connect to this line of thinking and relate it to her own experiences.

[14*] Amber: Some people are so worried to speak proper English around their friends because some friends are like, 'You sound so white.'
[15] Missy: Jenna, she like when we started she like said Ebonics but she like knows proper English, but she said what do think of Ebonics? What do you think it is? But you know proper English
[16] Amber: Or they're like why do you speak so proper? And then it is like when you're around your friends.

[17] Jenna: That happened to me when I went down South. And I don't know if they meant like by the words or I don't know. But I asked them, down there they like have a south-ern accent like.
[18] Mary: Southern
10:58 am
[19] Alissa: It's just like, why do people speak in an accent? But
[20] Amy: People have southern accents, western accents
[21] Alissa: Yeah
[22] Amy: Or eastern accents
[23] Alissa: Or French accents . . . actually Ebonics is sort of like an accent. Not really but sort of in a little way. Because everyone talks differently because different accents and stuff. Ebonics is sort of like an accent in a way
[24] Mary: You know what, I think it is a language in itself.
*line numbering is continuous for the purpose of this paper, additional turns in the entire transcript exist between the lines referred to here as 13 and 14.

The girls were exploring tough issues and seemed to use talk to make discoveries about their own thinking and life experiences. Amber's early two word assertion that Ebonics is "foul language" may have been her way of preserving a "confident, one-who-knows" identity in the presence of her peers. It may have been an attempt at avoiding issues of self as Amber often worked to mask her own uncertainties regarding the content of the conversation and/or her own standing as an African American girl. Whichever the case may be, these girls seemed to know the value of questioning, gathering perspectives, and using resources to inform their positions. Although they would say it is ok not to know things in this classroom, some of their contributions seem to adhere to a sense of certainty in hopes of claiming a powerful, safe, secure self in the company of others. Jenna knows Amber, she knew her life experiences, and she knew how she acted in school and with friends outside of school. Jenna also had an implicit understanding of the norms alive in this classroom. Weaving together these two funds of knowledge, she persisted in her pushing, wanting Amber to really think through her statements and realize everything that she is claiming with her two word statement that references Ebonics as "foul language." Jenna seemed to bring the issue into Amber's own life space as a means to help her think through and her feel comfortable letting go of her claim of being "one who knows what she is talking and thinking about" just long enough to contemplate what she might be saying about herself and to weigh this thinking against what society says is "right." The girls uncovered issues of social norms and language use that as they learned about Amber as well as themselves. Their social interactions allowed them to examine who they were and might become.

To Jenna, and others in this classroom, taking a stance is about more than having an opinion it was about taking risks related to the self and being particular kinds of people. Work within risk zones was not isolated to these three students, returning to students mentioned in the initial paragraphs of the Findings section there are references to other episodes which could be examined in ways similar to the analysis of Ana Crisitina, Mitchell, and Amber. Accepting feedback from peers that suggest Travis consult with his parents about life in Vietnam pushed Travis to relocate possible identities in a larger cultural sense. Making public feelings of injustice regarding gendered rules for noon hour football, called Alissa to take up a new-to-her position in advocating for change. Likewise, as Shelia interacted with peers studying Images of Mexico she began to see herself in new ways. The discursive spaces in which these students and their teacher lived seemed to invite these important conversations that not only addressed valuable content but facilitated interactions that were constantly asking and reasking who they were and who they might become in light of what they are learning.

DISCUSSION

What we learn from the children and teacher in Room 4 clearly links literacy work with identity work. As we watch what the students are doing in the process of becoming literate, we see that they have internalized the norms and discourses alive in this classroom to inform their actions. What is unique here is that the D/discourses in this classroom are significantly different than those available or enacted in traditional classrooms adhering to scripted or instrumental approaches to literacy instruction. In Room 4, you don't have to arrive at *the* answer or be the same as everyone else. Learning is not about acquiring a predetermined set of knowledge deemed necessary for all. Nor must everyone in the class learn Spanish or Hebrew, be adept at using all of the features of Point Point, or know how a CD player works; rather here one needs to recognize in oneself and others what they can do and where they might head in challenging themselves to grow. Important here is an understanding of the structural differences in discourses. D/discourse structure here suggests that literacy learning can be more than the apprenticeship into a particular discourse as advocated by approaches to literacy instruction that adhere to narrow understandings and autonomous models of literacy. Students here participate in discourses that resonate with those of therapy sessions as they revoice previous comments and actively listen to their peers. Students' talk and actions also tend to be oriented toward supportive and helpful interactions rather than always aiming to stake claims at being the best. They talk and act in ways that mirror legal discourses when they ask others to support their positions and take seriously the nature of each other's contributions. And, key to the work here in Room 4 is that the students have a sense of what they are doing. Because they are called to talk out their processes, reflect on their journeys, and work constantly work with others they develop ways of articulating what it is they are doing as learners. They learn to take positions that call them to deliberate on their relationships between themselves, others, and all available D/discourses. Take the scenario featuring Ana Cristina, students seem to align themselves with the teaching agenda and classroom norms by pursuing the work to position Ana Cristina as "one who can articulate what she is learning" while adhering to norms that support helping each other, taking risks, and communicating with intended audience. Ana Cristina and her classmates not only participate in implicit actions in line with process oriented norms, they participate in reflective conversations that bring actions to discursive levels.

Students, surrounded by the safety of their caring community, are encouraged to stretch themselves by trying on different "mes." They are encouraged to take on identities of "one who knows themselves as a learner" as "one who accepts their strengths and turns to others as resources" as "one who is flexible" as "one who is willing to reconsider" and as "one who is not tied to teacher affirmation or competition to be validated as a person or learner." These identities are not finite; students cannot "accomplish" them. Rather students experience these identities through their actions as they participate in classroom activity that values people-in-progress. And progress here stems from their interactions with others. Like in Amber's case, the students have taken what they know about interactions and learning in their classroom to push Amber to consider the identity claims wrapped up in her talk as they pushed her to step outside of a confident identity into one of confusion and difficulty. Interactions ask her to move beyond the safest place to stand, to step outside of a secure identity to try on a new way of being and doing so seemed possible because of shared understandings and persistent talk about what they are working to accomplish in this classroom.

Looking to the mediational moves by teacher and students with class members' risk zones offers ways to understand the participants' intentions, resistance, and collaborative work in pushing others to take risks and experience new ways of being. It seems that what one important factor that makes this possible is a difference in the organization of power relations in this classroom. We often see participants in peer cultures holding on tightly to one identity as a means to be recognized by others as "one who knows it all" or as "one who entertains" or as "one who is shy and doesn't participate." Such claims to singular identities allow actors to claim positions within in systems of power relations where being a valid person is equated with being "one who *can* do something" or "one who just hangs in the back." Living out such identities may be safe for particular persons, but it takes the position that one's identity is formed, rather than in flux. It also may assure a sense of security for the actor if the environment is such that risks to self seem too costly to assume an identity other than what is "expected."

Because the students in Room 4 are not all heading to one common destination and power isn't necessarily associated with a particular end, it becomes possible for students to participate in a culture where valuing process makes these sorts of risks possible.

Despite the differences in how D/discourse here in this classroom offer ways of being different from traditional classrooms, interactions are not always smooth. There is resistance here too. But the resistance is also unique. In thinking about Mitchell, he made moves to avoid entering into a risk zone suggested by his teacher. But his moves were not counter to the classroom norms. Resistant actions work within the recognized classroom norms where students manipulate acceptable actions within different contexts to avoid moving towards risks they feel unready to take. Resistance here took the form of reappropriating a D/discourse in a different context to accomplish different ends. In another part of the transcript not detailed in Amber's story included in this paper, Amber made use of other acceptable norms such as "all voices should be heard" and "multiple perspectives should be valued" as she continues to push her point without articulating further what she means by "foul language" nor by accepting a position of uncertainty. While she was resisting Jenna's agenda she was doing so by making use of claims to classroom norms that would be completely acceptable in other classroom contexts.

Therefore, in furthering our understandings of the how identities are important features of D/discourses, data analysis also suggests a seemingly significant structural difference in the D/discourses that permeate this classroom. Students here are not just learning to become comfortable with a different D/discourse. They are not just learning to take on a prescribed way of being, rather they are learning that their validity as a person need not depend on their affiliation with, appropriation or mastery of a particular D/discourse. Rather valid identities are connected with flexibility with respect to discourses of being not quite competent, of being honest about what one knows/what one does not yet know and/or what one can do well/cannot yet do well. As suggested by the data, the differences within the discourses here in this classroom do not vary by merely content alone rather by structures that allow different sorts of literacy practices that invite students' to live and learn in ways that are everything about who they are and who they are becoming.

As students collaboratively participate in the discursive practices of Room 4, their actions also punctuate the importance of carefully rethinking what is meant by social learning – here students learn not only from what Vygotsky would claim as the result of assisted performance by more capable others but rather students here learn about, with, and from their classmates in ways that challenge their conceptions of "how the world is." They unpack social and cultural meanings attached to the words they use or the cultural storylines enacted. Their classroom interactions seem to suggest the importance of intimate understandings of others, the need to create safe learning environments, and spaces where talking to think is used as a tool not only to develop content based understandings but also to develop fluid student identities. Together the teacher and students in Room 4 offer a window into ways of mediating each other's learning, and reconfiguring traditional communicative practices that invite students to take risks and move flexibly between tentative identities as they tryout and take on an array of possible "mess." Together they permit different ways of conceiving of what it means to be literate and how one may come to take up positions that question the way things are rather than enact socially constructed scripts for how things ought to be or who one should be within particular scenes.

Ana Cristina, Mitchell, and Amber's stories offer possibilities of what literacy learning in schools can be about. Putting words on the norms that make classroom interactions possible help us in creating other classroom cultures concerned with reshaping literacy practices that reflect understandings of the ties between schoolwork and identity work. The classroom norms that seem to open up space to make such mediational work possible, offer options for taking the learning from this classroom to new places. And inside of all that we can learn from activity in Room 4, the notion of the risk zone suggests that the development of a meta discourses in reimagining not only *what* happens within literacy practices but *who* one gets to be. It seems that too often students avoid identity related risks as attempts to maintain ties to peer or cultural groups and/or to protect their claims to power. By restructuring the D/discourse in classrooms we may offer students ways of being that value notions of continuous construction of identity and personhood – activity which we might refer to as "doing identities" in the process of becoming. And this flexible stance toward being and becoming with others offers open, honest communicative actions that embrace critical questioning of the world that surrounds us. Given such a stance toward literacy learning, students learn to read much more than the word. They learn to read the world – those that they share it with, the social narratives for particular identities inscribed within human interactions, and opportunities for action to create spaces where participants can continuously write and revise personal biographies as well as social landscapes – taking risks to the self and supporting the risks of others.

REFERENCES

Aboulafia, M. (Ed.) (1991). *Philosophy, social theory, and the thought of George Herbert Mead*. Albany, NY: State University of New York Press.

Adkins, L. (2002). Risk, sexuality, and the economy. *British Journal of Sociology*, *53*(1).

Bakhtin, M. M. (1994). *The Bakhtin reader: Selected writings of Bakhtin, Medvedev, and Voloshinov*. P. Morris (Ed.). New York: E. Arnold.

Bloome, D., & Katz, L. (1997). Literacy as social practices and classroom chronotopes. *Reading and Writing Quarterly, 13*(3), 205–226.

Carspecken, P. F. (1996). *Critical ethnography in educational research: A theoretical and practical guide*. New York, NY: Routledge.

Carspecken, P. F. (1999). *Four scenes for posing the question of meaning and other essays in critical philosophy and critical methodology*. New York: Peter Lang.

Comber, B. (2001a). Classroom explorations in critical literacy. In: H. Fehring & P. Green (Eds), *Critical Literacy: A Collection of Articles from the Australian Literacy Educators' Association* (pp. 90–102). DE: International Reading Association.

Comber, B. (2001b). Critical literacies and local action: Teacher knowledge and a 'new' research agenda. In: B. Comber & A. Simpson (Eds), *Negotiating Critical Literacies in Classrooms* (pp. 271–282). Mahwah, NJ: Lawrence Erlbaum.

Connelly, F. M., & Clandinin, D. J. (1990). Stories of experience and narrative inquiry. *Educational Researcher, 19*(5), 2–14.

Davidson, A. L. (1996). *Making and molding of identity in schools*. New York: State University of New York Press.

Dyson, A. H. (1993). *Social worlds of children learning to write*. New York, NY: Teachers College Press.

Fanelli, S. (1995). *My map book*. New York: Harper Collins Books.

Fariclough, N. (1995). *Critical discourse analysis: The critical study of language*. New York: Longman.

Gee, J. P. (1996). *Social linguistics and literacies: Ideology in discourses*. London: Routledge.

Gee, J. P. (2000). New literacy studies: From 'socially situated' to the work of the school. In: D. Barton, M. Hamilton & R. Ivanic (Eds), *Situated Literacies: Reading and Writing in Context* (pp. 180–196). London: Routledge.

Gutierrez, K., Baquedano-Lopez, P., & Turner, M. G. (1997). Putting language back into languae arts: When the radical middle meets the third space. *Language Arts, 74*(5), 368–377.

Gutierrez, K. D., Baquedano-Lopez, P., & Alvarez, H. H. (2001). Literacy as hibridity: Moving beyond bilingualism in urban classrooms. In: M. de la Luz Reyes & J. J. Halcón (Eds), *Best for Our Children: Critical Perspectives on Literacy for Latino Students* (pp. 122–141). New York: Teachers College Press.

Janks, H. (2001). Identity and conflict in the critical literacy classroom. In: B. Comber & A. Simpson (Eds), *Negotiating Critical Literacies in Classrooms* (pp. 137–150). Mahwah, NJ: Lawrence Erlbaum.

Jeffrey, B. (in press). Countering learner 'instrumentalism' through creative mediation. *British Journal of Education Research.*

Kucer, S. (2001). *Dimensions of literacy: A conceptual base for teaching reading and writing in school settings*. Mahwah, NJ: Lawrence Erlbaum.

Lawy, R. (2002). Risky stories: Youth idenities, learning, and everyday risk. *Journal of Youth Studies, 5*(4), 407–424.

Levine, J. (2002). Community: Risk, identity, and love in the age of AIDS. *Journal of Gay and Lesbian Psychotherapy, 6*(4), 23–44.

Levinson, B. A. U. (2000). Foundations of education in cultural transmission and acquisition. In: B. A. U. Levinson (Ed.), *Schooling the Symbolic Animal* (pp. 15–22). New York: Rowman & Littlefield Publishers.

Levinson, B. (2001). *We are all equal: Student culture and identity in a Mexican secondary school.* Durham, NC: Duke University Press.

Lewison, M., Flint, A., & Van Sluys, K. (2002). Taking on critical literacy: The journey of newcomers and novices. *Language Arts*, *79*(5), 382–392.

Luke, A. (2000). Critical literacy in Australia: A matter of context and standpoint. *Journal of Adolescent & Adult Literacy*, *43*(5), 448–462.

Luke, A., O'Brien, J., & Comber, B. (2001). Making community texts objects of study. In: H. Fehring & P. Green (Eds), *Critical Literacy: A Collection of Articles from the Australian Literacy Educators' Association* (pp. 112–123). DE: International Reading Association.

Moll, L. C. (1992). Literacy research in community and classrooms: A sociocultural approach. In: R. Beach, J. L. Green, M. L. Kamil & T. Shananan (Eds), *Multidisciplinary Perspectives on Literacy Research*. Urbana, IL: National Council of Teachers of English.

Möller, K., & Allen, J. (2000). Connecting, resisting, and searching for safer places: Students respond to Mildred Taylor's The Friendship. *Journal of Literacy Research*, *32*(2), 145–186.

New London Group (2000). A pedagogy of multiliteracies. In: B. Cope & M. Kalantzis (Eds), *Multiliteraices: Literacy Learning and the Design of Social Futures* (pp. 9–37). London & New York: Routledge.

Nieto, S. (2002). *Language, culture, and teaching: Critical perspectives in a new century*. Mahwah, NJ: Lawrence Erlbaum.

Olsen, L. (1997). *Made in America*. New York: New Press.

Orellana, M. F. (1994). Negotiating power: Critical literacy practices in a bilingual classroom. New Orleans: American Educational Research Association Paper.

Peacock, J. (1986). *Substance, the anthropological lens: Harsh light, soft focus* (pp. 1–19). Cambridge: Cambridge University Press.

Riessman, C. K. (1993). *Narrative analysis*. Boston: Sage.

Robertson, L. M., Harding, M. S., & Morrison, G. M. (1998). A comparison of risk and resilience indicators among Latino/a students: Differences between students identified as at-risk, learning disabled, speech impaired and not at-risk. *Education & Treatment of Children*, *21*(3), 333–354.

Shannon, P. (2002). Critical literacy in everyday life. *Language Arts*, *79*(5), 415–424.

Slavin, R. E. et al. (1996). *Every child, every school: Success for all*. Thousand Oaks, CA: Corwin Press.

Spradley, J. P. (1997). *Culture and ethnography, conformity and conflict: Reading in cultural anthropology* (pp. 18–25). Boston: Little, Brown.

Street, B. V. (1995). *Social literacies: Critical approaches to literacy development, ethnography and education*. London & New York: Longman.

Sumara, D. J. (1998). Fictionalizing acts: Reading and the making of identity. *Theory into Practice*, *37*(3), 203–210.

Thompson, P. (2001). *Turning on schools: Making the difference in changing times*. Sydney, NSW: Allen & Unwin.

Tulloch, J., & Lupton, D. (2001). Risk, the mass media, and personal biography. *European Journal of Cultural Studies*, *4*(1), 5–28.

Valenzuela, A. (1999). *Subtractive schooling: U.S.-Mexican youth and the politics of caring*. New York: State University of New York Press.

Varenne, H., & McDermott, R. (1998). *Successful failure*. Oxford: Westview Press.

Vygotsky, L. S. (1978). *Mind in society: The development of higher psychological processes*. Cambridge, MA: Harvard University Press.

Wells, G. (1999). *Dialogic inquiry: Toward a sociocultural practice and theory of education*. Cambridge, MA: Harvard University Press.

Wertsch, J. V. (1991). *Voices of the mind: A sociocultural approach to mediated action*. Cambridge, MA: Harvard University Press.

Willis, P. (1977). *Learning to labor: How working class kids get working class jobs*. New York: Columbia University Press.

Wolcott, H. (1991). Propriospect and the acquisition of culture. *Anthropology and Education Quarterly*, *22*(3), 251–273.

REDUCING INEQUALITIES IN FIELD RELATIONS: WHO GETS THE POWER?

Caroline Hudson

By giving up the power, you usually end up getting the power, honey.

(American friend, 1995, on real-life relationships)

MY DOCTORAL ETHNOGRAPHY

Over the twentieth century, there was a wide range of demographic changes in the family. Demographic shifts included a decline in the number of first marriages, and a rise in the divorce rate, the number of births outside marriage and the number of one parent families. Whilst ideologies (Eatwell, 1993; Seliger, 1976) of the family are many and varied, they tend to privilege the intact nuclear family as the natural, ideal and normal family form (Jagger & Wright, 1999) and as patriarchal, white and middle class. Other family structures, in contrast, can be seen as deviations from the norm. Such ideologies of the family are at odds with the changes in family structure outlined above. This tension between the ideal and the real can help stereotype children who live in families which deviate from the perceived norm of the intact nuclear family. This can disadvantage children who may be otherwise well-adjusted (Ferri, 1976; Mitchell, 1985).

I was interested in exploring, through my doctorate, how some of the macro changes described above were experienced at micro level, by a sample of young people. My doctoral ethnography (Hudson, 1999) questions whether commonly used categories of family structure (intact nuclear, reordered nuclear/step, single/one parent, and care) inform understanding of 32 young people's experience

Ethnographies of Educational and Cultural Conflicts: Strategies and Resolutions
Studies in Educational Ethnography, Volume 9, 255–270

ISSN: 1529-210X/doi:10.1016/S1529-210X(04)09012-6

of family and of schooling. Using a symbolic interactionist framework, the ethnography aimed to access the young people's voices on family and schooling. The 32 young people were in a mixed ability tutor group in Springfield School, a large urban working class comprehensive school in central England. The main part of fieldwork took place in 1996–1997, when the young people were in Year Nine (aged 13–14), though fieldwork continued until they finished Year 11 (the end of compulsory schooling) in 1999. The main methods of data collection were tape-recorded, semi-structured interviews, and informal conversations with the young people and observations of their experience of schooling, recorded in my research log. I conducted two sets of semi-structured interviews with the young people, the first in January to February, 1997 and the second in April to May, 1997. In addition to these, the young people could have as many extra interviews as they wished. In total, 237 interviews were conducted. All student interviews were conducted in lesson time. Other sources of data were interviews with staff and analysis of a selection of school documentation.

POTENTIAL POWER IMBALANCES IN FIELD RELATIONS

Field relations have received considerable attention in the methodological literature on qualitative research (e.g. Ball, 1988, 1991, 1993; Delamont, 1992; Finch, 1984; Mac an Ghaill, 1991; Measor & Woods, 1991; Pollard, 1987; Walford, 1991). It is axiomatic that power relations between researcher and researched are an important aspect of field relations. On the surface, a range of factors could have underlined inequalities of power between the young people and myself. First, I was an adult and they were adolescents. Second, I was the researcher and the young people were being researched. Third, the research took place chiefly in the context of Springfield School. Schools usually have a hierarchical structure and do not necessarily explicitly recognize the student perspective (Ruddock et al., 1996; Wallace, 1996). Fourth, my husband was in a position of authority in the school. He had worked at Springfield since 1994 (before my fieldwork began), first as Head of History and Year Head. From partway through my fieldwork, as will be discussed later, he was Assistant Principal responsible for discipline. Fifth, on some occasions the comments of teachers at Springfield potentially reinforced my position as adult to the young people. Whilst Lee (1993) argues that any research topic is potentially sensitive, it is likely that gaining access to private areas of experience such as family could be particularly sensitive, especially given the stereotyping of family structure pointed to above. In theory, the factors outlined above could have underlined power inequalities between the young people and myself and so limited the young people's openness with me on experiences of family.

On the one hand, it would be naïve to think that power imbalances in relationships, whether in research or real life, could ever be removed completely. On the other hand, it would be simplistic to assume that power relations are ascribed, and are not to any extent negotiated. My fieldwork was premised on the assumption that the more I reduced inequalities between the young people and myself, the more openly the young people would talk about their experiences of family and schooling. This chapter explores ways in which I attempted to reduce potential inequalities in field relations with the young people, to create a context within which to access their voices on their experiences of family and of schooling.

THE RESEARCHER AS "WHOLE SELF"

Woods and Jeffrey (Woods, 1996a, b, p. 47) highlight how teachers who treat pupils as "whole selves" rather than as "institutionalized clients" make "emotional connections" with their pupils, to the benefit of their teaching. I interpret "whole selves" as being broadly synonymous with treating pupils as people, with many dimensions to their personalities, rather than constructing pupils solely within the parameters of the school. Woods and Jeffrey (Woods, 1996a, b) make the point that by approaching pupils as rounded selves, teachers make bonds with students which transcend those of more instrumental, role-bound relationships. By implication, students welcome being treated as "whole selves" and teachers and students connect intuitively with each other.

It is almost a platitude that the researcher's self is the key instrument in qualitative research. Discussion later in this chapter will illustrate how I aimed to treat young people as "whole selves." I think that Woods and Jeffrey's (Woods, 1996a, b) "whole self" also has implications for the presentation of the researcher's self. I used the concept of the whole self to maximize my reflexivity about how I presented myself as researcher, to reduce inequalities between myself and the young people. I aimed to appear a "whole self" (Woods, 1996a, b, p. 47) to the young people in part by being with them in a range of contexts from, for example, maths lessons to the school disco, over a period of time. I also ensured that the young people saw me in a range of roles, such as someone who chatted to them, who laughed with them and whom they could also tease, who learnt alongside them in class, and who listened to their problems. I aimed to be someone in front of whom they could talk about drugs, drink, smoking and sex, and who would not be judgemental. Being with the young people in a range of contexts and roles reduced the possibility of being viewed by them as one-dimensional. More importantly, however, I always aimed to be myself, whatever the context or role. What was key was that none of the roles I assumed as researcher was sufficiently out of keeping with my personality to mean I was straining a role or situation.

CREATING CONNECTIONS

I spent the first couple of months of fieldwork with the young people, from November 1996 to the end of January 1997, building relationships with them, before starting the first set of tape-recorded interviews. Between November 1996 and January 1997 I sat in on lessons and had as many informal conversations as possible with the young people, in peer groups and on a one to one basis. I aimed to demonstrate to the young people that I was interested in them as "whole selves" (Woods, 1996a, b), in any aspect of their lives they chose to tell me about. What stands out from my research log is the range of conversations I was engaged in with the young people, often within a very short period of time. In one tutor time, for example, the subject of conversations with different young people encompassed cars, hair dye, what clothes to wear for a party, Christmas shopping, sharing bedrooms, and animals. The topics listed above indicate how much of the early interaction tended to centre around adolescent interests, rather than private experience. I aimed to show my interest in the young people by referring, over time, to previous conversations with them, to demonstrate that I had remembered what they had told me on a previous occasion. For example, a group of boys and I developed a long running joke about how could exchange my Nissan Micra for a car from one of the boy's father's garage. It is likely that the connections created through demonstrating my interest in the young people's concerns helped reduce potential inequalities between us, and laid the basis for the young people to open up on more private areas of experience in interview.

BEING EXPLICIT

In writing about the ethics of researching children, Alderson (1995) emphasizes that it is the researcher's responsibility to clarify the research to the children participating. However, I was explicit about aspects of the research not only for ethical reasons, but also to increase the extent to which I accessed the young people's voices. I assumed that if they were confused about any aspect of the research, then they might not feel confident about participating in the research. This in turn might make them less open with me. For instance, when I first met the young people in tutor time, I stressed that I wanted them to act "naturally" and "normally." I explained to the young people that I was interested in what they really thought, rather than what they thought it was polite or appropriate to say to someone. I reiterated this at various points throughout the research, such as before the first set of interviews. From November 1996 onwards, I referred frequently to aspects of the interviews, and I had what I thought was a detailed discussion about interviews with the young people in January, 1997.

However, in spite of my comments as above, just before the interviews began, Tom asked me what would happen if he could not answer a question in interview, and Brian asked me if an interview was like a chat show. These questions prompted me to give the young people the opportunity in tutor time, together as a class and individually, to ask questions again about interviews. Apart from the questions cited above, which were also repeated in the class discussion, other questions raised by the class included what would happen if there were a silence, whether I would ask another question if the interviewee could not answer a question, and what would happen if the interview finished early. I was also asked by some of the young people individually if they could swear and eat in interview. In response, I stressed that I wanted them to act normally. This indicates that it was important to be reflexive about the extent to which explicit comments did clarify the research to the young people.

CONFIDENTIALITY AND ANONYMITY

At the start of fieldwork, I told the young people that whatever they said, in whatever context, would be confidential, in that it would not be repeated to anyone in school, and anonymous, in that their names would be altered in any written account. I reiterated the confidentiality of the research to the class at various stages, such as just before the first set of interviews. I also reassured the young people about confidentiality on an individual basis, usually in interview, especially when I judged a young person had made a particularly sensitive disclosure.

There were various indications that the young people believed in the confidentiality and anonymity of the research. They coined a name for confidentiality, "the official secrecy." The room I usually interviewed in was known as the "confidentiality room." Indeed, it was interesting that when we went out of the more usual context of the school to the ice rink in a nearby town, the young people checked that they were still "under the official secrecy." At the same time, belief in confidentiality sometimes transcended context. When the young people were in Year 10, I was employed by the school to conduct a short-term piece of research on attendance. They were part of the sample. When I started to explain about the confidentiality and anonymity of an attendance questionnaire I was about to distribute, I was interrupted by Charley with:

> We know all that! We've been through all that last year. (Research Log, 1998)

Some comments suggested that the young people had grappled with the implications of anonymity and confidentiality. The following was part of a conversation with a group of girls one breaktime:

Sara: Even if you change all the names, my mum'd still recognize me. After all, I've told you the story of my life. If my mum reads it, I'll get done. She'll kill me. Do you think you could make your book too expensive for my mum to buy?
CH: How much is too expensive?
Sara: £6.99.

Belief in the confidentiality of the research is likely to have increased the young people's openness about their experiences of family and schooling and so increased the quality of data constructed.

CHOICES

It has been argued (e.g. Ball, 1988, pp. 39–40) that children usually have little control over the research process. Pollard (1987, pp. 107–108) comments that the quality of data from children is related to the amount of control they feel they have over the research process. Giving the young people a range of choices was important in reducing power imbalances between researcher and researched. For instance, at the school's request, I gained written parental/guardian consent to interview. All parents/guardians consented except for one. However, the young people, with the exception of the student whose parent refused to allow her to be interviewed, had the final say about whether to be interviewed, and how many interviews to have. This meant that the number of interviews per individual student varied greatly, from 29 to 0. The young people could opt in and out of the research, if they wished. They could choose about when to be interviewed; they decided which lesson they signed up to be interviewed in. They also had the choice about how much to say in interview. I told them they need not answer a question they felt uncomfortable with. I talked through collectively with the students ways in which they could say no, to avoid answering a question. Constructing semi-structured interviews around topic areas enabled the young people to have considerable control over the development of conversation in interview. Indeed, some of them were impressive in their skill to direct the interview to their own agenda.

THE DEVELOPMENT OF FIELD RELATIONS

Various markers indicated the progression, over time, of field relations with the group as a whole. One marker was the interview. On the whole, students talked more openly in the second set of interviews than in the first. As the research progressed, more young people requested additional interviews. Another indicator of the development of field relations was the increasing frankness with which young people spoke to me. First girls, and then, more slowly, boys started telling me about their sexual activities and their experience of smoking, drink and drugs. Then there were perhaps predictable requests for me to buy alcohol and cigarettes for them. Another marker was where the young people felt comfortable talking to me. After a short while with the tutor group, the students started talking to me outside the classroom. Then they began to ask if we could walk together from, for instance, the tutor room to the interview room or to class. By Easter 1997, the young people were speaking to me outside the nearby shop, where they used to congregate to smoke. From Easter 1997, I was also invited on various occasions to the school ditch, where they also used to smoke, and to their parties.

At the same time, there was considerable variety in the development of individual students' relationships with me. This diversity suggests that the young people felt empowered to make choices about their interactions with me, as the three contrasting examples indicate. Sara is an example of rapid development of field relations, Sammy is an example of fluctuation in research relations, and Tim is an example of slow development in field relations.

Sara

Although Measor and Woods (1991, p. 65) comment that:

> Access in the sense of trust only develops slowly in research, as it does in any relationship,

Sara needed little time, either to trust me or to become a key student gatekeeper in facilitating my access to other students. From early in the fieldwork, Sara would invite me to join her and her peers, in lessons. For example, when I went into a Health, Home and Community (HHC) lesson (the equivalent of Personal and Social Education (PSE)) Sara loudly hailed me with, "Miss! Miss! Come and sit with us!" When I introduced myself to the young people in November 1996, I stressed that I wanted them to act "naturally." From very early on, Sara would remind both staff and students that I wanted the young people to, in her words, "act natural" or "act normal." When, for instance, the students were told off for their behaviour in a maths lesson where "the writer" (me) had been present, Sara was sent out of the room for saying, "But she wants us to act normal" (Research Log, 15.1.97). When Sara's friend Anna overheard the tail end of Sara telling me how the two of them had almost been caught smoking in the school ditch at lunchtime, Anna said, alarm in her voice, "You haven't told her that, have you?" Sara responded, "She wants us to act normal" and Anna joined in the conversation. This example illustrates how Sara was important in developing other students' trust in me.

Sammy

Sammy wanted to be interviewed at the start of fieldwork, and, in the first set of interviews, she talked with apparent ease and openness. I felt we had established a good rapport (Research Log, 23.1.97). Consequently, in April, 1997, I was surprised first when Sammy said she did not want an interview and second, as she was usually forthright, that she was reluctant to explain why (Research Log, 25.4.97). When she did explain why, she said she felt she had disclosed too much about her life to me, and that she would rather get on with life, than reflect upon it (Research Log, 28.4.97).

Rereading my research log, I thought it might not be coincidental that in a previous English lesson (10.3.97) Sammy had double-checked with me about the anonymity of the research, saying:

> My mum would kill me if she knew what I'd said.

From April until July, 1997, Sammy ignored me completely, to the extent that she would even avoid eye contact with me if I was with her peer group. Although my supervisor Geoffrey Walford suggested that I should encourage her to be interviewed, I kept my distance. I was pleased that Sammy felt able to express her wishes. Then, in July, 1997, Sammy suddenly started talking to me again, going from the extreme of a perhaps hostile silence, to opening up at great length about being in trouble for defacing the school's new cricket wicket (Research Log, 16.7.97). I do not know what prompted her to reopen channels of communication at that particular moment. I still did not ask her about being interviewed; if any initiative were taken, I wanted it to come from Sammy. Months later, Sammy asked for an interview, saying:

> I've got lots to tell you! (Research Log, 11.11.97)

Tim

The positive development of Tim's relationship with me hinged on, over time, his realization that he could control our interactions. Initially Tim said he did not want to be interviewed and was uncommunicative with me. After an HHC lesson, I wrote:

> Started to talk to Tim and immediately got a 'wall'. I decided to leave him alone, and so talked to Charley, who was sitting by Tim. Interesting that after a while Tim voiced a comment about Charley and then joined in the conversation with a little bit about himself. Finally, Tim dominated the conversation!

It was perhaps fortuitous that, in one humanities class, the teacher sent me to sit at the back with Tim. Tim buried his head in the curtain at the prospect of sitting by me, and I had to coax him out. At the end of the class, however, Tim asked:

> Are you still accepting offers to be interviewed?

To an affirmative, he replied:

> I'll think about it! (Research Log, 13.1.97)

Two days later, in a design technology (DT) lesson, he engaged me in conversation in the middle of the room. On being told to sit down by the teacher, Tim declared impatiently:

> 'Ang on! I'm talking to Miss!' (Research Log, 15.1.97)

On 27.1.97. Tim asked to be interviewed, and subsequently had extra interviews.

Sara, Sammy and Tim indicate how different young people expressed their voices at different moments of their choice, over time in the field. The examples illustrate the value of giving young people space over time. I did not know whether I would ever interview Sammy again, or whether I would interview Tim even once. However, both my intuition and my underpinning approach of listening to the young people's voices told me to hold back from pushing them. Data constructed from interviews they had requested were likely to be of higher quality than from interviews they had been propelled towards.

MY HUSBAND'S ROLE

Pollard (1985) discussed the problems and possibilities of doing participant observation in the school in which he taught. Whilst a key issue was combining teacher and researcher roles, Pollard comments that "much to (his) surprise" (1985, p. 226) this was less difficult than he had anticipated. My husband Richard's role at Springfield might, in principle, have helped maintain or even increase power imbalances between myself and the young people, and so have limited the quality of data I constructed, particularly as he was well established at Springfield by the time I started fieldwork. In theory, it might be assumed that the young people might associate me with Richard, and so put me in an official teacher role.

I aimed to use Richard's role to increase my reflexivity on the extent to which I was reducing inequalities in field relations and accessing the young people's voices. At the outset of fieldwork, I decided that I would not introduce the subject of being married to a teacher, as I did not want to suggest to the young people that this might be significant to the research. At the same time, I decided that, if the young people raised the subject, then I would answer their questions openly. It was not long before the subject arose. One break early in fieldwork, some of the girls realized I was married to a teacher. Initially, they confused "Mr. Hudson" with another teacher with a similar name. Girls crowded round in a flurry of sympathy. Anna, exclaimed:

> What, not that tall bloke! Poor you! What's he like at home? (Research Log, 24.1.97)

Her remark suggests some sympathy for my perceived position, rather than constructing Richard and myself as a couple, separate from the young people. Indeed, over fieldwork, the young people's comments tended to suggest they had a much stronger sense of my relationship with them, rather than any relationship I might have with my husband. For instance, later in fieldwork, when Sara was reading the school newsletter in December 1997, she turned to me and exclaimed:

> Miss! Did you know your husband's been made Assistant Principal? (Research Log, 12.12.97)

When Sara telephoned me at school during the summer holidays, 1998, my husband answered the phone. Sara must have heard us finish a conversation as he handed the receiver over to me. Despite the explicit reminder that I was married to someone official, when I asked how she was, Sara immediately launched into a diatribe about a boy she had "shagged" and described the prospect of returning to school as "crap."

Furthermore, some of the young people asked me to collude with them against my husband. For example, after a school production of *West Side Story* at Christmas, 1998, Andrew came up to me. The following conversation ensued:

> CH: How are things going?
> Andrew: Okay. There's just one problem.
> CH: What's that?
> Andrew: Your husband. He keeps comin' up the field when there's only 20 minutes of break and we want to 'ave a fag and e' just stands there. D'ye think you could have a quiet word? (Research Log, 2.12.98)

The apparent incongruities of my husband's official position, juxtaposed against the openness of the young people's accounts and requests, served to highlight the extent they felt empowered to express their views and wishes, and also, on occasion, perhaps to manipulate me to their advantage.

NEGOTIATING BOUNDARIES IN FIELD RELATIONS

Hammersley (1995) makes the point, almost scathingly, that facile contrasts between dilemmas and inequalities in real life and in research should be avoided. It is realistic to expect limits to form part of any interpersonal relationship, whether in the field or real life. It would be simplistic to assume that such boundaries are necessarily at odds with the aim of accessing and listening to another person's voice. Because I encouraged the young people to behave "normally" and "naturally" it is unsurprising that I placed myself in some situations that required careful handling.

In some situations, I altered some decisions, to respect the young people. For example, at the start of fieldwork I had told the young people that I planned to end fieldwork in July 1997. I reiterated this at various points during the fieldwork. In July 1997, I again talked to the young people about leaving the field. I explained that I was going to be writing up my "book" and we talked through the ways they could keep in touch with me, if they wished. However, Hammersley and Atkinson (1995, p. 121) rightly stress that leaving the field is not always unproblematic. At the beginning of the new school year, the young people demanded that the fieldwork should continue. I reversed my decision and extended my fieldwork in September, 1997. In my view, not to respect the young people's wishes would have been unethical; I would have been exploiting them for the perceived benefit, in terms of timescale, to the research. In actuality, the data were enriched because my relationships with the young people developed further during the unexpected extension to fieldwork.

Most situations requiring careful handling concerned peer group activities, such as smoking, drinking, drugs and sex. In some instances such as the "spit test," I colluded with the young people. On an HHC trip to the local maternity hospital, a group of the students asked me to find out from their Year Head, Karl Price, whether the much dreaded spit test, used to attempt to detect illicit drinking, was to be used that night at the school disco. With apparent casualness, I started a conversation about the school disco with Karl Price, asking him what problems were likely to arise. The first he mentioned was that of alcohol. I asked what measures Karl would use to deal with this. The spit test was not mentioned. I checked that Karl had not forgotten to mention it, by asking if there were any additional measures he would use. The answer was negative. I let the young people know the outcome. I colluded with the young people for a range of reasons. These included the strength of my relationship with the young people, lack of respect for degrading measures such as the "spit test," and the view that, as a researcher, I was not working for the school. However, I also colluded with them for a strongly pragmatic reason; I did not think I was likely to be caught. Had there been a strong risk of getting caught, my course of action might well have been different.

On other occasions, I put up boundaries in my relations with the young people, and demonstrated that how I chose to handle a situation was not necessarily synonymous with what the young people wanted from the situation. For example, I was frequently invited to the young people's parties and to the school ditch at break and lunchtime, with my tape-recorder. The school ditch was viewed by staff as frequented only by reprobates and as the site of activities which were against school rules. It would probably have yielded a valuable seam of data; I could have triangulated the young people's accounts of ditch activities, with my observations. However, although Pollard (personal communication, 1997) advised me to go, I never took up invitations. Whilst Measor (informal taped discussion with Ball, in Ball, 1988, p. 43) said she did not enter students' private spheres because she felt she had no right to, I felt uncomfortable about such direct collusion with the young people. I also thought the risk involved was too great. I would have had to walk directly past the staff room window on my way to the ditch. Discovery could have jeopardised my access in school. I also did not want to compromise my husband's position at Springfield. The young people responded to my refusals by offering to keep me informed about ditch activities and even to take photographs as supporting evidence to their accounts.

When the young people asked me, on a number of occasions, to buy alcohol for them I did not collude with them. This was because buying alcohol for them would have been illegal. Had I been caught, I would probably have got into considerable trouble with the school. On the first occasion I was asked to buy alcohol the students even offered to pay me. I responded by saying that I was sweet and innocent, and the young people were trying to corrupt me. Charley saw through this straight away, responding with:

> Don't give us that one! You're not sweet and innocent. You've been through it all before. (Research Log, 16.5.97)

I had attempted to deflect the situation, when it is more in keeping with my character to be direct about an issue. I resolved to behave in character by being straight with the young people and so treating them with respect, as individuals who can see through sham. On subsequent occasions, I accompanied my refusal with the explanation that, if caught, I would be thrown out of school. Whilst this did not deter the young people from repeating the request, they appeared to respect my decision. For example, on the next occasion I refused, Malcolm said:

> It wouldn't really be fair on you, would it? (Research Log, 22.5.97)

THE YOUNG PEOPLE'S GAIN

I aimed to ensure that gain from the research was not one sided. There was evidence that the young people benefited from the research in a range of ways.

The fact that most students requested extra interviews indicates they perceived they were benefiting from the research. Measor (informal taped discussion with Ball, discussed in Ball, 1988, p. 37) comments on how the students were always pleased to see her. Indeed, if I appeared in the tutor room on a day for which I had not previously arranged appointments, students would rush towards me, often almost knocking each other over and even almost knocking me off my feet, clamouring for an interview. When, on a few occasions, I double-booked students by mistake, the young person who was not interviewed on that occasion was visibly disappointed, even though I always fixed up replacement appointments. Another indication that the young people felt they were benefiting from the research is that they were always punctual for interview, whilst they were often late for lessons and most, at some point, truanted from school. There were also indications that the young people remembered what they had said in previous interviews to me, whilst they often could not remember what had happened in lessons earlier in the same week.

Pollard's (1985) account highlights how his student research team enjoyed his research. The young people in my research also found aspects of it fun. For instance, McDonald's vouchers generated great excitement. I held raffles for McDonald's vouchers when, for instance, parental consent letters were returned and when the young people had completed the first set of interviews. In the raffles, the young people competed with each other about who was going to draw the winning names out of the bag. There was also heated discussion about whether winners in the first raffle should be excluded from the second. Several students offered me money for vouchers. One boy even offered me £15, which he flashed surreptitiously before me in a humanities lesson, when the teacher's back was turned. I think all involved enjoyed this drama.

Some teachers commented that participation in the research helped the young people feel more positive about themselves. It is likely that they enjoyed the extra attention and the fact that they were listened to, in a sustained way, over time. It was clear that for some of them the research was therapeutic. For example, I heard Leanne comment as follows to her friends about being interviewed:

> It makes you think and it really helps! (Research Log, 10.4.97)

Whilst Louise said, during an interview:

> I enjoy comin' 'ere to tell like someone. It's good to talk! (April, 1997)

Perhaps the young people's gain is best encapsulated by two examples. At the end of a morning's interviews, four boys were watching me label tapes used that morning. They asked me where the other tapes I had used were. I explained they were at home, locked up in case of burglars. One of the boys, Matty, exclaimed:

> Let's go and burgle Miss' house! Then we can do it all again!

When the young people were asked, on finishing Year 11 (aged 16) in 1999, what they had gained from most in their school experience, many cited participation in the research.

GAIN TO THE RESEARCHER

Because I aimed to reduce inequalities in field relations as much as possible, the young people were encouraged to express themselves openly to me. As a consequence, the young people brought a liveliness and a vitality to their interactions with me. They almost ran some aspects of fieldwork and our relationships developed in ways I could not have predicted at the outset of fieldwork. I constructed a breath and depth of data I had not envisaged at the start of fieldwork.

Woods has argued that the "ring of truth" should be a criterion in assessing the quality of data (personal communication, 1996). Implicit within this is that is for the reader to judge whether data have the "ring of truth." To enable the reader to judge whether interview data from my research have the "ring of truth" an extract from one interview is cited below. Chris is Louise's half brother who has cystic fibrosis. Louise's step-father has moved out and Louise's mother's boyfriend has moved in. In the following, Louise's tone is laden with anger:

Louise: I hope my mum will get a lesson taught her.

CH: In what way?

Louise: That she'll learn not just to love Chris. I know I might say that just 'cos that's how I'm feelin.' Like the other day, she brought back a whole pack of cheese straws, just for Chris. A whole pack of cheese straws like about four in the pack. 'Mum, can I have a cheese straw?' 'No, they're Chris'.' 'Mum, can I have a drink of water?' 'No, it's Chris'.' Mum, can I have a chocolate bar?' 'No. it's Chris'.' 'Mum, did you buy us any cheese straws? Mum, did you buy us any chocolate bars?' 'An it's like, 'Chris 'as gotta 'ave 'em. 'E's five years old. Chris 'as gotta 'ave 'em. 'E's got cystic fibrosis.' An' I think sometimes, 'I wish I 'ad cystic fibrosis.' I'd never want it, but the other day she was sayin', 'Yes, cystic fibrosis does have a better life span. They do live till longer.' There she is goin', 'E's gotta 'ave chocolate.' 'E's just a spoilt little brat! Oh, an' my mum's always with her boyfriend. (Sighs.) Just always with 'er boyfriend! I'm gettin' fed up!

CH: Why are you getting fed up?

Louise: Because he's just always with her. An' it's, 'I think of you kids first.' An' it's like, 'Oh yeh, you think of us first so much that after my dad you let another man in.' Because after my dad left it was, 'I'm never ever having another man in this house' (June, 1977).

If the reader wishes to draw on more interviews to assess whether the data have the "ring of truth," s/he should refer to my thesis (Hudson, 1999).

In my view, my American friend's comment cited at the beginning of the chapter was indeed borne out in my fieldwork. By attempting to reduce inequalities in field relations, the research met a range of the young people's needs and my needs as researcher. Both the young people and I benefited.

CONCLUSIONS

This chapter has explored my field relations with 32 young people in my doctoral ethnography. The chapter first outlined the chief potential inequalities in power relations between myself and the young people. It was argued that, in theory, potential inequalities could have made accessing the young people's voices on a private area of experience such as family particularly challenging. The chapter then discussed ways in which I attempted to reduce power imbalances. These were treating the young people as "whole selves" (Woods, 1996a, b); aiming to appear a "whole self" to the young people; using a preliminary period before starting interviews to make connections with the young people; being explicit about aspects of the research to the young people; respecting confidentiality and anonymity; and giving the young people choices. Case studies of the development of relationships with the young people were discussed. The chapter also explored how I used my husband's role in school to increase my reflexivity on the extent to which I was reducing inequalities in field relations. The issue of negotiating boundaries in field relations was considered. Finally, the ways in which the young people and I benefited from the research were discussed. It was argued that my American friend's comment, cited at the beginning of this chapter, was borne out by my fieldwork. By aiming to reduce inequalities in relationships between researcher and researched, gain was mutual.

REFERENCES

Alderson, P. (1995). *Listening to children: Children, ethics and social research.* London: Barnados.

Ball, S. (1988). Participant observation with pupils. In: R. Burgess (Ed.), *Strategies of Educational Research.* London: Falmer.

Ball, S. (1991). Power, conflict, micropolitics and all that! In: G. Walford (Ed.), *Doing Educational Research.* London: Routledge.

Ball, S. (1993). Self-doubt and soft data: Social and technical trajectories in ethnographic fieldwork. In: M. Hammersley (Ed.), *Educational Research: Current Issues.* London: Paul Chapman.

Delamont, S. (1992). *Fieldwork in educational settings: Methods, pitfalls and perspectives.* London: Falmer.

Eatwell, R. (1993). Ideologies, approaches and trends. In: R. Eatwell & A. Wright (Eds), *Contemporary Political Ideology.* London: Pinter.

Ferri, E. (1976). *Growing up in a one-parent family*. Windsor: NFER.

Finch, J. (1984). It's great to have someone to talk to: Ethics and politics of interviewing women. In: C. Bell & H. Roberts (Eds), *Social Researching: Politics, Problems, Practice*. London: Routledge & Kegan Paul.

Hammersley, M. (1995). *The Politics of Social Research*. London: Sage.

Hammersley, M., & Atkinson, P. (1995). *Ethnography*. London: Routledge.

Hudson, C. (1999). *Young people's experience of family and schooling: How important is family structure*? Oxford: University of Oxford Department of Educational Studies. Unpublished doctoral study.

Jagger, C., & Wright, C. (Eds) (1999). *Changing family values*. London: Routledge.

Lee, R. (1993). *Doing research on sensitive topics*. London: Sage.

Mac an Ghaill, M. (1991). Young, gifted and black: Methodological reflections of a teacher/researcher. In: G. Walford (Ed.), *Doing Educational Research*. London: Routledge.

Measor, L., & Woods, P. (1991). Breakthroughs and blockages in ethnographic research: Contrasting experiences during the *changing schools* project. In: G. Walford (Ed.), *Doing Educational Research*. London: Routledge.

Mitchell, A. (1985). *Children in the middle: Living through divorce*. London: Tavistock.

Pollard, A. (1985). Opportunities and difficulties of a teacher-ethnographer: A personal account. In: R. Burgess (Ed.), *Field Methods in the Study of Education*. London: Falmer.

Pollard, A. (1987). Studying children's perspectives – A collaborative approach. In: G. Walford (Ed.), *Doing Sociology of Education*. Lewes: Falmer.

Pollard, A. (1997). Personal communication.

Ruddock et al. (Eds) (1996). *School improvement what can pupils tell us?* London: David Fulton.

Seliger, M. (1976). *Politics and ideology*. London: Allen & Unwin.

Walford, G. (1991). Researching the City Technology College, Kingshurst. In: G. Walford (Ed.), *Doing Educational Research*. London: Routledge.

Wallace, G. (1996). Engaging with learning. In: G. Ruddock et al. (Eds), *School Improvement What Can Pupils Tell Us*. London: David Fulton.

Woods, P. (1996a). Personal communication.

Woods, P. (1996b). *Researching the art of teaching ethnography for educational use*. London: Routledge.

ABOUT THE AUTHORS

Lawrence Angus is Professor is Head of the School of Education at the University of Ballarat. His most recent book (with Professor Terri Seddon of Monash University) is *Reshaping Australian Education: Beyond Nostalgia.* His publications include several books over 50 refereed book chapters and articles in academic journals. His particular research and teaching interests include education equity and policy.

Eve Gregory is a Professor in the Department of Educational Studies at Goldsmiths' College, University of London She joined the Department of Educational Studies in 1987, after having taught for nine years in schools and two years at Nene College, Northampton. During her years at Goldsmiths, she has co-ordinated language and literacy programmes for the BA Ed, taught across Early Years programmes and established student exchanges in France, Spain and Austria. Recent research has included studies on family literacy history, on siblings (both funded by the ESRC) and children's home and school literacy practices (funded by the Leverhulme Trust).

Kathleen Gwinner began her career in education as a high school art teacher in rural areas near Kansas City, Missouri and El Paso, Texas, and then in Houston's urban schools. Travel and a continuing interest in art history prompted her to return to university for a Masters degree in European history, and she subsequently taught history and art history courses at private and public schools with a great variety of student populations. Her doctoral research was conducted at a specialized vocational school within the Houston metropolitan district where she was a teacher. She now teaches at a school for the gifted and talented where she is continuing her research on high achieving girls.

Martyn Hammersley is Professor of Educational and Social Research, Faculty of Education and Language Studies, the Open University. His early work was in the sociology of education. Much of his more recent work has been concerned with the methodological issues surrounding social and educational research. He is currently investigating the representation of research findings in the mass media.

He has written several books, including: (with Paul Atkinson) *Ethnography: principles in practice* (Routledge, 1995); *The Dilemma of Qualitative Method* (Routledge, 1989); *Reading Ethnographic Research* (Longman, 1998); *What's Wrong with Ethnography?* (Routledge, 1992); *The Politics of Social Research* (Sage, 1995); (with Peter Foster and Roger Gomm) *Constructing Educational Inequality* (Falmer, 1996); *Taking Sides in Social Research* (Routledge, 1999); and *Educational Research, Policymaking and Practice* (Paul Chapman, 2002).

Sam Hillyard is a lecturer in sociology at the Institute for the Study of Genetics, Biorisks and Society and a member of Nottingham's Institute for Rural Research. Her research interests include ethnographic research and theorising; the Sociology of Education; the history of symbolic interactionism and the sociology of Erving Goffman. At Nottingham, she teaches rural sociology and recently finished a research project studying images of farming in children's literature.

Caroline Hudson is Basic Skills Advisor in the Home Office National Probation Directorate. Caroline has published on offending and education, evidence-based policy, and family structure (intact nuclear, reordered nuclear, single parent and care) and young people's perceptions of family and schooling. Her principal research interest is issues related to social exclusion. Prior to working in the Home Office, Caroline was a researcher at Oxford University Department of Educational Studies and Oxford University Centre for Criminological Research. Before doing a Master's and doctorate at Oxford University, Caroline was a secondary school English teacher for 12 years.

Bob Jeffrey's ethnographic research at The Open University has focussed on the effects of policy reform and managerialism on the creativity of primary teachers in England. Together with Peter Woods, he has identified their dilemmas and tensions, their creative responses, identity reconstructions, and changes in professional role. He has, together with Geoff Troman, and Dennis Beach, established an extensive European network of ethnographic research interests and his current research project involves ten European partners focussing on the student's perspectives of their learning experiences with particular reference to their creativity. He has maintained a regular flow of articles concerned with ethnographic methodology.

Susi Long is an Associate Professor in Early Childhood Education and Language and Literacy at the University of South Carolina in the U.S. Her research interests include language and literacy learning in marginalized populations and teacher education. In 1997, she received the National Council of Teachers of English (NCTE) *Promising Researcher Award* for her ethnographic study of cross cultural learning in Iceland. She continues similar work in the United States with projects that include a study of professional development at the

University of South Carolina's Children's Center, a six month study of Mexican American kindergartners, and a long-term study of new teachers during their first three years of teaching. Key publications can be found in the journals, *Research in the Teaching of English; The Journal of Teacher Education; Reading, Language and Literacy*; NCTE's *Primary Voices*; and in an upcoming issue of the NCTE's *Language Arts*. Her most recent work is coedited with Eve Gregory of Goldsmiths College and Dinah Volk of Cleveland State University. The volume, *Many Pathways to Literacy* (Routledge Falmer, 2004) is a collection of studies that illuminate mediators of language and literacy learning in the lives of young children across a range of cultural settings in the U.S. and in the U.K.

Colton Paul worked as a primary school teacher for a number of years in the London Borough of Haringey and Tower Hamlets. He is now employed as a lecturer at Goldsmiths College educational department. Colton Paul is primarily concerned in his research with culture, identity and education, in particular the ways in which notions of race, power, and representation interact to influence cognitive development. his current area of research for his PhD thesis is focused on the effects of mythologies and power relations on the educational development of children of Caribbean heritage.

Ilana Snyder is an Associate Professor in the Faculty of Education, Monash University, Australia. Her research focuses on changes to literacy, pedagogical and cultural practices associated with the use of information and communication technologies (ICTs). Four books, *Hypertext* (Melbourne University Press & New York University Press, 1996), *Page to Screen* (Allen & Unwin and Routledge, 1997), *Teachers and Technoliteracy* (Allen & Unwin, 2000), co-authored with Colin Lankshear, and *Silicon Literacies* (Routledge, 2002) explore these changes. In collaboration with Simon Marginson and Tania Lewis, her current research includes a three-year Australian Research Council-funded project examining the use of ICTs in higher education in Australia. The focus is on innovation at the interface between pedagogical and organisational practices. She is also working on the application of Raymond William's ideas about technology and cultural form to a study of the Internet.

Ruth Silva teaches at the College of Education, University of North Texas having completed her doctorate in teacher education at the University of Houston. She has been a teacher and administrator in high schools in Australia and an administrator with the Department of Education (Independent and Catholic Schools) in Sydney. Her research focuses on the role of the classroom teacher as researcher, instructional supervision, and pre-service teacher education.

Katie Van Sluys is a doctoral research student at Indiana University.

Ilana Snyder is an Associate Professor in the Faculty of Education, Monash University, Australia. Her research focuses on changes to literacy, pedagogical and cultural practices associated with the use of information and communication technologies (ICTs). Four books, *Hypertext* (Melbourne University Press & New York University Press, 1996), *Page to Screen* (Allen & Unwin and Routledge, 1997), *Teachers and Technoliteracy* (Allen & Unwin, 2000), co-authored with Colin Lankshear, and *Silicon Literacies* (Routledge, 2002) explore these changes. In collaboration with Simon Marginson and Tania Lewis, her current research includes a three-year Australian Research Council-funded project examining the use of ICTs in higher education in Australia. The focus is on innovation at the interface between pedagogical and organisational practices. She is also working on the application of Raymond William's ideas about technology and cultural form to a study of the Internet.

Wendy Sutherland-Smith is a lawyer turned teacher and an Associate- Lecturer in the Faculty of Business and Law at Deakin University. She has taught in secondary and tertiary institutions for the past fourteen years. Currently, she is teaching Corporations and Business Law to international students, whilst also undertaking doctoral studies in the Faculty of Education at Monash University in Australia. Her Ph.D is a cross-disciplinary investigation of notions of plagiarism, from perspectives of Legal and Literary theory. She is particularly interested in the Internet literacy practices of tertiary undergraduate ESL students. In her doctoral work, Sutherland-Smith is focuses on Bourdieu's notions of symbolic violence, cultural capital, habitus and field. She applies these critically in analyses of international ESL students' academic writing, both print-text and Web-text based, with respect to plagiarism and intellectual property. She has published articles in *The Reading Teacher* (2002), *Prospect* (2002), and *TESOL Journal* (2003) on her research of international students' reading practices in paper-text compared to hyper-text environments. She has also published in the broader area of the nexus between linguistic and legal theory. Her email address is wendyss@deakin.edu.au.

Dinah Volk is a Professor and Coordinator of the Early Childhood Program, Cleveland State University, Cleveland, Ohio, USA. She has taught young children in the U.S. and Latin America and her research interests include sibling and peer teaching and the language and literacy practices of young bilingual children and their families. Volk is co-editor, with Gregory and Long, of *Many Pathways to Literacy: Young Children Learning with Siblings, Peers, Grandparents, and Communities* (RoutledgeFalmer, 2004) and is co-author, with DeGaetano and Williams, of *Kaleidoscope: A Multicultural Approach for the Primary School Classroom* (Prentice Hall, 1998). Her articles have been published in *Research* *in the Teaching of English*, the *Journal of Early Childhood Literacy, Reading: Language and Literacy*, and the *Early Childhood Research Quarterly*.

Geoffrey Walford is Professor of Education Policy and a Fellow of Green College at the University of Oxford. He was previously Senior Lecturer in Sociology and Education Policy at Aston Business School, Aston University, Birmingham. His recent books include: *Affirming the Comprehensive Ideal* (Falmer, 1997, edited with Richard Pring), *Doing Research about Education* (Falmer, 1998, Ed.). *Durkheim and Modern Education* (Routledge, 1998, edited with W S F Pickering), *Policy and Politics in Education* (Ashgate, 2000) *Doing Qualitative Educational Research* (Continuum, 2001) and *British Private Schools: Research on policy and practice* (Woburn Press, 2003, Ed.). His research foci are the relationships between central government policy and local processes of implementation, choice of schools, private schools, religiously-based schools and ethnographic research methodology. He is editor of the *Oxford Review of Education* and has recently completed a Spencer Foundation funded comparative project on faith-based schools in England and the Netherlands.

Sue Walters completed her DPhil research in the Department of Educational Studies at Oxford University and is now a Research Fellow in the Faculty of Social Sciences, The Open University, Milton Keynes (researching Ethnicities and Contemporary Rural Identities). She was previously a Secondary School English teacher and an English as an Additional Language specialist and has academic degrees in Literature, Women's Studies and Educational Research Methods. Her current research interests lie in issues concerning academic achievement and Bangladeshi pupils, ethnic minority and bilingual pupil's experiences of schooling and ethnicities and identities.